Praise for *Painting the Digital River*

"This book is as much about painting as it is about the digital world. But beyond both it's really about visual intelligence. What makes it a joy to read is the lovely match between Faure Walker's subject and his style of writing: apparently artless, just making itself up as it goes along, but actually always with a witty spring, and never slack."

— MATTHEW COLLINGS, *artist, critic, author, and television host*

"As a painter himself, James Faure Walker opens up a provocative dialogue between painting and digital computing that is essential reading for all painters interested in new technologies."

— IRVING SANDLER, *author, critic, and art historian*

"Faure Walker has a distinguished background as both a painter and digital artist. He is an early adopter of digital technology in this regard, so has lived the history of the ever-accelerating embrace of the digital. On top of this, he is a good storyteller and a clear writer who avoids the pitfalls of pretentious art-world jargon."

— LANE HALL, *digital artist and professor*

"Using a wide stream of fresh water as a metaphor, Faure Walker depicts a flow of ideas, concepts, and solutions that result in digital art. All the core elements of an art-style-in-making are here: ties with mainstream and traditional art, stages of technological progress, and reflections on the bright and varied personalities of digital artists. With a personal approach, Faure Walker presents vibrant, exciting, emotionally overpowering art works and describes them with empathy and imagination. This entertaining, sensitive, and observant book itself flows like a river."

— ANNA URSYN, *digital artist and professor*

"Something like this book is overdue. I am not aware of any comparable work. Lots of 'how to do,' but nothing raising so many interesting and critical questions."

— HANS DEHLINGER, *digital artist and professor*

"Here is the intimate narrative of a passionate yet skeptical explorer who unflinchingly records his artistic discoveries and personal reflections. Faure Walker's decades of experience as a practicing painter, art critic, and educator shine through on every page. The book is an essential resource for anyone interested in digital visual culture."

— ANNE MORGAN SPALTER, *digital artist, author, and visual computing researcher*

Painting the Digital River

Painting the Digital River

How an Artist Learned to Love the Computer

James Faure Walker

PRENTICE
HALL

Upper Saddle River, NJ • Boston • Indianapolis • San Francisco
New York • Toronto • Montreal • London • Munich • Paris • Madrid
Capetown • Sydney • Tokyo • Singapore • Mexico City

 Arts & Humanities Research Council   The research for this book was supported by the Arts and Humanities Research Council of the UK.

The publisher offers excellent discounts on this book when ordered in quantity for bulk purchases or special sales, which may include electronic versions and/or custom covers and content particular to your business, training goals, marketing focus, and branding interests. For more information, please contact:

US Corporate and Government Sales
(800) 382-3419
corpsales@pearsontechgroup.com

For sales outside the US, please contact:

International Sales
international@pearsoned.com

Visit us on the Web: www.prenhallprofessional.com

Library of Congress Cataloging-in-Publication Data
Walker, James Faure.
  Painting the digital river : how an artist learned to love the computer / James Faure Walker.
    p. cm.
  Includes bibliographical references and index.
  ISBN 0-13-173902-6 (hardback : alk. paper)
  1. Computer art. 2. Art and technology. I. Title.
  N7433.8.W36 2005
  776—dc22
                                                                                2005030006

Copyright © 2006 Pearson Education, Inc.

ISBN 0-13-173902-6
Text printed in the United States on recycled paper at Courier in Westford, Massachusetts.
First printing, January 2006

To Vivien

Contents

CONTENTS

Illustrations

Preface   **River Gods**

Make friends of all the brooks in your
neighbourhood, and study them ripple by ripple.
—John Ruskin, *The Elements of Drawing*

Not so long ago only a handful of painters knew anything at all about computers. Now, like everyone else, most painters have a computer, a Web site, and a cell phone. They know about Photoshop even if they do not use it. They know you can "paint" through the computer. They know there is virtual paint and real paint. What they are less sure about is what all this means for the art of painting itself. What happens when painting goes digital? Something must be gained, but what is lost? Does painting switch over into another art form? Or does it falter on the edge and somehow remain intact? Or—this is just a hunch—has it always been digital anyway?

It is enough to keep a painter like me in a state of panic and in need of therapy or at least something like a comfort blanket. It has all become so strange. That, I suppose, is a good excuse for writing a book. I first got hooked on digital paint in the mid-1980s. The program was Dazzle Draw, and I was dazzled, not just by the color I painted on the screen, but by the ideas set loose in my mind. Was I converted? Did I become a digital painter? Yes and no. I blinked, but could not make up my mind. I still paint with both real and digital paint. Gradually, it occurred to me that this is quite an interesting place to be, half in the digital art world, half in the painting world. On one side I hear brave talk of the new media, of Net art, of interactive art, of highly energetic art forms poised to take over from "traditional" painting; on the other side I hear—and see—painters thriving, absorbing what they need from the digital, toying with video, with photography, but in no mood to slink away. The paradox is that new technology has come up with the painting tools that Renaissance artists dreamed of, yet old-style paints are still preferred by most leading artists. Amazing art is being made with no more than a pencil, a brush, and some pigment. But here I go, rushing into the question of what is or isn't significant, advanced, retrograde, brilliant, or dismal in art. That would be art criticism, hinting how painting, or digital paint-

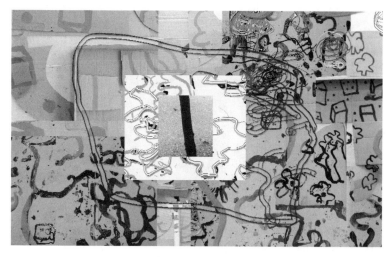

James Faure Walker, *Pigeons Kyoto*, 2002, 29" × 43" (74 × 109 cm), giclee iris print. (See also Plate 1.)

ing, could flex its muscles in this new landscape. Actually, it is a great time to be a painter and to be thinking about painting.

If I were to write an essay that was more a meditation than anything else, I needed an image to come back to as a symbol. Why the river? Some ten years ago I was at a private view of the sculptor Eduardo Chillida and found myself talking with a fellow enthusiast for all things digital. He invited me to visit the small company he worked for, called the Zap Factor. For some reason he didn't show up at the office, but I did not mind waiting there. The office happened to be in an old warehouse on the Thames. In fact, I knew this space and its fabulous views already, because since the 1970s these warehouses, then semi-derelict, had been co-opted as artists' studios through an organisation called Space, started in 1968 by Bridget Riley and Peter Sedgeley. (For the record, I have been in the same Space studio since 1971 and must be about its longest-lasting tenant). I forget exactly what Zap Factor did, except that it was pre-Web, overoptimistic, and started by someone inspired by swimming with dolphins. I must have been staring for an hour at the grimy greys of the Thames as it gently ebbed while the office buzzed behind me, and I kept thinking about the absurdity of us humans scurrying around excited by our toys while the Thames just flowed on as it had done for centuries, unconcerned.

I kept thinking of Turner, and went back to my own studio. Within a week, I had made a moody, quite spare painting out of those same greys. Looking back, I believe that my experience epitomised the dilemma of any painter aware of the new "paints" emerging in software, the dilemma of being part of this new cult while at the same time staying loyal to the old gods of painting. It was only much later that I realised that it also made sense to think of the stream of images, messages that come to us through TV, mobile phones, the Internet, screens here there and everywhere as—metaphorically—a river. In other words, this digital river could itself be the subject, the phenomenon, that a painter attempted to understand—I won't say "represent." Turner was fascinated not only by water, waves, and storms, but also by speed, and was one of the few painters in the first half of the nineteenth century to depict a steam train. I speculated about the type of painting that should be made, whether it should itself be made from this digital substance, be itself part of the river.

Some years later, when wondering how I could find a shape for my meandering thoughts, I realised the river was just the right image. I recalled this episode. As a painter I am still ambivalent. Do I jump in and try to become part of this digital river? Or do I linger on the side watching it flow by? Rivers are fecund symbols: They change all the time and remain the same; they divide territories, have bridges, provide frontier crossing points between old and new worlds; they have pure sources and muddy deltas, main currents and tributaries; from a plane they look like veins of silver threading their way round obstacles; they have secrets and histories and invite journeys into the unknown. I should not overdo this symbolism, but this just might work out as an essay plan. Painting has always had some connection with water, either as the medium for pigment or as a subject—lake, river, sea. The challenge of digital paint is whether painting can swap pigments for electronic colour and still be painting. Can it cross from the predigital to the postdigital? Or could this be quite the wrong way of thinking?

This is neither a how-to-paint-digital book nor a survey of a dozen "digital masters," but a book about painting written from the inside, from the inside looking out. I may already have digital eyes. Ruskin famously spoke not of teaching to draw, but of teaching to see.[1] One side effect of using the new technology is that your eyes adjust to seeing in a different way, and—in my case—a whole period of medieval art becomes vivid and accessible. It looks digital. This also works in reverse. Professionals in computer graphics, even video-game addicts, here and there turn to painting; they relearn how to draw. They realise how drastically we underrate the sensitivity, the sheer intelligence, of the human eye. I want to speak to the experts about the details of software. No, no, they say, painting is much more interesting.

I have arranged the book into sections, which roughly follow the river theme. I begin by posing the problem of how a painter copes with the blinding confidence of the high-tech-art hypothesis. I recount some of my own difficulties in reconciling the solid ground of the "painting culture," its history, and its technical foundations with the flux of the new thinking. I am tempted to say that the existing conventions of painting amount to a shaggy orthodoxy, and this orthodoxy is under siege from born-again zealots, but that is not quite how it is. The new does not stay new forever. I have felt the pressure from both sides, have seen the establishment entirely miss the point of painting with the computer, and have also seen the digital fraternity missing the point, or rather missing out on the pleasure of painting. In later pages of this book, I have included sections that are more about inaction than action, about how as an artist you fish for ideas and, one way or another, learn to make something of them, and how even the fastest computer only helps you so much. So there are limits, and when it comes to how you rate what you do, how you reflect critically, then again the software is not where you will find the answer. I allow myself to dream about how software might be different and more in tune with the way painters actually think, or don't think in some cases. Certainly, the way you work and the tools you use shape the sources you look for. After this I sketch out some of the "strange plants" upriver, suggesting some elementary classifications for types of digital drawing and digital painting. The final section returns to the initial questions. What are the fundamentals, the elements, of digital painting? What should students study to become the artists of the future? Software principles as well as art history? Could it be drawing? Can painting remain painting, a blend of old and new?[2]

My motivation throughout has been to throw some light on a subject that has been unfairly left out of the reckoning—why has so little been said about computers and painting? I hope it is a tolerable read for computer people, who will forgive my amateurish grasp of computer science, and I hope aesthetes will tolerate my lapses into technobabble and my name-dropping conference anecdotes. It is also a book about uncertainty, little comfort for students, fellow artists, and friends of art who are expecting some weighty conclusions. I am trying to work out what I think, but in the process—on my river journey—the encounters make it less easy for me to settle down in one or other position. I remain an agnostic. Perhaps that is the point of the metaphor: The river changes, and if it is the Thames, it is tidal. It flows first this way, then that way. Whatever. If one or two artists stop complaining about the lack of essays on digital painting with any awareness at all of "the art scene"—of what makes painters tick, groupies crowd out art fairs, and critics scream in pleasure or pain—then I shall consider my mission half accomplished.

James Faure Walker
September 2005
j.faure-walker@camberwell.arts.ac.uk
www.dam.org/faure-walker

Acknowledgments

This book was written with the help of a three-year Senior Research Fellowship awarded to me in 2002 by the Arts and Humanities Research Council (AHRC) of the UK, undertaken at Kingston University. I must thank the AHRC for this invaluable opportunity, and for backing the principle of artists working as researchers. I have also benefited from colleagues at Kingston, and at Camberwell College of Arts, University of the Arts, London. For their longtime support and willingness to share ideas, I thank Anne Morgan Spalter, Hans Dehlinger, Wolfgang Lieser, Keith Watson, Roman Verostko, Matthew Collings, Sue Gollifer, Andrew Carnie, Victor Acevedo, Wolfgang Schneider, Cynthia Beth Rubin, Annette Weintraub, Ken Huff, Yoshiyuki Abe, Anna Ursyn, Rejane Spitz, Lane Hall, Lisa Moline, Joan Truckenbrod, Mike King, Karla Loring, Greg Garvey, Carole Robb, Cher Threinen-Pendarvis, Jeremy Sutton, Jeremy Gardiner, Dennis Leigh, Mark Zimmer, Perry Hoberman, Erkki Huhtamo, Lev Manovich, Mike Wright, Teal Triggs, Leo Duff, Angela Rogers, Janna Levin, Irving Sandler, and many others. I thank the production team at Prentice Hall, particularly Tyrrell Albaugh and Patty Boyd for their tolerance and meticulous attention to detail. Finally, I must express deep appreciation to my editor,

Peter Gordon, for his patience, encouragement, and such pleasant working lunches. My initial ideas were, to say the least, unformed, but he seemed to have faith in this project when it might so easily have come to nothing. I must also thank my wife, Vivien, and children, Josephine, Eddie, and Dulcie, for their unerring good sense and for now and then turning down the TV next door.

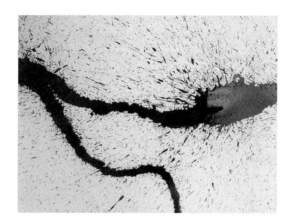

Chapter 1 **The Mud of the River**

Dipping into the Digital River

Rich Gold was as interesting a character as his name suggests. He was one of the best speakers I have ever come across. It was a shock to find out that he had died in 2003. I recall a long conversation we had in which he was complaining how the avant-garde of loft artists in New York were always aligned with the very poor and the very wealthy, but somehow no one was making art for the vast majority, the ordinary middle class. This had been the theme of the talk he gave at the ISEA (Inter Society for the Electronic Arts) conference in Rotterdam in 1996. Contemporary art was infested with the virus of snobbery, albeit an

1

inverted snobbery. It was a provocative point, and I pressed him to spell out what he meant and asked him, what would such an art be like? Perhaps we have it already—though when he said this, there was no Tate Modern, Bilbao Guggenheim, or revamped MoMA, and the phenomenon of the gigantic installation, the immersive, almost theme-park-like art experience was more talked about than real. At the same time, his point still holds, in that the top-rank art fairs present an extraordinary mixture of the superrich and the relatively impoverished. His point was that the dress code for "artist" still conformed to the Bohemian milieu, yet this was not the actual world artists lived in. In some respects he was out of date because even then younger artists were dressing in Armani suits instead of denim.

Among other talents, Gold was a jazz musician and a brilliant cartoonist. He had also been the instigator of artist-scientist research in the PAIR program at Xerox PARC (Palo Alto Research Center).[3] In 1993 he gave a cartoon-illustrated talk at the ISEA conference held in Minneapolis. The talk was entitled "The Ubi-Lunch-Box," where the lunch box served as a communications centre, sensor, computer, phone. The subject was really ubiquitous computing, which in 1993—in a pre-camera-phone and pre-Web era—was nothing like as routine an idea as it is now. He began his talk with a quotation: "We make art from the mud of our own river." The quote sounded familiar. In fact he had made it up. He had a good point. One way or another it would be absurd if our generation—our tribe—could not make significant art from the mud of our digital river.

But how could this be achieved? Would I need to work in a computer lab or a painting studio? At that time, computer art was still on the fringe and the significant works were like prototypes, suggestions of what might be possible a decade or two into the future. I wrote a report on the conference. Published in the mainstream journal *Modern Painters,* the article centred on the lunch-box idea and conveyed, I hoped, some of the excitement surrounding the first virtual-reality projects, such as Brenda Laurel's *Place Holder* and new modes of cyberart, such as biohacking. Like almost everyone else, I failed to notice that the big story was the emerging Internet.[4] The problem of finding the right form—or format—for shaping this "digital mud" was more open and speculative then—nowadays every college, museum, and art magazine has its circle of new-media experts. At that 1993 conference, Stephen Wilson, whose *Information Arts* is a formidable compendium of every conceivable branch of science-based digital art, spoke to a handful of fellow artists on how artists could cross over into research.[5] Arguing that the creative-genius stereotype of the artist was no longer credible, he predicted that artists in the new century would work directly in fields such as genetic engineering. They might create pet bacteria, patterns of green and purple slime moving round the living-room walls.

If you thought of committing yourself to that route—to work with virtual reality if not circus bacteria—this would have meant gaining access to lab equipment completely out of reach for any individual. You would need to worm yourself into a corporation or a campus research lab. From the opposite point of view, from someone deeply sceptical about the very possibility of computer art, given what then existed, you might think the only hope was to import a squad of "good artists" and let them loose on whatever equipment was available. This point was actually made by Jan Hoet, the keynote speaker and recent curator of *Documenta* in Kassel, Germany, the most influential art survey you could find anywhere in the world.

I was left somewhere in the middle, fascinated but also sceptical of all the attempts to force a new art into existence— aside from virtual reality, the other hot topic was artificial life. I

3

was repelled by the virtual-blob look of the simulated sculpture and by the simulated paper textures, while at the same time caught up in the attempts to get beyond the computer-art stereotype. Yes, much in the exhibitions had the look of art, but somehow it was not working as art. When I returned home I shuffled around painting exhibitions with some discontent. I found myself asking the same critical questions that I had asked of those electronic prototypes. I found the whole culture of contemporary painting not up to the test, and though pigments are literally mud in some cases, I saw that there was less of a challenge in making art from materials bought at the art store than from electronic components. I saw that Rich Gold did have a point.

Through the Studio Window

Some twelve years later, I am no clearer on how to mould this digital mud into something worthwhile. The digital-art movement—if it was a movement—has lost much of the momentum and coherence of that phase, and the mood now is considerably less utopian. *Digital art* is hardly a usable term, as it covers anything from Web art to printmaking, software to video. Blends of traditional and digital forms blur distinctions. Digital art is now also much less of a pioneering, or elitist, pursuit, and there are numerous Adobe Photoshop user groups and do-it-yourself magazines catering to hobbyists. You no longer need to go to the labs, but can, with a modestly priced laptop, run the programs that mesmerised those audiences. The digital part of digital art is nothing special now.

In my case the fundamental question is still the same: how to make substantial art and avoid the parody, the simulation-of-art effects—how to connect, so to speak, with the soul of art.

I am no saxophone player, and obviously, without that instrument, jazz would not be the way it is. But it is as if we were all missing the point in a big way, looking obsessively at what the fabulous instrument—the computer, the visual processor—could do, and not noticing that instead of a song, there was just a tinny cackle. Don't get me wrong; I am as excited as ever with what the upgrade can deliver. But given all the confident talk of new media conquering everything in its path, I am a little surprised that painting still looks a good bet. Incidentally, I don't like to see the term *traditional* applied to all painting, that is—if you like—predigital painting or pieces at least made out of actual paint, as if all those who work this way are thereby conservative and backward-looking. Yes, of course, there are tired and awful paintings everywhere, but equally, if you look up *digital painting* on Google, you find cat paintings and velveteen abstracts. If I think of the smartest, most innovative ideas around—even ideas about programming—they turn up in remarkably fresh-looking paintings.

Instead of working in my studio, I find myself turning over question after question about painting and the computer and often end up sketching out the next idea on the screen via my Wacom tablet. Why? Well, I can walk across the park to my painting studio, or I can sit at this desk in my digital paint studio. Unfortunately—or fortunately—this computer is also full of e-mail, news updates, cricket scores, and photos, and this is where I set down my thoughts. I shall soon have to give up on handwriting, as I cannot decipher my own scribbles. Let me think about this a little ... Am I going digital stage by stage without realising it? Are the paintings on canvas I am doing becoming less and less legible, even to me? All murky corners and unresolved mess, while the digital pictures I make through this machine are ultraclear, crisp and legible? Hardly.

I look out the window, daydream a little. It is apparently no bad thing to be "creatively" idle. (In jazz they call this wood-shedding.) I am surrounded by gadgets for inputting—the keyboard, a graphics tablet, a mouse, a microphone I rarely use, a camera (I don't actually have a scanner), Internet connectors—and it occurs to me that these are all substitutes. The data flows in and out of the memory, lingers a while, trickles away at shutdown. But these gadgets see nothing, hear nothing, remember nothing. As far as I know, they are not conscious. They are not aware. It is up to me. I am the only conscious sensor here. I have to be sure I absorb what I need, stay alert, keep in training. Keep to one drawing a day, keep taking photographs, keep playing around with that paint software. Is this what a painter does? Observing, responding, staying connected, but connected to what? Have I missed something?

> *Remember when creating art meant canvases and paint?*
> *And seeing art meant physically going to museums? Of*
> *course, we still have those options, but digital media have*
> *made computer graphics and virtual museum tours*
> *everyday modes of creation and viewing.*
> "Fine Art: Dramatic Digital Expression,"
> Web page for Apple Education, Digital Campus

It occurs to me that in dithering around in this state—don't get me wrong, sometimes I really do work relentlessly, blindly, along a straight arrow of determination, like a soldier on a mission—I may be part of something much larger. I don't want to speak of a widespread shift in painting culture; nothing connected with this is visible out my window, and how would you know if it was occurring or not? It sounds like lazy journalism. The point is, there are few activities that have not been shaken out of their old habits—banking, shopping, gambling, dating, dentistry—and there is nothing special about the digital invading painting, producing a cloned and virtual version, which threatens to replace the real thing. Just as the bank clerk fears being transferred to a call centre, with no face-to-face contact, so a painter like me worries about becoming abstracted and eliminated from the physical dimension. So I keep in contact, breathe the studio air—the turpentine fumes. Is that a reason for persisting?

Painting and new media? Some of my colleagues would not accept that. They work on the edge, without the warmth of nostalgia, without compromise. I recall one curator, a curator of new media at a major museum in Chicago, saying that painting was simply "over." Yes, there was plenty of activity in the area, even vital activity, but it was just going over old ground, repeating ad nauseam what had long become overfamiliar.

James Faure Walker, *Ideas and Music: Curiosity,* 2002, 68" × 92" (173 × 234 cm), oil on canvas. (See also Plate 2.)

Fine, I said, but can you point out the works in new media that carry that sting of real innovation? Quality, too? Difficult, she said. Like me, she had seen, or been immersed in, most of the works often cited as classics—*Osmose* by Char Davies, *Legible City* by Jeffrey Shaw, *Interactive Plant Growing* by Christa Sommerer and Laurent Mignonneau—but had reservations about all of them. These were simply not up there with Picasso or Pollock. Her point, quite a forceful one, was that they were prototypes, leading the way, shots in the dark. Once the next generation had come to terms with them, the real stuff would emerge. Just be patient. For now it was promise, not delivery. You could say the same of early-twentieth-century classics—I think of Malevich and Duchamp—not for what they are but for how they turned familiar ideas of art upside down.

Yes, new-media art is a gift for anyone wanting to start a combative seminar about the future of art. It is a tangle full of the wildest speculation and imponderables. I do find much less of a challenge in conversations with my fellow painters. Images of dogs, patterns, flags, or splodges of colour . . . who cares? Painters just feel besieged, unnecessarily ingrown, and defensive about their art form. They are always talking of how "the art world" is ignoring painting in favour of video, installation art, and new media. Whether this is really the case or not, it has led to a mind-set that is resentfully detached from the idea of progress. Not in all cases—there are many bright sparks—but when painters complain that opportunities are denied them, they sometimes have only themselves to blame. They have boxed themselves in. Ordinarily, I try not to think of painting as something old and worn out, something tarnished and appreciated—like a vintage car—only because of its complete irrelevance to modern life. It can be difficult. For some visitors to a painting studio, the smell of turpentine and linseed oil is enough to trigger instant nostalgia—the equivalent of old

THE MUD OF THE RIVER

leather and engine oil. But I think of painting as an art form that can capture, and exist in, the present moment, so that at its best we see through the same eyes that Cézanne looked through to paint those trembling views of Mont Sainte-Victoire.

Of course, it is not the format of painting that makes it resilient, and ever renewable, but the life that resurges through it, the very idea of what a painting can be, and in painting, generation after generation of new talent finds fresh points of view. The question then is how the next generation will deal with this prospect of digital painting. I can't imagine the technology will be ignored. But how the digital and the painterly come together is the tough part. As I write this I check what is happening in the run of electronic festivals that fill the summer months. At ISEA, held this year in Finland on a ship, the theme is the Sonic, Wearable, and Wireless Experience. The focus is on the video jockeys, networked sound projects, fantastic worlds just round the corner—no place there for painting, thank you very much. Painting is not exactly the hot topic of the moment. I get an e-mail from a painter friend who has been working in Venice and whose work is steeped in art-historical resonance. She has just sold a set of gouaches to a museum—which seems to complete another kind of circle. It bears out too what my curator friend was suggesting, that painting is no longer a vital force, it just plays the old favourites over and over and picks up the rewards. To get out of that closed circle, you have to make a radical leap. Wearable networked painting, cell-phone images? I won't rule that out just yet.

Charts

Realising that this essay could grow alarmingly, I look around to see where I might be heading. I can only start out with a handful of visual metaphors, which may well be discarded along the

9

route. First, the whole culture of painting up to the 1960s could be represented as a map with many radiating centres, edges fading away into prehistory, with ebbs and flows of influence ... Siena, Florence, Bruges, Paris, New York, till the present landscape, where all kinds of networks overlap on a global scale. But by zooming right in and going backward and forward in time, you could see that the studios themselves had not changed so very much over the centuries and that art education had not altered very much till the 1960s. By and large, learning to paint involved years of practice with materials, handling the brush, learning the techniques of the old masters, and understanding the iconography, the history, stage by stage. It could not be hurried or compressed into a six-week course. In fact, as late as 1960, students in Britain were still following the ancient system of first drawing from plaster casts of classical sculpture for a year or two, then graduating to drawing the live model, and only at the end moving up to paints. Roaming around the map, you could see that painters' prospects were driven by the church, by trade, by the vanity of patrons, by fashion, by doctrines, by the artists' own wilfulness.

Then, with digital technology, a map with a quite different set of patterns is laid over this ancient parchment, with its stains and scars and meandering paths. Sometimes the new template fits; sometimes it just doesn't correspond at all—it has no historical dimension, no depth. I am thinking not just of the Web, the incredibly intricate network of connections that now links millions of artists instantaneously, but of the changing architecture of studios, even their disappearance. Studios have been customised workspaces for generations: old leaking sheds, sometimes grand salons or minimalist galleries to put a client at ease. Can that whole dense culture of painting be contained in a shrink-wrapped pack of software?

It is not so far-fetched to imagine a human skill being

replaced by a box. Some years ago I was interviewed for a job teaching digital art at a college in Cornwall. When being shown round the studios, one of the candidates asked what had happened to the previous tutor doing the job. The answer was evasive: She had run off with the printer. I imagined a couple eloping hand-in-hand over the hills along the cliff top. But no. The equipment had been pinched. I still think of the studio printmaker as someone wearing a brown apron, coping with shelves of arcane chemicals. On the desktop, the printer is the machine housed in a beige plastic box.

Pre and Post

One way to think about the mismatch between the pre- and postdigital is to concentrate on the difference. First, it is the speed. We can produce paintings and other images incredibly fast, in minutes, whereas "real" oil paintings can take days, weeks, months, years, because of drying times. Of course, you can work physically at the accelerated pace of a digital drawing, making an image in a few seconds. This is one simple lesson I have learned from painting digital, though it does not mean you cannot also work on a much-extended timescale. I look at drawings with more attention to the pace at which they were made. I recreate the way a line has travelled, often preferring an efficient and economic line to one full of mannerisms, indecision, and dutiful in-filling. Critics generally have preferred the economy of a seemingly casual elegance, but I have caught myself going round exhibitions of drawings with the eyes of a typographer or graphic designer, for whom redundant information is a no-no. I even begin wondering whether some methods of drawing and painting seem dated and unsatisfactory to me, not just because I find the style tired and irrelevant, but because the technique is so gratingly inefficient. This attitude is, of course, quite unreasonable, but it is also an interesting exercise, like expecting paintings to compete directly with photographs, and I would guess that manuscript scribes had to undergo some traumatic retraining once the printed book became the norm. But when a museum collection has an agenda, such as Tate Britain, which is dedicated to British art, and where the quality at some periods in the twentieth century slips embarrassingly below par (such as an exhibition of Augustus and Gwen John, painters highly regarded in their own time), the comparison is handy. Though the "Is it art?" question is regularly thrown at contemporary art and digital art, we should sometimes ask this question about reputations that in their own time looked rock solid.

Painters a hundred years ago might not have thought of oil painting as a particularly slow method. Impressionists had completed paintings in a day, or in a morning, but the nature of oil paint would dictate that the brushing would be dabs of wet paint applied individually and not overlapping too much, or the technique of working thicker paint over a thin, wet layer in a technique known as "wet in wet." There would not have been much else on the menu of options, and then you would need to wait a few days before that layer was dry or could be "dropped." In comparison, drawing (except drawing in ink or watercolour) is a dry and instantaneous medium. Drawing could be done in a hurry, in seconds on the back of an envelope, and painting required more time—preparing a canvas could take six months if using a lead white ground.

Though the "brushes" and "paints" on a paint program can be called oil, watercolour, crayon, and charcoal, their characteristics are really evened out and they can be made to behave the same. Oil "dries" at the same rate as the graphite of the pencil. This may not be significant initially, because any painter familiar with the behaviour—I can almost say the psychology

12

associated with these differences, some impulsive, some requiring patience and great care—would use the paint in an equivalent way. It is interesting that paint software is the ultimate step in fabricating "convenience" paint. Artists' materials have long been produced in different grades, with the student range being the cheapest and easiest to use, and the artist range the most expensive. Student pigments are mixed so every colour has roughly the same covering power as every other. The more expensive pigments in the artist range each have their own peculiarities: Cobalt blues, greens, and violets have a granular, translucent quality, which can be wrecked in mixtures; the green from the oxide of chromium is a dead, heavily opaque pigment; Indian yellow looks like a brownish ochre, but stains as a luminous yellow. The same is true of media and brushes, with numerous peculiar specialist brushes available outside the standardised range made available for the student or hobbyist. But if eventually the paint of the paint program became the norm, the different behaviours of oil paint and charcoal would be unnecessary knowledge and the connection with physically real materials no more than a distant association. The terms would refer simply to a different look, a different visual texture, a different number on a dial. You could as easily describe the different paints as different fruits, countries, insects.

When a new paint appears and artists take to it, then painting does seem to turn a corner. I recall the excitement over acrylic paint, which became generally available in the 1960s and could dry within the hour. The magazine *Studio International* would carry back-page advertisements featuring artists on ladders completing murals that would have been impossible with oils—acrylics were much simpler to use, the colour was more saturated and covered better, and the paint was more durable. The murals were actually quite uninteresting in themselves. In fact, the development of acrylics had made possible the large-scale "stain paintings" of Helen Frankenthaler and Morris Louis a decade earlier, at which point the artists found it more effective to pour the diluted paint directly onto the unprimed canvas, controlling the paint's spread with sponges or by suspending the loose canvas between trestles. These paintings were to have a huge influence and initiated what became known as colour field painting. There is not a perfect analogy here with the new "paint" of the paint program, but it does demonstrate how, given the need, a new technology can play a part in opening up an art form. One technology that was also advertised, but on the back pages of *Art News* in the 1950s, was the completely artificial acrylic canvas, with a lifespan of hundreds of years. It never caught on. Moreover, after the surge of interest in acrylics, oil paint is still the preferred medium for most painters today.

Even an acrylic painting, and especially a thin stain painting, which is one-shot with no possible revision, is no match for the speed at which a digital painting can be made and manipulated, its colour inverted and corrected, its forms collaged. True, this is only a model, a virtual painting, but at the rate that inkjet and other printers are both improving and becoming more affordable, the virtual nature of digital may become far less of an issue. As Photoshop becomes second nature for painters, a corresponding way of looking at paintings in terms of "filters" and "layers" may emerge as a sensibility. Seventeenth-century Dutch interiors seem to have become easier to see, and to appreciate, with the advent of photography because they had a photographic look to them. Perhaps I won't be alone in finding the clarity and vacuumed atmosphere of much medieval and early Renaissance painting particularly appealing because the works have that deliberate, piece-by-piece "assemblage" structure of primitive 3D-rendered visualisation. Marketing has given us such phrases as *real time* and *air*, which mean the ability to collage clips of video and text live during a news broadcast. It is not painters—the fine-art lobby—who have driven this demand for speed. We have to thank the TV, film, and games industries.

The digital is different in a fundamental sense; it is in a different category. Even if it is a perfect simulation, it is still a simulation. This may be blatantly obvious, but it is worth always bearing in mind. In the earlier phases of computer art, the difference would be self-consciously underlined, either through the staccato repetition of line or through science-fiction fantasy. The images were strange, often strange in the extreme, and announced clearly that they were not real. They were immaterial, of the same substance as mathematics. Jasia Reichardt, the curator of *Cybernetic Serendipity* at London's Institute of Contemporary Art (ICA) in 1968, has often emphasised that the exhibits were not necessarily intended as works of art. They were to be seen as experiments, prototypes. In the Computer Art Society's journal, *Page,* John Lansdown, a founder of the society, takes issue with Frieder Nake (one of the first computer artists to exhibit in an art gallery, in 1965) for falling into the trap of "equating computer art with computer graphics. . . . [H]is whole argument seems to be based on conclusions drawn from the output of computer graphicists."[6] Lansdown makes the point that as a "proceduralist," he and most of his colleagues are interested in the process going on inside the computer as much as the object produced. *Output* is a dirty word. What they were after was the distinctive, creative contribution that happened in the processing. For them, that was the mud.

I met John Lansdown a few times some years after this, in the 1980s, and owe him a debt, simply for his encouragement. I also recall with some embarrassment a complete clash of cultures, taking issue with him over whether computational logic really had much to do with creativity. He would cite the way Mozart might begin by throwing the dice. My perspective, like that of most other wide-eyed newcomers, was only made possible because we could buy off-the-shelf software and plug the processor into a printer. We could superimpose our painterly way of thinking over the simulation. To purists like Lansdown, it must have seemed no more than a superficial diversion, a preoccupation with output at the expense of process.

From the 1970s to the 1990s, it seemed that whatever emerged from the experimentation would be significantly different and a step away from the existing way of thinking about the art object. Computer artists believed that "traditional" artists would carry on in a state of computer illiteracy; whatever you could do with a computer would stand in contrast to the dumb, handcrafted painting. Computer-generated images would run alongside the mainstream, but the two streams would never flow together. But once it was possible for a nonspecialist, a nonprogrammer, to find his or her way round a paint program—literally in my case, since the early programs had huge program route maps pinned to the wall—the balance would shift. Painters could become expert users themselves and challenge the notion that the automated choices made in coded procedures amounted to anything special. Artists would begin by looking and thinking about output and work backward, to see what they could do. *Postdigital* applied to painting is best understood as having sufficient know-how to choose the appropriate method.

All the same, using the accumulated ingenuity of several generations of programmers and engineers—all this expertise— to help produce something as conventional and "dumb" physically as a painting is probably not what the pioneer computer artists had in mind. It would be like admitting that human intelligence was already implicit in the art of painting, its raison d'être, its patterns of images and symbols, and these patterns were too subtle for the robot's thinking process. And how would the robot artist ever cruise its way through the private views and make bitchy small talk? Ironically, after all the high-speed processing and incredible gadgetry, we might end up where we started: The pigments reconstituted from the mud of the river itself become the output.

It happens to be one of the neglected questions, because one naturally assumes—it is what all the marketing says—that the traffic is one way: Why, when you have tasted the digital, would you want to go back to old-world ways? Well, perhaps you preferred the real thing after all and you wanted to figure out how to incorporate the new and the old, a combination that somehow makes something interesting out of the difference.

Thinking again of that second layer, that template of digital culture imposed on the older map of painting culture, we see that a further difference concerns direction and chronology. In the predigital map, the part that gave you a rough idea of where you were according to the contemporary landmarks, you could work out how you were connected to the past and where you were heading. There were these vague zones: abstract, figurative, photorealist, postmodern, pop, minimal, conceptual, expressionist, surrealist. You can still follow those routes in digital simulations, but now the whole landscape has found itself reshaped. Distances, even the time lags (like the echoes of a transatlantic phone call), seem to have disappeared. When the CD first appeared in the early 1980s, one of its surprises was that you could switch instantly between tracks without messing around holding the stylus arm. The switch from analogue to digital is only a tiny factor in flattening out historical perspectives—often tagged by the catchall phrase *postmodernism.* In the 1990s, art museums themselves seemed to lose confidence in art history, as if any step-by-step chronology was an imposition of an outmoded master plan in which history equals progress. When Tate Modern opened for the first time in 2000, the rooms were arranged by headings: Landscape/Matter/

Environment, History/Memory/Society, or Nude/Action/Body. Paintings and objects from quite separate places and periods were juxtaposed. The stately procession of art history gave way to a scattergun seminar of arbitrary compare-and-contrast exercises. At the time, the gallery was heavily criticised for being "look and learn" and patronising. It became like surfing through an online gallery—a student has been given a theme in an art history essay—and the Web had been reproduced in the real gallery. Every artefact is accessible from anywhere.

The past decades have been a confusing period, because at the same time that the sense of progress was being shaken out of art history by well-meaning curators and opinion formers, the evidence of progress in technology was staring you in the face on your desktop. Twenty years ago the monitor would probably have shown you chunky green text on a black background. The Apple G5 that I use today has a speed of 2 GHz; two years ago the Apple PowerBook had a speed of 867 MHz.[7] Six years ago the G3 was 350 MHz, before that the Apple PowerPC 7100 was 33 MHz, before that the Commodore Amiga was 7 MHz, and the one I used twenty years ago had a speed of 1 MHz. From twenty years ago to now is an increase by a factor of two thousand. From eight or sixteen colours, I now have millions.

So this mud is not quite the unchanging, washed-through silt or spongy clay that I might have expected. Each year, its chemistry, or at least its molecular clock-speed, goes off the chart. Meanwhile the elders in the village all say that history is an illusion, nothing really changes. Art is art whatever it is made of.

Good-Bye Futurism

How can a painting possibly compete with that flat-screen TV? It is like the wall furniture of another epoch. Should painting adapt and "go digital" in some way? Become something else?

18

Dive into the Internet? How would a painting be recognizably a painting, rather than a page of Web graphics? Why should it be a still, silent, and noninteractive image? Or should it carry on much the same, indifferent, as if Photoshop, Google, and the Sony PlayStation did not exist? Perhaps it should. That could be the point of continuing to paint: to stand solid against the techno future, to stand for something earthy, something rough and agricultural—pigments, oils, canvas, hog-hair brushes. Painting doesn't fit the digital lifestyle. The brush mark is human and imperfect, something unrepeatable that cannot be simulated. Ask a painter who dislikes computer images why; the answer is always the same: the absence of touch, of texture, of feeling.

In my case, when those friends ask whether I am "still painting," they must suppose that it is only a matter of time before my digital conversion is complete. I should be able to put a coherent answer together, but I can't. I don't know what to say, except that I am comfortable using both digital and physical paint; one does not necessarily replace the other. But I am not comfortable. I am indecisive. There are too many points of view, too many questions. But this also intrigues me. I like to think there could be a dialogue across the divide, but it happens rarely. It is a fundamental rift.

Though digital artists do it all the time, it is not helpful to speak of painting as a totality, blurring any differentiation between past and present, professionals and hobbyists, and ignoring the deep divisions between conservatives and radicals. Nor is there a clear consensus among critics as to which direction painting may be heading, and every potential tendency claims to be at the centre. There are ultracool abstract painters and photorealists who have no problem at all with joining the digital club. Some expressionists, some primitives, self-conscious "slackers" owing something to performance art, value directness above all, and they oppose computers on principle. Retired art teachers use the PC for painting. There is no mess, the computer takes up little room, and it is altogether more convenient. There is some expense, but not the expense of building that extension on the back of the house for a studio.

Not so long ago, talk about art and the computer was futuristic. You were gazing across the horizon and up into the sky: What happens to art when it goes into cyberspace? Ten years ago John Browning, the editor of *Wired UK* asked me this question when discussing an article I was doing. It was a reasonable question. Art might shift up into that realm, that semi-material state, and still be art, but it might have had its molecules reconstituted, as in *The Fly*. Now the question strikes me as one that no one today but a sociologist or an economist would think to ask. *Wired UK* was a short-lived offshoot of *Wired*, a magazine that in 1995 seemed to encapsulate the utopianism of the Web—it was the magazine for and by the people "defining the future." Uploading art into cyberspace would be just another day's work for the revolutionaries. But art has not changed very much, not on the surface. After a flurry of energetic Internet art and online museum collections, the novelty has passed: As with banking and booking a flight, the Web is just "there." People talk as engagingly about eBay as they do about the "paradigm shift" of the disembodied art work. You can shop for your groceries online, but the groceries—you hope—will be real. That is all there is to it.

In the 1990s the new millennium loomed ahead as the horizon line, with a new civilisation just on the other side. Initiated by the millennium bug was a new form of art, labelled *new-media art:* interactive, virtual, and immaterial. Mutation was the buzzword, *Mute* the magazine. For a while digital art seemed to be all about envisioning the future. It would look beyond traditional art in the same way that science fiction looks beyond science. The new art would be exotic, mind-blowing, quite unlike boring, noninteractive, static, "old" art. That was the theory. Naturally we—the brave pioneer technoartists—would be right at the centre carrying the flag. A new consciousness!

Well, nothing quite that spectacular has happened, so far. Instead the more noticeable changes have been small-scale and allow us a more mobile lifestyle—camera phone, laptop, iPod. In the mid-1990s, a TV series called *Wild Palms* foresaw virtual reality at play everywhere. Before then, some artists were excited that with the brand-new CD-ROM player (initially it was separate from the PC) they could be piping their pictures into every sitting room in the country via the TV screen. They thought of the work as being ultimately static paintings on large, flat screens. Instead, the PlayStation arrived, and you could argue that that is a kind of art, too. One painting student I taught some years back—when the Royal College of Art still had a Computing department—went into that world. He used to explain to me the elaborate pretesting involved in getting the visuals right for the game (this in lengthy calls from California to London). Some years later, he was calling about the painting shows he was in.

How can a digital artist—perhaps a dilettante, perhaps a really committed painter—find a format, a technology niche, something that won't be swept aside by the next wave of lifestyle marketing? Can't we be active participants in this, not just consumers looking on? Is the best we can hope for to be providers of content for a Web site or for a cute image on a cell phone? The "painted" sets in a car chase game? Even if a painter wants nothing to do with computers, the world outside the studio is not what it was. Conservative artists have cell phones and Web sites and use scanners and inkjet printers to reproduce watercolours of Elizabethan cottages. TV news is instant and global; tourists send back photos on cell phones, and children gossip by text messaging. Nor can the digital artist afford to stand still and miss two upgrades in a row. Year by year another part of the vocabulary becomes a cliché—*fractal, cyberspace, virtual reality, bit stream,* and probably *digital* and *wireless* will soon become too embarrassing to use in an exhibition title. Before 2000, digital shows had titles like "the future is now." Not anymore.

Floating

"Floating Window" sounds like a good title for a long essay on the subject of the ambivalent and inconclusive thoughts of a digital painter or someone trapped between the ancient and the modern. It has a mystical, even Oriental, tinge to it—Edo, the Floating World. I would like to think that any linkup between the nongravitational, mathematical optics of computer graphics and the muddy, wet, dripping pigment of old-style painting did not have to end up as a weakened mixture. Perhaps the images would float before your eyes; perhaps they would be inscribed and splashed in the most insistently heavy material you could imagine, something in the manner of one of Tapies's great paintings or the more theatrical and overdone Kiefers. I would hope that the digital window would be first and foremost about release, freedom, a way out, an opening onto a new space.

I would also start thinking of the sense of detachment and distance in painting and how the window on the desktop or a layer in Photoshop can float from one context to another. Painters often block out the windows of a studio to get more wall space and to avoid distractions. A window is also an opportunity, a hole in the schedule. In that broader sense, computer graphics offers the painter a completely new window, as dramatic an innovation as perspective or photography. I want to touch on "wicked problems"—problems that aren't too easy to define, but are always kicking around somewhere just out of reach. Just as books on popular science provide windows onto landscapes as weird as anything in science fiction, be they the vertiginous dimensions of the universe, the tiniest particles, the unpredictability of massive prime numbers, or the world of the trilobite, so have computer graphics created windows that must excite anyone with an interest in painting.

These windows open on the past as much as onto the future—the early Netherlands painters would have windows on either side of the Virgin Mary, so that the earthly contemporary landscape outside is the setting for the sacred interior. In so many respects, the devices, the optical controls, the rectilinear logic of the paint program, have the character of a Renaissance drawing machine. I cannot help wondering what earlier generations of artists would have made of such technical marvels. Paradoxically, the PC crept into the home just when—generally speaking—artists least needed it, when the mechanistic and fiercely visual painting of the 1960s had been superseded by the monochrome self-denial of minimal art. Technology and optimism gave way to the uncertainties, the pessimism, the ideological hectoring, even the romanticism of the postmodernism of the 1970s and 1980s. "Real paint"—or a simulation so effective it is called "natural media"—arrived just when many serious painters were putting their paints away for good.

One potential use for a paint simulator would be to train and rehearse what you might do on the real canvas afterward. This would only make sense if there were no question of the virtual's replacing the real. In a sophisticated virtual studio, the painter, like the pilot on a flight simulator, could learn to anticipate all the possible contingencies and disasters and then, with all that expertise absorbed into the reflexes, paint—or fly—the real thing. If you book a flight to the other side of the world, you don't worry that the cockpit has an autopilot and computers monitoring every function. But you do mean to travel somewhere. You wouldn't want the whole thing to be virtual, spending twenty-four hours sitting behind a pilot in a simulator. By the same token, you might prefer a "real painting" to an image on a screen, an inkjetted canvas, a print, or a projection on the wall. In a painting, you would not necessarily want something flawless and accident free—though that is just what you want from air travel. That is one point of view. But I am not convinced by the analogy, because a painting itself is a simulation, a pretend window, an illusion. Even when the painted surface is emphatically physical, emphatically opaque as though the view through is blocked—literally so in some abstract paintings with blocks of colour looming forward—you tend to look at that surface with a special kind of attention, as if it were some kind of window.[8] A landscape painting may be technically primitive in comparison with the view through a virtual flight deck, but both attempt to take viewers out of themselves to another place.

As a device, the window is common to a painting and the computer desktop, a device for framing your attention and organizing information. Without computer windows, there would be no way to differentiate, to sort categories, functions, effects, yet alone to work intuitively with them. Take them away, go back to the pre-windows epoch, to the pre GUI—graphic user interface—and we would stumble to a halt as we reached for the manual to remember the commands we had to type in to make anything happen. In painting, we think of the canvas as a window, a view onto a landscape, into a room, into some imaginary world, or even a view denied as a flat surface. In the paint program, the canvas is the window you work on, and if, like me, you lack self-discipline, you may well have other windows open—BBC News. Before anyone ever had a radio or a computer in a studio, I expect there was always something going on next door, somewhere to break for lunch. These desktop windows, these screens, have a dual role: You may be connected by e-mail and can visit exhibitions all over the world, but you are also isolated, physically disconnected.

Chapter 2 **A Bend in the River**

Beginners

None of us starts out as an expert, in art or in software or in the art of combining the two. We all start as beginners, and some of us never lose those first impressions—thrill, bafflement, exasperation, boredom, triumph. It doesn't matter that we begin loving art—or technology—for the wrong reasons. In my case it was first of all the smell of hog-hair brushes in the village art shop in Sussex and the white impasto of seaside paintings. Then much later, after drizzly greys and greens, it was Colour!—on the fizzing, pixel-jagged Apple II. Nor does it matter that we turn against art from time to time. What matters is that the enthusiasm remains and carries us forward, makes us curious about what lies round the corner. I confess that I get excited by each upgrade and rush to try out the new gizmo; I also get excited in the art store when I find an exotic brush or a pigment I have never seen before. Shopping may not be an art form or the kind of research that earns you a PhD, but I would never have learned about painting, or about computers, without a great deal of window shopping.

I learned about both painting and computer graphics first as a complete outsider, by looking at the tools, the way things were made. It is curious that when we are young we probably only think of painting as something we can do ourselves— *painting* means pots of colour—and it is natural to become fascinated by the mixture of tools in the painter's studio. Asked about painting and the computer, the seven-year-old is more likely to connect with something the child himself or herself has "painted" on the screen. The only way to learn about it is to do it. And yet when it comes to adulthood, there lies this sharp division between the makers, the interpreters, and the consumers. There are the insiders, the intermediaries, and the outsiders, professionals and amateurs: on the one side the boxes of paints, or the boxed software, with their how-to-do-it instructions; and on the other the catalogues, the anthologies, the critical writing that signals what is in, what is out, and what it all may or may not mean. Before the gramophone, the radio, and the TV, many households would have only known live music through the piano; even if you didn't play yourself, or played appallingly, you would know instinctively how music was made. Player and listener were connected—both of you would be in the same room. The household computer is both a medium you can use passively—download music or images—or actively as an instrument. By reading and playing by sight the sheet music sold weekly in the 1920s, you could say the piano was also a machine for reproducing music. But by learning to play bit by bit you gain a different kind of knowledge from what you learn by slipping the CD in the player and reading the sleeve notes.

So it was the *paint box*—a term used for Quantel's paint system—that held all the secrets: the rows of colours, the clean brushes, and the bottles of turpentine and linseed oil. There are people who collect artists' materials and never use them. They don't want to mess up that initial impression. I can understand that. Other people collect software far beyond what they need, just because they are fascinated.

The major annual computer conference, SIGGRAPH, is held at a different US city each year but now most frequently at the Los Angeles Convention Center. The conference is divided into a commercial exhibition of hardware and software, an academic conference with papers on new research, and exhibitions of emerging technology, art, animations, and games. So you have machines, theories, and playtime. Sometimes the machines win out. Nothing else is as bizarre. Gadgetry that was dreamt up in the laboratories becomes a consumer product in just a few years, but there is a peculiar halfway stage where it is neither one thing nor the other, and no one knows quite what the consumer is going to make of it.

Learning How to Move

A gentle way of establishing your authority when lecturing to a fresh group of students is to ask if there are any Photoshop experts present. You have to make clear, first of all, that your own knowledge is quite limited. If the experts do volunteer, they can be a help to their fellow students, but in practice it usually turns out that they know considerably less than they think they know. I found out early on that there is an unspoken etiquette in this field: Don't overreach or claim to know what you don't know; admit your ignorance. That makes sharing knowledge easier.

The SIGGRAPH conference is fascinating in this regard. I could be sitting having a coffee and find two people opposite earnestly discussing chip design. Joining the conversation—and this is something I know next to nothing about—I realise there is a distant connection with my field, in that the better the drawing tools for designing the circuits, the better the chips, the faster the processors, the better the tools, and so on. How could a sculptor be useful in a courtroom? The answer, I discovered, was in 3D visualisation, because 3D animation, sometimes mixed in with real models, is used to reconstruct traffic accidents. In the 1980s, few forecasters would have predicted any connection between puppeteers and computing, but once motion capture arrived, puppeteers were in demand in the animation industry. So, the changing use in tandem with the changing technology keeps the ecology turning over. Experts sometimes do not realise they are experts until someone else discovers that their expertise is just what they need.

My initial reaction to finding several live drawing classes— that is to say, life drawing except that the model was in a bikini— at the SIGGRAPH conference was that this showed we had passed the high-water mark. The classes took place on the commercial exhibition floor, right beside booths promoting high-end 3D animation software, graphics cards, and motion-capture suits. The pencil-and-paper method seemed like a return to basics. The technology can do all this, but you still need to draw. That was a superficial reaction, but also a half-truth. Several of my colleagues who teach computing to art students had come to the same conclusion. Unless they can draw from observation and learn to persist and get better, the students will have a hard time grasping even the most basic design principles, such as figure and field, foreground and background, composition, light and shade, and the flow of line.

Life drawing is something of a cult in art schools, something either done for its own sake, an act of faith in "traditional values," or something to scoff at; it no longer has a direct function, as for example a preparatory study for a figure composition. But I was wrong to look at these elementary drawing classes—elementary to say the least in that the instructor reduced the figure to a cylinder for the torso and a circle for the head—as art therapy. I have a friend, Jeanine Breaker, who for some years has been teaching life drawing in the leading animation studios in Los Angeles. She speaks of the limits of realism in animation, of the human, the boy in *Toy Story,* and how unconvincing he is compared with the toys. The way he moves around is all wrong. That is how she began getting work. She showed the animation studios that you need to know some anatomy, to understand the way the body shifts according to whether the weight is through the right or the left foot; you need to know what happens to the shoulder muscles when the head turns. These were lessons drummed into you when life drawing was still taught by elderly "experts" who would think nothing of erasing your whole drawing before showing you how the thorax connected with the pelvis. It was as if the studios expected the technology to do it all, but by the time they discovered how much the software could not do, it was too late. They had lost the intuitive understanding you acquire through drawing the figure as a routine, day after day. They relied on the visualisation alone. They had lost the knack of seeing where and how it went wrong.

Jeanine herself is neither an animator nor an academic realist, but a painter. It interested me that someone dedicated to the still image should be able to help out so much with the moving image. I would normally think of any sustained piece of animation, especially a fully 3D piece, as an impressive technical feat, even if the narrative or the actual aesthetic quality did not win me over. I have dabbled enough in animation to know what is involved. She tells the story of a friend who has a well-earned reputation for her commercial animations and who is used to considerable success. This friend decides she is really a painter. She rents a studio space, spends several months making some carefully produced and, to her mind, equally professional paintings, and arranges a group exhibition where they can be seen. At the opening she is distressed. No one is looking at her work. They don't even notice. Their backs are to it while they chat. Paintings are just wall furniture. Background. Welcome to the real world, says Jeanine. Animation catches the eye; you don't have to work for the attention.

Another Admirable Invention

Digital shortcuts take much of the labour, the chores, out of painting. Whether you think this cheapens the art form or opens up an entirely new universe depends on your point of view. It could be doing both. In Japanese the ideogram for opportunity is the same as the one for problem. No one could expect to modify long-established methods without some disruption, but those traditional methods may not have been as permanent as they seem with hindsight. We see rows of paintings, century after century, in solidly built museums and imagine equally solid traditions to have been laid out for the old masters and pioneers of modern art. But that is an illusion. For the most part they worked amid rival schools and styles, with as much uncertainty, in ramshackle studios with all kinds of technical recipes and gadgetry, old and new. What we see is the tiniest percentage of what went on. If there were traditions, academies, and dogmas, there were also disputes and professional rivalries, generations that overlapped and misunderstood each other, and old and new "technologies" that could happily run alongside each other.

In 1854 Eugene Delacroix was fifty-five. He was shown the photographic etching process. To a friend he wrote: "How sorry I am that this admirable invention should have come so late, as far as I am concerned."[9] Photography permeated the world of the nineteenth-century painter, and it is a truism to say that its influence was as much in the way these painters perceived their surroundings as in the technical shortcuts that came their way. As with the emergence of the home PC, nothing changed overnight. It was not the core invention itself that made the difference, but the availability of affordable and convenient cameras: the equivalent of today's peripherals like scanners, printers, and digital cameras, which we now take for granted but which twenty years ago were "high end." Though photography came to be recognised, eventually, as an art form in its own right, its impact on painting was complex and diffuse, and in part the impact was the effect of photography on society as a whole. Photography did not replace painting wholesale like a universal upgrade—though its impact was irreversible. The camera was much more than a useful studio accessory, a gadget for capturing scenery and snapping portraits, churning out reproductions of paintings. The Kodak camera may not have "caused" impressionism, cubism, surrealism, abstraction, and postmodernism, but if a time traveller went back and uninvented the camera, then art in the twentieth century would have been a completely different story.

The impact of the computer on painting may or may not be following a similar pattern, but it is useful to bear some of these parallels in mind. An art form need not disappear because a new technology comes along and takes over its functions. It can be reinvented to accommodate the technology, and it can find new functions. The roots of painting, like the roots of dance, music, theatre, and literature, go back a long way. The digital technology that can now simulate paint is awesome, but the problem—or opportunity—of absorbing that impact may itself be an old and familiar problem.

The Road to Extinction?

Digital painting does already exist as a hybrid genre, with how-to books, star artists, anthologies of expert practitioners, and user blogs debating the relative merits of digital and traditional brushes. But digital painting tends toward commercial illustration and leisure painting, and the fantasy dragons, cybermen, and proudly authentic Messerschmitt 109s of World War II comics would send a shiver through the aficionados of "real" painting. Not a shiver of terror but a shiver of laughter. The typical images presented as the work of experts, as the most accomplished digital art, can look no better than the direst clichés; they don't connect with the "informed" end of art at all—except as a kitsch form of antimatter. The contemporary shows you find at Tate Modern, MoMA, or the Pompidou Centre would only admit these works as "popular culture," a kind of folk art. Yet when that world of *biennales* and critical discourse peers into the digital world, its view is clouded by its own ignorance: For years the digital would crop up as something futuristic, weird, alienated, and too exotic to understand.

Postdigital painting is a label that might get round the difficulty; at least it would if the term meant anything. It was the title of an exhibition at the Cranbrook Museum in 2003. It prompted these observations from a reviewer:

> Is traditional painting on the road to extinction? First there
> was the photography revolution that resulted in pictures

being made by pressing a button. Then came the computer to codify vision electronically. Can handcrafted painting on canvas survive such radically changing technology?[10]

I am normally involved in the day-to-day problems of making paintings, and I happen to love the way cameras, projectors, printers, software, can all work together. I don't see that any of this makes "handcrafted painting" obsolete, or digital painting better, more advanced, or more radical. I actually become more enthusiastic about the characteristics of several favourite brushes and try all sorts of unorthodox techniques—a drop of spirit in watercolour, for example, or an old electric toothbrush—to make some digital ideas work on the studio floor.

As far as I know, there is no panic in the galleries and no sign that a supercharged, high-performance kind of painting is pushing everything else to the side. Anything but. Most of the digital painting I come across is embarrassing only in being—in painting terms—terrible. It is pretentious, and predictable. The argument in its defence has been that its time will come and that we haven't yet learned either how to make it properly or how to look at it. It is an argument that after a decade or two sounds hollow. How long do we have to wait? Centuries? Or perhaps next week an exhibition will make me eat these words. Perhaps there could be much better ways of bringing together the knowledge of painting and the knowledge of the digital paint.

Blinking, Thinking

I spend much of my time wondering how best to combine the baffling freedom of the digital palette with "real" painting. Sometimes I think my generation has stumbled across the ultimate painting machine, the perfect instrument, but we haven't a clue what to do with it. Does it replace the haute cuisine of traditional painting with convenience food? It could just be a passing fascination with speed and novelty. Quality goes out of the window.

Now that there is the digital alternative, I feel extra affection for the paints and brushes in the art store, the labels, the smells, the messy space of the studio, the feel of fresh oil paint on canvas, the quiet concentration, no monitor, no e-mail. But nostalgia is not enough for the tough-minded artist: You are supposed to have something to say, to aim for, some compulsion. There was more to the art of the Renaissance, of the impressionists, of the cubists, than just savouring the paint. So, yes, painters collectively may accommodate themselves to a completely different studio setup, a studio you can carry around wherever you go, and "paintings" that, strictly speaking, are not objects at all. Or perhaps this art of painting will survive intact in the world of much smarter media. Perhaps on a planet a few light-years away they have figured that out. For the moment, I keep my hand in both fronts, tinkering around with both physical and digital paint and seeing what happens when one is played off the other.

Actually, I doubt whether the painting process can be translated into the digital without something vital dropping away. I am not a fan of printed canvas—at least not at the moment; it costs too much. Nor would I want to become more a printmaker than a painter. And as for any kind of automatic, computer-generated painting or drawing, I still think of it as a party trick. I usually prefer to make the decisions, the marks, myself. I cannot see video projection, or a flat screen on the wall, or Web art as serious contenders. I have been a digital junkie and paid my dues at the "art of the future" electronic art festivals, but I still linger with the Holbeins in the museum.

At the same time, the painters curious enough to look into this digital window may have found themselves transformed: This is not just a kaleidoscope of effortless visual creativity; it is a responsive, volatile, sensitive instrument. From now on, to paint will be to *continue* to paint; to stand still in old media amid the rush of new media. Still painting? say my friends.

If we want to know what time it is, most of us don't worry about the clock's being electric, or electronic, and we take the accuracy of such timekeeping for granted. Clockwork clocks needed winding and were never as reliable. If painting were about delivering a message as straightforward as "it is 5:35 P.M.," then pigment and canvas would be a cumbersome and futile way of getting the information across. The favourite parallel for the impact of the computer on painting is the effect of the camera on nineteenth- and twentieth-century painting, and some observers go back further still to speak of perspective and realism. The trouble with all these analogies is that they lead us to expect a steady trickle of evidence year by year: the paintings in national galleries being taken away and replaced by digital displays, much as DVDs are being swapped for videos in Blockbuster. If nothing much happens—some inkjet paper on sale in the art store, yes—we go back to the old studios and shrug: so much for the digital revolution.

Buying a laptop is not like joining a highbrow think tank, where we all become Renaissance all-rounders conversing via wireless at the court of the Medicis—except we are liberals to the core. An optimist like Ben Schneiderman in *Leonardo's Laptop* seems to believe in a new age of enlightenment:

> The new computing software that supports innovation will provide exemplars of excellence for you to build on, templates for getting started, and processes for guiding your creative experiences. Even as a novice you'll be able to perform better than today's experts.[11]

Alternatively, laptops are just accessories. Deep-rooted social problems, questions of climate change, third-world deprivation, AIDS, political conflicts, or the relatively tiny problems

of writing novels or painting pictures are not solved by pur-
chasing new software. Unless you take some initiative, unless
you recognise the opportunities that stare at you through the
laptop screen, then this metaphorical window will be as much
use as a blank screen. It won't exist. Opportunities are there to
be recognised and taken up. That is something the laptop will
not do of its own accord. But some opportunities are so trivial I
would have missed them before I had the hardware. The painter
can work on impulse, from something glimpsed that will vanish in a second or two—the rain trickling on the windscreen.
With camera and laptop you can turn this into a "solid" image,
the first stage of a drawing. For example, if you photograph the
rain at night and invert the image, you have something that
looks like ink on paper. I only hit on this because one evening I

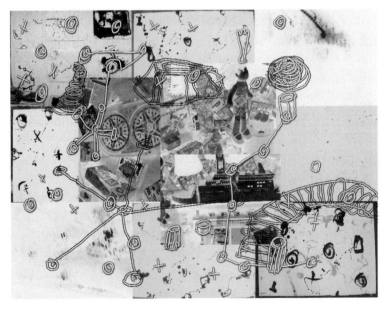

James Faure Walker, *A Song for Upper Street,* 2004, 26" × 33"
(66 × 83 cm), inkjet print. (See also Plate 3.)

had been drawing in gouache with a stick and a brush on paper on the floor of my studio, drawings that I would photograph and then feed into a parallel drawing made in Adobe Illustrator or Corel Painter. Instead of driving off straight after doing this, I was sitting in my car listening intently to some political debate on the radio. That is how my thoughts became lost in the pattern of rain on the windscreen, the reflections of the street-lights. The way peripheral ideas can feed into a process fascinates me, the way that painting and digital gadgetry can be brought together, not necessarily blended, or collaged one onto the other, but it means details become visible that might not have been picked up so readily before.

Too Quiet

Sooner or later a museum will mount a vast exhibition about the impact of the digital on painting. Every week, I come across something unforeseen—a conceptual artist of the 1960s with intriguing movies and JPEGs on his site, a Hollywood effects artist painting space cruisers, a Photoshop user club producing gorgeous colour work with feathers. Piecing all of this together, identifying the significant themes, the sources, the leaders and the followers, would be quite an assignment. It probably could not be done. If such a survey were to reflect the sprawl of the subject—even a day researching through Google is exhausting—you would be hard put to wedge the various aspects of digital into distinct categories. Any category you can think of—real versus digital painting, for example—raises more questions than it answers. What of Web art, CD covers, video games, video installations, the programs themselves, or even the virus as an interventionist art form? Whatever line the exhibition curator took, it would be contentious and divisive. If digital art as a whole could be conceived as one coherent category, then to juxtapose it with half-digital or nondigital art would be stirring a family row, and a dysfunctional family at that. The younger, "advanced" art form would be in competition with its parent— a fraught relationship. Yet it is not a straightforward story of the young challenging the old. For one thing, most of the noise in favour of "putting the record" straight about the contribution of the digital comes from an older age group. The PlayStation generation moves more easily between digital and nondigital. So to date there has been no such exhibition. Perhaps that is the point. As Sherlock Holmes said to Dr. Watson, the significant fact is that the dog didn't bark.

There are already enough books on art and the Internet to fill a shelf. They may not define the subject the same way— there is Web design at one end of the spectrum and tactical media at the other—but it is a genre that already has been assigned archaic, classic, and baroque phases. The year 1994 is a date in the archaic period. 1994? If painting proper is to be part of the digital-painting chronology, and we have to think about what painting is now and how it started, then 1294 is quite a conceivable point on the time line. Some art historians would put that date as shading into the dawn of the modern period. So this could cause some trouble for our curator. Digital painting originates with the invention of the paint program. But if—for the sake of argument—*painting digital* is defined as the synthesis of real and digital painting, then we are peering into the darkness of prehistory to find our true ancestors. How far is any innovation in painting tied to a new or modified technology? Art historians certainly call attention to the origins of oil paint—available but little used before the Van Eyks used it to the full—and to the practicalities of pigments in tubes, combined with rail travel for the impressionists. But histories of painting are not usually phased according to developments in paint technology. Different methods tend to coexist in any one period—fresco alongside oil paint, watercolour alongside Photoshop. If anyone expected painting as a whole simply to "go digital" because the technology is so much smarter than a pack of acrylic paint, then he or she may be in for a long wait.

Many artists must find themselves—like me—in this in-between state and more than a little confused. What does it mean to be artists, experts at what we do? Do we need to be software engineers? Paint technicians? Do we need a deep understanding of art history? Where do we go to keep up with the pack: to the Venice Biennale, to the Frieze Art Fair, to Ars Electronica, to SIGGRAPH, or to none of these? The subject is in danger of expanding in every direction. You need to know both something of painting—its past, its present state, the critical fray—and something of the digital. Knowing about the last few decades of digital art would be more useful than essential, and you would certainly need to know your way around the programs. Even knowing which is the right hardware and software is a skill in itself, and you could only acquire this by trying out the alternatives. Adobe's Creative Suite, for example, contains five programs, and until you have some experience of Photoshop, Illustrator, or the suite's other programs focusing on Web and page design, you won't know which is for you. Corel's Painter program is the best in that it is designed specifically for a painter. And then there are the 3D and animation programs: programs like Flash, which is essential for animation on the Web; Director, for interactive graphics; and Final Cut, for video. Even this sampling, I should add, is only scratching the surface. But it would be wise to take a tour round what is available before deciding where you are going to specialise; trying out a high-end digital camera, for example, usually involves quite an investment of time and cash. It is a conundrum, and learning about the development of Flemish painting and studying museum collections is not going to help you with file formats. But perhaps in a generation or two it won't seem quite so odd to be learning complex paint software one moment and studying Rubens the next.

I have already touched on the metaphor of the window. Before Microsoft Windows, the window was a device to keep the wind and rain out while letting the daylight in. In painting, the window has long been a symbol, a source of illumination, sometimes the light being symbolic, the light of divine revelation. The view through the window shows also an "out there" world, the distant view, even the far away and exotic. The allusion to travel to exotic lands can be extended by a globe, a map on the wall—as in a Vermeer. On the desktop the travelling is more virtual than symbolic. A click takes me out from my paint program and I "look" through another window: It could be an e-mail with an attached JPEG file from across the Atlantic, or I might find a live close-up of a boulder on Mars. In his 1857 *Elements of Drawing*, Ruskin said go out into the road and pick up a stone—it's tarmac on my road now—and put the stone on the table and draw it; observe the way it is worn, how light and shade define its form. I wonder what would be the equivalent exercise today. This was meant as a lesson for the beginner, and today we would have to decide between drawing from observation, drawing through a program, or using a camera. If we decided on drawing from observation, should we rule out these "windows" to distant places? Should we insist on daylight or candlelight, or allow electric light? Some of my college tutors used to insist on using natural light, even when it was almost completely dark. Much as I might want to go back to the tradition of landscape painting, the view through the window, I cannot go back to that period before air travel, before city centres were blazing with neon, before half the globe was watching the World Cup, all in the same split second. But I still find sense in the principle that with repeated practice, drawing is a discipline that helps you see. The question becomes how drawing can be redefined to take account of both changing drawing implements and the changing scenery outside the window. I wonder how Ruskin—he recommended copying photographs, so he was not technophobic—would have updated his "elements" as the digital elements of drawing.

For all the attention given to Net art, digital art, and other new media, to my mind there is something missing from the digital-art bookshelf. There are good anthologies and catalogues; there are rigorous texts of theory; there are the practical how-to manuals. But there is little that tells you what it feels like to be part of this collective experiment. The answer may be simple: Half the time you feel lost. On all sides there are experts, but few seem to have any doubts. Who is catering to the agnostics? They tend to keep quiet. They stumble along finding out what they can through trial and error. You can pick up so much from a software manual or an exhibition catalogue. But this information has an inbuilt bias. I have only once come across a technical manual that admits, "this may not work," and catalogues tend to be economical with the truth when it comes to the artist's shortcomings. The best resource to help you find your way is probably the casual conversation, the sharing of experience you find within the milieu of like-minded souls. I was struck once by an artist who one moment was vigorously publicly defending the innovations of digital art and a few minutes later was amiably but privately admitting that 90 percent of it was "slush." But this did not make him—or any of us—any less passionate about what we were after. He knew firsthand the formidable difficulties of making anything

41

worthwhile as art and was as dismissive of facile techno-solutions as anyone else.

There is a case to be made for keeping quiet. Any artist should be content to let his or her pictures speak for themselves. Well, of course, but sometimes it is not so easy for the pictures to be seen. For years computer art was such a low-ranking category that the only showing opportunities were the dead areas at computer trade shows. That was then. Now, uncritical acceptance of digital genres may be as much of a problem, in that digital painting slips out of the reckoning. Even if the shift turns out to be only a sideways one, the evolution from predigital to digital in painting could prove an extraordinary episode in its history. It would be a pity if there were only a few eyewitness accounts. This is David Em writing in 1988:

> While I was away from the high-tech lab, I became extremely conscious of how much the tools we use determine the physical and social environments we live and work in, and how much these factors influence our perceptions and ideas. How tedious and time consuming it must have been for Rembrandt's studio assistants to grind up a tiny quantity of paint for the master's daily work, compared to more recent times when an artist like Jackson Pollock, alone in his studio, could take advantage of drums of commercially produced paints to develop new creative directions. Now, by eliminating paint entirely from the initial creative act, the computer is pushing the envelope of imaging a little further, opening the way to a vast new and unpredictable visual territory.
>
> How physically and spiritually removed sitting in front of a computer terminal is from the experience of a prehistoric cave painter making a red handprint on a cave wall. Perhaps if the prehistoric painter were presented with Velazquez's paint box and brushes it would take him a little while to

grasp what had been delivered into his hands. And perhaps it will take us a little while to appreciate that the computer, which has so suddenly appeared in our midst, is likewise a wonderful and mysterious gift.[12]

I have had friends who achieved something quite special in art, in critical writing, in digital art, but they never condensed their perceptions into a book. When they died, their singular way of seeing was lost. I don't put myself in their class, but I hope that some of the lessons I have learned could be passed on. Most of us are self-taught in computer graphics. When we were students this field did not exist. We have patched together a ramshackle bridge between the old and the new. Much of what I

Hans Dehlinger, *Kreise_7.3sc,* 2003, 24" × 20" (60 × 50 cm), plotter drawing.

43

know of Durer I have learned from the pioneer computer artist Hans Dehlinger. Sometimes the new provides a route back to the old, just as the old provides the window to see the new.

Being on Both Sides

The demise, the eventual disappearance, of painting has been on one or another avant-gardist's wish list for more than a century. Painting has been accused of being bourgeois, self-indulgent, or old-fashioned. These attacks on painting have been led by painters, or former painters, needless to say. An analyst might recognise something Oedipal about slaying the father art form. Presumably, the failure of old-style painting to survive the digital makeover would finish off the story of twentieth-century art. Object-based art would come to an end, would become dematerialised, not as envisaged by the conceptual artists in the 1970s, but courtesy of Apple.

One recent development on London buses has been the flat screen at the front of the bus giving passengers views of themselves on the security cameras, the evening's TV schedules, their horoscopes, news, advertisements, and travel features. On a 277 bus in February, I found I was watching surfing in Brazil while it was snowing outside. Could I have made any sense of this with a sketch pad and a pencil? Sometimes I take photographs from the bus with a digital camera, but that can hardly do justice to the ambience of the bus as TV lounge amid a moving panorama. Part of me knows that in terms of visual communication, or even just to divert passengers from their worries or boredom, a painting would be no match for these screens. If nothing else, the fact that the images move and cut from scene to scene holds the attention. I may be confident that painting will survive as an art form, but I have to admit that it will have to trade on its limitations—don't expect messages.

Like photography the digital seeps into our lives and we take its "information windows" for granted. This affects how paintings are made and how they are viewed. Digital culture permeates almost everything we come across—the look of TV, newspapers, logos, the way we talk and send text messages, the way we hold cameras, even the way art materials are manufactured, packaged, and marketed. The influence in painting is even more direct. A paint program re-creates painting methods— methods that have been refined over centuries—and substitutes the digital for the physical. It takes a while to master the intricacies of watercolour, let alone gouache, oils, acrylics, silkscreen, lithography, etching, and photography, and now these "skills" are no longer required—or so it seems. Just buy the software and thumb through the manual for a few minutes, and any of those "looks" is yours for the taking. Now you are the expert.

In the 1960s, painters really did talk about advances in the art form. Studios changed. No longer found in backrooms, basements, or attics, studios moved to former industrial premises of hangarlike proportions, with vats of acrylic paint, chugging compressors for spray paint, tangles of used masking tape, and teams of assistants in engineering overalls. Led by Frank Stella, or Warhol's Factory, the new painting was spoken about in terms of components, units, systems, series, assembly. This was not the solitary, meditative shrine immortalised in Georges Braque's great studio works, where the stove, the table, the palette, the symbolic bird, were like half-formed thoughts in a shadowy dream world. Now the colours were bright and flat to the eye, and nothing was hidden. Long before it was taken up as the WYSIWYG acronym of "true" vision in computer graphics, "what you see is what you get" was the slogan of the painter who dealt in the literal, in facts.

As with the factory-style studio, on the face of it, painting that identifies itself with "advanced" technology should be

45

moving the art form along in a progressive direction. But this is not necessarily the case, and there can be anomalies. In one studio, a painter studies the nude model and re-creates in oil paint diluted with turpentine the seated figure. Every proportion is carefully measured, the tonal steps are exactly matched, and the planes subtly harmonised by the daylight wafting across the forms. A solid 3D rendering takes shape over a couple of weeks. You might say that by painting this way the painter rejects the main theme of twentieth-century art, which, from Picasso to Pollock to postmodernism, sought other ends than "straight" realism. Meanwhile, in a studio a block away, another "artist" is at a work station putting the finishing touches on a fully rendered (hair, skin pores, the works) model, a virtual actor, for a major movie. There is no live model, just a plastic one with articulated joints. There are 3D scans and video clips and data from motion-capture sessions. Here absolute and total realism is the goal, not the signature style of the artist, not the pictorial harmonies, not an existential reflection on perception. Lighting, viewpoint, and expression are again crucial. But though the processes of building the figure have points in common—modelling hair in a digital world is complicated, but so is rendering it in paint—the contexts and the uses of the image are worlds apart. If the phrase *advanced* means anything in contemporary painting, it doesn't normally include such naive realism undertaken for its own sake, not unless there is a sprinkling of irony and double takes on the genre. In other words, advanced technology can be used and has been fine-tuned in the service of old-fashioned art ideals. And for that matter, the most "advanced" painting can be made with materials and technologies—paints, brushes, canvases—that are premodern.

Much of what you come across in any art form is modest, intimate, and about everyday matters. I don't mind reading a novel that is about the form of the novel or that reinvents the format, but I am glad that there are plenty of novelists who do more than bang on about The Future. Perhaps it is in the nature of painting, an art form that has always played with illusion and ambiguity, to be reflective, to slow things down, to hide some of its inner secrets. Yet technology questions have practical ramifications. Every so often, artists have to make critical financial decisions. Do they need a better printer or more paint? Do they need to rent "wet" studio space? If they don't upgrade, will they be left behind? If you were deciding which course to take at college, studio art or digital, or if you were in charge of an art school and had to decide between the two, it would be an even tougher call.

There are the questions about equipment, about how to become competent in both physical and digital painting, and about the different meanings of *advanced,* depending on the context. Likewise, *computer graphics* has a varying meaning depending on where it is used. In the graphic design world, you would be talking about page layout, packaging, design as design; in the hardware world, it means making information visible, whether the information were the statistics of a lending library, a weather map, or a photo of an old master painting; in the painting world, *graphics* emphasises the artificial and synthetic, the geometric as opposed to the more natural and "painterly." In the painting world, the phrase *computer imagery* can crop up as if the neon, blocky, pixel look of the 1980s video game was all there was. For their part, the specialists who look after paint software can be just as out of touch, at least with contemporary painting, and might not be able to name a single painter who has emerged in the last twenty years.

There are other sources of misunderstanding. In the digital art world a reputation can build through a few appearances at specialist exhibitions and academic journals. Nothing need be sold. In the world of film production the "artist" is the

47

illustrator who creates the *treatment,* the atmosphere for a spe-
cial-effects project, a gothic refuelling depot for intergalactic
cruisers. This would be the *concept artist.* For the *loft artist,* the
term *conceptual* applied to painting means sophisticated detachment—you copy, or "appropriate," sci-fi images, but would
never make them as a gullible fantasist. Software lives or dies in
the marketplace and depends on reaching its "artist" consumers. In the software manual, the artist is the end user, be it
an eight-year-old or an eighty-year-old, amateur or professional. The more users the better. It's democratic. It depends on
high-volume sales. The marketplace for fine art works on a
quite different principle. It depends on the rarity of the product. Galleries command high prices for living artists, provided
there are not too many of them. A top gallery must give the
impression of being an exclusive zone where only a handful of
the international A-list exhibit. The rarer the product, the
higher the price.

Chapter 3 **Big Pixels, Small Minds**

Strange Country

I count myself one of the lucky ones because when I stumbled into the world of computer graphics in the 1980s, I already had a decade of painting and exhibiting behind me. I could take it on without feeling overwhelmed, but I was far from being an established artist who would be wary of a complete makeover. It took some faith to view the blocky pixel forms of the eight-bit system inaccurately printed out onto tiny sheets as a mighty challenge to the art of painting. But I did sense that once I let this silent "assistant" into my studio, nothing would ever be the same again. Some of my dearest theories about painting would be stood on their head. For a start this was a way you could watch yourself thinking visually—and it was easy to contrive errors, which often turned out to be improvements.

I was attracted too by the way you could be so engaged in the actual orchestration of a picture space. For years it had been hard to find any way of arranging the formal vocabulary of abstract painting that was not an instant cliché—the shapes, colours, textures, patterns, symmetries. Every extreme position was already overpopulated—from the ultrasimple one-colour, one-surface painting, to the ultrabaroque pattern painting. The intellectual and inventive input was channelled into clever titles, parodies, knowing references. Occupying the middle ground was fine, but from the 1970s onward no one expected much to happen here, just a handful of "good" practitioners to emerge once in a while. It soon turned out—this was my view—that abstract painting as a raison d'être was not going anywhere, or rather it was going round in circles. It needed something outside the fence to aim at. It could be an image, it could be a concept, it could be a different technology. So I was well primed to give it my all. I also had another advantage—which only became clear to me much later. I had behind me quite a few years of writing criticism, including a decade of editing a leading art magazine.

I knew my way round the art world, how things worked, how reputations could be made and unmade. I knew that the vast majority of artists worked outside the limelight. It was difficult enough just surviving as an artist—starting a magazine had been like creating your own biosphere—let alone nursing your own ideas till they could compete on a professional, even an international, level. To the outsider, to the reader of the magazine feature on the art world, all that exists is this glossy exterior, the world of exhibitions and profiles of successful artists. But none of that would exist without the less visible activity going on lower down the pyramid. Everyone starts out at the bottom, and though there can be quite a scuffle just to get a foothold, no one gains the respect of his or her peers without reason. Occasionally I run into "digital" artists who complain about their lack of recognition in the art world, and I wonder whether they have any idea at all how rough it is in there. Even calling yourself an artist is pushing it. Many digital practitioners have academic positions and are in effect part-time artists. Many of my neighbours in my studio complex support themselves by driving vans, working in galleries, or waiting at table and have little chance of landing an art school job, let alone getting to academic conferences on new media. In such studio complexes there is less talk of being an artist than there is of survival, and how to remain visible. Prestigious open shows of digital art tend to accept something like one out of two to ten entries. Some shows accept every entry they get. The ratios for the equivalent shows of painting are more like one in fifty to one in two thousand.

Public and Private Views

> *The art world, with its traditions of personal dealing and secrecy, its intimidating spaces, and its dizzying mixture of ineffable values and effable bucks, rouses anxieties that are allayed by suspicions of cabal. The main fact missed by "outsiders" is not that the "inside" is an assembly of angels, but that the inside does not exist. The art world is a balkanized anarchy, with lots of little insides, lots of little games, better and worse people, hierophants and hustlers. Meanwhile there is art, available to anyone who has a personal use for it. Love of art and hope for it are the only solid ground in this swampy, fecund craziness.*
> —Peter Schjeldahl, *The Hydrogen Jukebox*

Sometimes it is impossible to avoid using a phrase like *the art world* or *the mainstream art world*. By using it you imply there is some coordinated operation involving every conceivable outcrop, from antique dealers, museum directors, avant-garde artists somewhere, to collectors, critics, and so on. The reality is that certainly within major cities there are numerous groups and inner groups that have little idea of each other's existence. What began as a cluster of like-minded digital artists began to define itself by alluding to "the mainstream," the big river that ignores the little tributaries. Because so much of the initial effort was made—for logistical reasons, since computers were only available in military and scientific establishments—outside any art context, it took a long while for the basic critical concepts, that is, ways of telling the good art from the not-so-good, to emerge.

Without feeling they belonged inside this larger art world, and without a string of masterpieces of the past to judge by, the digital art world periodically spoke of needing its own critical language, even its own critical system. But reputations in art emerge in quite a curious way—it is not like the exhaustive peer review, publication, and cross-checking of the scientific community. You do not have recourse to that brand of objectivity. In art the private view is a central ritual, a kind of subliminal court. As the new arrivals wander into a private view, their eyes first check out who is already there and who is important, and then they scan the works on show. You can walk in and deliberately ignore the other people and get straight to work on the exhibits, but this is itself a social statement—"I haven't got time for chitchat, I am here to look at the art"—and a kind of defiance. I confess that as a young art student I would march into a gallery and look at the painting on the wall very close and sideways, to see what kind of staples, canvas, and stretcher was used. I thought this is what the professional would do. Eventually you learn the form and some uncomfortable truths. Of the thousands of would-be artists out there, the vast majority are on the outside looking in. Being inside is something to savour. At the private view the work is the one thing you don't talk about, except in passing. Even if it is only through the glance, the shrug, or the jealous aside, you can usually tell whether a show is making an impact or whether the response is just polite acknowledgment.

Hanging in the National Portrait Gallery is a work painted by Henry Jamyn Brooks in 1889. It is a painting of the 1888 private view at the Royal Academy of an exhibition of the old masters. What strikes me first about this painting is how the

Henry Jamyn Brooks, *Private View of the Old Masters Exhibition, Royal Academy, 1888*, 1889 (includes Sir John Everett Millais, William Holman Hunt, George Richmond, William Powell Frith, Sir Lawrence Alma-Tadema, Francis Montague ("Frank") Holl, George Frederic Watts, William Gladstone, Sir Edward John Poynter, and John Ruskin), 23" × 42" (60 × 106 cm), oil on canvas. Copyright National Portrait Gallery, London. (See also Plate 4.)

exhibits are clearly left to the background. They are dimly lit and out of focus, and viewers find themselves much more interested in the characters leaning on their umbrellas, holding or wearing their top hats, looking this way and that, hardly at all at the marvellous canvases—Rubens, Veronese. From a useful key provided in the gallery you can identify the leading British painters of the day, pre-Raphaelites like William Holman Hunt and Millais; prominent figures such as Alma-Tadema, Poynter, Leighton, Watts, Frith, Burne-Jones, and Ruskin; but also Gladstone, the prime minister, and numerous aristocrats and other VIPs of the day. The atmosphere is full of the same deference, reserve, rituals of introductions, greetings of old friends, that must have happened at countless exhibitions ever since. Of course, this is a painting that one treats as a reliable document because it has the feel of society photographs blended into a group portrait. For its time it was a remarkable research feat, partly inspired by the social documentary realism of William Frith, who had painted a similar subject a few years before. Brooks had to work within official restrictions. He wasn't allowed to sketch the old master paintings in situ, because of a vigilant resident "detective"—presumably enforcing copyright—so he had to rely on his visual memory. And the whole assembly was stitched together:

> Such a picture as this is never painted now entirely from life sittings, but . . . photography is used to save time and spare the patience of those invited to form the group.[13]

It means much more if you know that these ladies and gentlemen were the powers-that-be of the London art world. They in effect were the art world. If by some chance some of them had been discussing what the future of painting might be, I wonder what they would have said. Bear in mind their air of self-confidence, but remember that by this date, the impressionists had had their final exhibition, Seurat's *La Grande Jatte* remained unsold, Van Gogh had two years to live, and the very first films were being made just down the road in Piccadilly, by William Friese-Green. Today, art lovers wait in line outside the Royal Academy to view impressionist paintings—the old masters of our time—in those very same galleries. A contemporary audience looks with eyes attuned to impressionism, pop art, postmodernism. We are much less interested in identifying themes, or significant detail. In an impressionist painting, we are not concerned with the moral message of what the distant figures are up to on the banks of the Seine. Our way of seeing is different. What we expect from a painting is—generally speaking—not what they expected. They didn't do irony. We expect it. We don't expect likeness, an exact representation of what we see. Few now would look at this picture and savour its aesthetic qualities. Only the occasional portraitist might do so, or a digital artist on a day off.

This painting provides a roundabout way of showing how at any given date there can be quite varied and incompatible versions of what art is, what it should be, where it is going, and how it is to be judged, all going on at the same time. Thinking of contemporaneous Paris, it would be tempting to say that the "real" art was going on outside the salons and the academies, and that new technology would somehow bring about "modernism." It was not that simple. The impressionists, like any avant-garde milieu, had their own petty in and out crowds. Opinions were divided. The new tech of the moving picture was appreciated just as much by academic artists and in no way led to a cutting-edge art form straightaway. Modernity, the question of who is or isn't "advanced," can be argued this way and that. There was never a time when painting was universally a settled, technical matter, where everyone agreed about its future.

Small Minds

It makes more sense to speak of a variety of art worlds, some identified with cities, continents, parishes, colleges, clubs, all in some way interlinked and intermingled. The most noticeable common factor is that the art world is always a "they." So when digital artists speak in disgruntled tones about the art world's not appreciating their innovatory art form, they are not voicing anything that hasn't been heard a thousand and one times before. But are they a special case? Has the critical reviewing process let them down?

Again, it makes little sense to speak of "the critical process" as if there were just one such thing, or even a process at all. Published criticism is the conspicuous part, but much is also decided through the influence of galleries, collectors, editors, committees, fellow artists, and sheer accident, being in the right—or wrong—place at any given time. Moreover, everyone makes mistakes or no longer stands by some opinion that looked incontrovertible a few years back. I recall with embarrassment some of the poor judgments I made. I completely missed the point of several artists I subsequently came to see as crucial influences—such as the geometric fantasies of the sculpture, drawings, and performances by Paul Neagu, who became a good friend and who died in 2004. But that can be the way a true original works on you. At first you just do not see it at all—and this is not necessarily because the medium is familiar or unfamiliar. I began writing reviews in 1974 for *Studio International,* and from 1976 to 1983 for *Artscribe,* the magazine I cofounded. I was also the editor of *Artscribe* for seven years. It was an artists' magazine in that it was written and produced for the most part by artists, but it also came to be the leading contemporary art magazine in Britain—it did not fold till 1992. It was a team effort, and if there had been a "critical system" at work, I should have known about it. In fact our aim—apart from survival—was to be as fair and comprehensive as we could be, which meant checking through a large number of exhibitions at home and abroad and deciding what should take priority. I mention this because in retrospect I do not think that we were mistaken in giving computer art a low priority. In relation to everything else, it just wasn't that interesting. There were always a dozen other art events, emerging talents, controversies, competing for attention. There is a convenient myth, or half-truth, that early computer work was overlooked out of prejudice or ignorance. The reality is that critics may be fallible, but there are always half a dozen subgroups of enthusiasts lobbying for attention, and computer art would have ranked alongside textile art, glass art, mosaic art, printmaking, landscape painting, and photography as a category. Presented as a blanket category, that kind of lobbying was usually counterproductive.

At the time, all you can do is trust what your eyes are telling you. I knew some art that could make you jump out of your skin. But always in play were other expectations and subliminal influences that meant that no one's eyes were completely innocent. Speaking generally, the 1960s was a period when novelty in art was prized—kinetic art, op art, and computer art—and the 1970s was a period of recession and guilt-inducing ideology—the Puritanism of conceptual art. The 1980s began with a resurgence of extravagant and oversized painting, coinciding with the emergence of a new breed of collector, new money, and the massive expansion of the audience for contemporary art. The 1990s was an imperial decade, with bursts of energy here and there, but dominated by power: by the power of the collector, the curator, and architecture, the exquisitely tailored modern museum—MoMA, the Bilbao Guggenheim, Tate Modern.

In the 1970s, it was possible for a small bunch of artists to produce a magazine and send ripples throughout the system. The museum curators took notice and invited you to lunch. If you were a potential inside reviewer of a show, you got to drink the champagne. And yes, power within that world is exciting, exhilarating even. I did meet some of the most influential critics, but my impression was that they were insecure and troubled creatures, less certain of their observations than their acolytes were.[14] If for a period you function both as an artist and a critic, you suffer a personality split, one side the uninhibited creator, the other the repressive schoolmaster. You also have the stress of time management and thoughts from one part of the brain invading the other. Of course, artists have to function as their own critics and are as fascinated by power as anyone else—in my experience they can be just as vain as any critic.

It took a friend and old *Artscribe* colleague, the mercurial critic Stuart Morgan, to prompt me to see how different the artist's power could be from the critic's. To produce something that still holds an audience's attention ten, twenty years after it is made gives you a gentle buzz of satisfaction. It is still alive, working on the eye. This has little to do with the longevity, the "archival" properties, of the material, by the way. It is to do with its qualities, or lack of qualities, as art. The critic's writings, the magnificent critical theory, the bon mots, the devastating critiques, the scoop interview, the smart put-down, can have tremendous potency at the time they are published. Some artists can be made, some destroyed. But let five, ten, twenty years pass by, and few of these critics will be remembered. Their phrases will have no sting at all. Eventually they can be resurrected from the archives in the art school library, but they are diminished and faded by the perspective of time.

We may feel we have left the period of small-minded critics behind. We may feel that if we have "gone digital" and linked up with computer science, we can float free of the mood swings of contemporary art. Perhaps digital art can circumvent the normal system and appeal directly to the viewer—through the Web, through direct interaction, through delivering "the aesthetic experience" undiluted, unmodulated by such trivia as what is on the cover of *Frieze* magazine. I am of two minds on this. I would like to believe that this alternative is feasible, but I note that everything that is promised is vague and abstract. I just cannot believe in this cultural vacuum, with just one kind of viewer, one kind of consciousness, and nothing else filling it except an appetite for a fix of electronic art. I suppose, though, that this is what Mondrian might have believed. At least he believed in the power of painting to cut through the mirage of everyday life to some Platonic world of perfectly balanced harmony.

Published criticism can help shape opinion in its own time. The drawback can be that it stays on the record. In 1927 Nelson Junius Springer was reviewing the "New Primitives," an international exhibition put on by the Societé Anonyme in New York, for *The Studio*. He praised several pictures by artists now little remembered except as provincial social realists, which "seem to have gone the furthest toward rendering new methods articulate, and perhaps eloquent." But his conclusion was not as prophetic as probably he hoped:

> There is one man, Mondrian (The Netherlands), praised very highly by the Societé Anonyme, whose work frankly exasperates even my open mind. Two straight, black lines, intersecting at right angles, cannot, by any stretch of my imagination, be conceived as art, and certainly cannot be conceived as experiment. (I seem to recall the same thing's been done before). But if one excepts "Mondrian from Holland with his International Group standing for Clarification", as he is enthusiastically described in the catalogue, one feels

that here is an exhibit which presents modern art in the light of unusual promise. It definitely feels after an expression of important realities in forms familiar to our contemporary consciousness; and, at times, it definitely lays hold on them.[15]

If he could have travelled in time would Mondrian have been passionate about electronic art? In 1938 he came to London from Paris and moved to Upper Park Road in Belsize Park. There he became fascinated with the underground, and presumably its famous map, which was designed by Harry Beck in 1933 and is still in use today. The map was based on an electrical circuit diagram, with a different colour for each line, and influenced subway maps throughout the world. Mondrian painted *Broadway Boogie Woogie* in 1942–1943, after he moved to New York in 1940. The piece pulses with the syncopation of boogie-woogie, almost like an animation, and also has the look of those maps. In London he had sent postcards and letters to his younger brother Carel in Holland. The postcards were of "Doc" and scenes from *Snow White*. Despite his Calvinism, Mondrian was quite a Disney devotee.[16]

With queues round the block to see any show of Matisse today, it takes some effort to recall how "modern art" was for so long a controversial topic, and perhaps it still is. Sometimes I start thinking that electronic painting is some great leap forward, as though buying the fastest machine and putting some ingenious piece of animation on the Web is the equivalent of synthetic cubism. If a sufficient number of enthusiasts felt the same way, I suppose they could form a consensus in which "traditional" modern art was shoved aside as inadequate. I find it fascinating to look through these issues of *Studio* from the 1920s and 1930s, since the art world it represents is so unreachably different from what we know today. I wonder how our own assumptions—especially our feelings about "new" technology—will look in seventy years' time.

We cannot assume we are immune from the cultural influences that are so apparent with hindsight. In those *Studio* pages two aspects stand out. First the ethnocentrism: the number of portraits of racial types, the nationalism, the feature on the rigid portraiture and heroic style of Mussolini's Fascist Italy—praised for its discipline and its rejection of the slovenly values of modern art. And second, the lack of correspondence between what we now value from the period and what—according to its coverage—was valued by the magazine's readership. The publication betrays its provincialism: Although the pioneers—as we would call them—remain in the background, the favoured artists all tend to make a feeble compromise between, say, the traditional family group, or society portrait, and a smattering of cubism. It is worth, just for a moment, opening up the ill feeling that went into the case against modern art. This is the editorial of December 1936, entitled "Is Modern Art a Sham?"

> The layman says that the modern artist cannot draw, that his work often appears to be careless and incompetent. Against this has been urged the value of freedom of expression, of the greater expressiveness of distortions which give the appearance of bad drawing. But how far has this plea proved valid in practice? A rough sketch does not constitute a picture and a good deal of modern painting seems to hesitate between the rough sketch on the one hand and on the other the limited form of architectural design known as abstract art. They may have their merits, but they cannot be considered as anything but the beginning of an art or as a small part of its possibilities. Is it likely that a panel of living artists would be able

to mention more than a very few among the moderns who can really draw? How many among modern artists are aiming to be masters?[17]

In the following issue there was a flood of letters, most from artists, supporting this view at a ratio of about eight to one. This is a typical excerpt:

> The "modern" artist sees nothing but gloom and morbidness, he has lost his vision and has no ideals, he has no hope in the future and sees nothing before him but death and putrefaction.[18]

You could have said that the recommended dewy-eyed optimism was misplaced in 1936, and perhaps the pessimists had got it right. Moreover, some of these arguments about being unable to draw, about unpalatable subject matter, are still with us today. However, I don't think there is as much distrust of sketchiness, abstraction, or distortion—few people would now mention the "distortions" in a Matisse or Picasso. These painters are now accepted without question as "the masters."

Digital art is a less coherent term now than it was in the 1990s, both because it has split into groupings like Web art, or virtual environments, and because "mainstream" artists more readily use digital media. Digital painting is a special case because—so it may seem—the entire art form is being simulated, infiltrated, replaced, by an electronic surrogate. The issue of how, or whether, digital paint should be used is more disturbing. Blaming "the art world" for its small-minded attitudes and missing the point used to be part of the small talk at any gathering of digital artists. But now the more pressing question is how the high points of digital art fit in with the larger picture. Many of the greatest works by Picasso, Braque, Matisse, Léger, Miró, and Mondrian were made at the same time that many cultured people considered modern art a sham. This is hard to believe when I see those works in elegant museums and nowhere more impressive than in New York's MoMA. Many of us must take their apparent visual authority for granted. Do I believe that digital art, often in the past disparaged if not actually called a sham, is waiting in the wings? Actually, no. If anything, digital artists are in danger of being the small-minded ones, missing the point of the mainstream. Peter Schjeldahl spoke of the "love of art and hope for it," and I would add the power of art. Allen Ginsberg said a good poem was like a radio station that kept transmitting for all time. There may be a little moral in this for the digital artist: There is processor speed; there is the power of art. They are not the same.

Hooked on Pixels

I was disoriented when, in the 1980s, I first wandered round a commercial computer graphics fair held in London's Alexandra Palace. The event was certainly buzzing with vitality and was ten times more powerful—literally and visually—than any equivalent art event. There were giant screens of the palest fluorescent greens and purples, and though by today's standards the images would look appallingly jagged and pixel-grained, the idea that you could so liberally manipulate and squirt these forms across the TV monitors was absolutely captivating. People stood around with their mouths open. No one was fretting about whether it was true art or not. No one cared. And I was hooked.

I have been addicted to computer graphics ever since, but not at the expense of painting. From my first plunge into this extraordinary new world, I felt I might be knocked sideways. I wondered whether the entire culture of painting could be overwhelmed from top to bottom. Here was the painting studio shrunk into a grey box with a TV screen on top—my first machine was an Apple II. Tasks that would normally take weeks to complete could be achieved in minutes. Within a few years the CD, and then the Web, meant you could "visit" an art gallery from home and exhibit your own work on the Net.

True, electronic paint is not real paint, and it is easy to go along with an appallingly shallow idea of art—menus that list the Van Gogh brush-stroke or the instant watercolour effect. That can trouble the purist in me. But these are just badges. We have Rembrandt-brand paints, the Citroen Picasso, and mobile homes called the Cézanne, the Renoir, the Matisse, and even the Lautrec. There is no reason why the advertising and entertainment industries should be more sensitive than anyone else about a postimpressionist brand name. This is really my own misconception. The software has grown up using familiar metaphors—brush, canvas, paint, sculpt, photo—that take the complexity out of image manipulation. I recall eight-bit paint programs that were painfully simple in performance—like making pictures with Lego—compared with today's Photoshop, Illustrator, or Painter, but were also painfully complex to use. They lacked the paint metaphor to wrap around the computer code. Sometimes you could only navigate through following a flow chart on the wall, and even in the excellent Deluxe Paint on the Amiga, you had to remember effects by terms like *XOR* rather than anything to do with real paint. By building the friendly interface around an artist's studio or a photographer's darkroom, you could work without checking the manual every ten minutes. This was a colossal advantage, though at the time the ease of use was deeply resented by some hardheads because it took away their raison d'être: If the program were impenetrable, you would need the guide—be it person, manual, or map on the wall. I recall a technician who hid the drawing tablet, on the grounds that it encouraged a misuse of the computer. There was a protestant work ethic, something that still permeates the psyche of a certain type of artist who finds virtue in difficulty, especially unnecessary and esoteric difficulty. So I should not complain. It may turn out to have been a happy accident that "painting" became one of the key sources for icons and menu items. But it was only a means to an end. You didn't need to know anything at all about Matisse to use the Matisse system; all you needed to know was how a brush was different from a crayon.

From the 1980s on, I became one of the many thousands attending computer graphics conferences, but all the time I also felt—or the painter part of me felt—torn between painting and the new technology. I recall a technical talk at SIGGRAPH, the Mecca of the conferences. The speaker had devised ingenious software that turned video footage instantly into "paintings." A video of the New York subway became an instant Monet-in-motion. Having visited a museum and found the dappled impressionist surfaces "cool," he took them as his model. If I had had the presence of mind to ask a question it would have been, Why do you have to use art in this way? Why does it always have to be an imitation? Cannot we make art directly without using these dreadful clichés? This plea was the mantra of the hundred or so artists—émigré painters, performance artists, full-fledged digital artists, who hung around.

But looking back I can see there were contradictions aplenty. If our own art works were to be intelligible, they would also need to be dressed up to some degree as recognizable art. One problem was that the actual way in which data, or more or less raw images, was processed was so fascinating in its own right. It was not as if a latter-day Marcel Duchamp could drop by, hire a few top-end machines and technicians, put the objects in a smart gallery, and declare them art. It is one thing to get hold of a bottle rack, shovel, toilet, or whatever and look at it as if it were sculpture, but this stuff was too hot. You couldn't pick it up from a skip or a hardware store, and you probably could not afford the insurance premium to put it on display for a week. In art schools the conceit of moving something out of a nonart context into an art context was called *appropriation.* If you made a faithful copy of someone else's picture, you had "appropriated it." The trouble here was that it was appropriation in reverse. In some cases, actual artists were being hired, absorbed, and "appropriated" by this new mega industry. Wandering around with saucer eyes, we sometimes forgot that all these booths with their roaring, warring robots were not installations in an art show but demos in a ruthlessly competitive trade show.

Another problem was that if as an artist you wanted to get your hands really dirty, to work in the mud of this software revolution, then you would be competing not with a handful of like-minded artists but with thousands of computer science graduates, who were completely focused and not distracted by events at the Venice Biennale or Ars Electronica. You would be an amateur in a professional's world. One way or another you would need to find a balance, a compromise between being an artist and a computer expert. It was a dilemma, and a dilemma complicated by the constant use of "art" as the default subject sample. Scanners are now so taken for granted that they no longer crop up at commercial computer-graphics fairs, but when they were exotic novelties, the picture scanned more often than not was a painting masterpiece, a Constable reproduction, something with a rich colour range and plenty of detail to show off the printer's resolution. The first inkjet printer I bought, a Xerox 4020, could not manage anything as fine-grained as a photograph. The demo image was a Swiss chalet with the optical texture of a knitted sweater. As soon as printers became capable of handling gradated colour without tidemarks and irritating textures, the demo went into reverse. You started with the holiday snap on the scanner, put it into Photoshop, filtered it back into the desired crude and smeary textures of "impressionist paint"—or the knitted-jumper look—and again, coming out of the inkjet was the "painting." That was progress.

Paint programs moved from blocky pixels to simulations of slick oil brushwork. Once I saw the benefits of the friendlier interface—from the start, Painter was fixed up like a smart studio with "drawers" of different brushes and grainy paper—I forgot the advantages of the cruder interface. For example, one of my favourite Mac programs was Studio 8. The menu did not differentiate between marks or lines that you could make with a real set of paints and ones that you couldn't. You could draw with a freehand line, but you could also draw playfully with ellipses or use the "airbrush" to spray gradated colour. You can also do this with most "naturalistic" paint programs, but it was the emphasis. In the "natural media" program the truly weird methods take second place.

All this equipment, this software, has a much shorter lifespan than a set of conventional art materials. I must have some little-used colours that are fine after ten, twenty years or much longer. I even have a set of watercolours from the 1880s that looks OK. You don't need a new "platform" every four years to run your oil paints. And each upgrade costs most artists more than they can afford. But the new features and the increased productivity and work flow are irresistible. The fear is that if you miss out on this upgrade you will never catch up. You, and your art, will be left behind.

I also wonder sometimes what else I am in danger of leaving behind, whether unconsciously I become so acclimatised to the *metaphor,* to the substitution of the simulated palette for the messy reality, that my senses, my reflexes, become numbed. Like

67

someone conditioned to junk food, would I become incapable of recognizing, or even caring about, the real thing? Already I have beside me a printer that can print my "painting" superbly on dedicated canvas. On the other hand I do have my physical studio, and I try to keep to a routine where I am always reasonably in touch with both modes. I am not leaving the old life behind, at least not yet. Walking back from my studio and noticing a gym being built in a new set of apartments, I realised that this feeling of being stranded on the threshold of a different lifestyle, with physical exertion becoming a folk memory, must keep psychotherapists in business. Real physical labour is replaced by a hi-tech substitute. The rows of stationary running figures I see through the windows of the gym are engaged in virtual running. As I write this, my son, a good tennis player, is playing Virtual Tennis Pro on the PlayStation. A three-part shop called Empire DJ sells nothing but DJ mixing decks, and gradually the vinyl, "real" analogue method is giving way to CDs and to virtual vinyl, where the record does nothing but emit a constant note and all the mixing is done digitally. The need for physical contact, physical resistance, friction, the interaction of touch, is behind the principle of the Wacom table, the feel of drawing with the pressure-sensitive stylus, or playing the keys of the Midi. In all these cases, there is a compromise between the physical model and the digital process.

But what of the quality—the quality of the experience, the quality of the art? If you search in Google for *digital painting,* you may well come across an avalanche of what is best described as kitsch— from soft porn to fantasy castles. On this evidence, digital painting means a catastrophic drop in quality, what you might expect to happen once the hard-won "skills," the cuisine of the painter's studio, is packaged into accessible software. You can always argue that it is entirely a matter of taste, and no one has the right to impose his or her supposedly "good" taste. You can also argue that there is something refreshing in the naïveté, the lack of restraint, the lack of art-world knowingness. But my tolerance has gradually been worn away, and I find it difficult to be that reasonable, especially after browsing through a good number of digital-art competitions and even occasionally being on the jury. In my bleaker moments I am convinced this is a genre poisoned at birth by overkill and by cliché, an awful kind of self-conscious originality. Why use one effect when you can use fifty? Why not collage those dog heads on the cactus? To some participants this combination—revolutionary technology (the PC) plus quirky imagery (from Dali) makes the art form visionary. In fact, the artist statements I came across in one competition where the art was modest, to say the least, were extraordinarily immodest, as were the prices. It is the visual equivalent of the local community newsletter with half a dozen typefaces and blurred photos stretched to fit the already crammed page. If typography is an art, the art consists in the judging as much as in the assembling, and also in the art of concealing the artistry. Yes, there is plenty of do-it-yourself painting, typography, and Web design, and little of it is any more significant artistically than a karaoke evening. But I shouldn't blame technology. It is not the technology that produces the dross, and who knows, there could always be that odd nugget of gold.

Hotel Pixel

Digital artists are not normally molested by critical radar. There are no quality checks, apart from the juries and gallerists who say yes or no. If digital artists spout pretentious nonsense in a catalogue, there are no reviewers around to ridicule it in a magazine column, because the magazines don't exist and the art magazines steer clear. So digital artists have long felt neglected—what artist doesn't?—and they cite technophobia as the cause of their stigma. Sometimes they overcompensate and imagine they project creative radiation that knows no bounds. In abandoning the old formats, we are liberated from the constraints of conventional thinking. If the larger art world dismisses what we do—fools!—it is because they are not technological prophets like us. We need a new kind of art criticism—actually anything a little sympathetic would be fine, but preferably one that puts us at the top of the heap.

There was a defining moment at that 1993 Minneapolis ISEA (Inter Society for the Electronic Arts) conference. The keynote speaker was Jan Hoet, the director of the recent massive Documenta survey and the director of the Museum of Contemporary Art in Ghent. He had also, I heard, once been a boxer. He did not hold back in ripping the claims of electronic art to pieces. It was not art at all, it did not touch his emotions, it had no bearing on the human condition. The response of a good portion of the audience was sheer outrage.

My own loyalties were divided, and looking back, I am sure Hoet saw his role as a provocateur, but sadly few of the questions he raised have ever been fully thrashed out since that confrontation. At the time, some in the audience must have felt confident that with their avant-garde data-gloves they were in the front line. This art was as hot as the technology that powered it. Up to that time, art could only trigger the imagination. Here were art forms that could make the imaginary as real as you wanted. Build your dream. Float in the sky, visit the future. You wouldn't be just staring at a flat landscape picture. You would be there right in the middle, feel it, smell it, interact with it. The exotic dream world of Douanier Rousseau would come to life—Rousseau's primitive cardboard cut-out jungle was an ideal source for the low-resolution virtual-reality (VR) panorama. A grand corporate demo became an art environment by association. That was the theory. A giant step forward for humankind. If art from the Renaissance to the present were Art I, said Roy Ascott, this would be Art II, the "being there" genre.

Yes, but. Missing from this theory was the elementary consideration that if the imaginary is filled in with literal and photorealistic detail—like those French salon paintings of the 1870s where the angels have buttons on their costumes—it rather loses its point. It is no longer an imagined image. Suggestion can be more effective than laborious photorealism. (And who made the buttons for the angels' outfits?) Art II sounded like a pretentious Disneyland theme park. The star work at that conference was Brenda Laurel's *Place Holder,* whose bird and snake forms were the first VR piece I had come across. What was actually shown was a video documenting what the "subjects" were experiencing, obviously a fuzzy approximation. It fell far short of the ultrarealism of VR predicted as one branch of Art II, but it was awesome in what it hinted at. In a sense the project itself was the "image," the stimulus for the audience to imagine a future art form—this was pre-PlayStation, pre-Web.

There was much excited talk about what was to happen once "artists" got working with this hallucinogenic illusion system. Again, there was this crucial blind spot. Half the point of most of twentieth-century movements had been to dispense with illusionism to reach a solid core: the authentic, the innocent, the pure. The visceral handling of the expressionists, the iridescent primary colour of the Fauves, the muted harmonies of Braque's and Picasso's early cubism, and the echo of African sculpture—all this was emphatically low-res and low-tech. Instead of the smooth virtuosity of Victorian painting, instead of the panorama of ancient Greece, *being there* in this modernist sense meant being physically aware of the artwork in front of you—it was not just a window for an escapist fantasy. In one sense the proposals for Art II centred on virtual reality,

71

on suppressing the viewer's normal awareness and substituting a fake universe, and this would have been a retrograde step. It meant that artists would become IMAX engineers like the various forms of being-there cinema of the 1950s and 1960s.[19] They would be even more out of the loop of the critical debate. The rest of the art community was negotiating its way through the maze of postmodern mirages—even the local park was regarded as an ideological construction, a fabrication, a "representation." The postmoderns had read Barthes. The leading artists were poring over photographs and TV images, but with a questioning frown. But here in ISEA were self-proclaimed VR gurus high on new-age therapy. They were after the Garden of Eden art theme park. And they weren't joking. A collision was inevitable.

The "realistic" simulations, with their time lag and chunky pixels, would not seem so convincingly realistic today. Like a museum of early video games, the primitive early VR works—Jeffrey Shaw's bicycle ride through a city is another iconic piece—live on, not so much as art experiences, but as self-documenting curiosities, as evidence of an exploration for a different kind of art. Ironically, such exhibits now exist primarily in the mode of art history, in a museum like the ZKM Center for Art and Media in Karlsruhe. They are not really "there," but become evidence of past explorations, the documented performance. The documentation is in the 1970s format of grey photographs plus text, factual commentary bracketed by time and place, events that took place and that you can read about but don't need to witness—like a walk though the Kalahari desert. These early VR works appear to be about an experience, but an experience that is only available vicariously. Your interface becomes the handout from the new-media history centre—a smudgy photo, educational prose.

The idea that Art II would blow away the limitations of

traditional media and thereby liberate the imagination lingers on, despite the conspicuous absence of mind-blowing art. Some artists refer to this phase as the demo art period, where it did not matter that the immersive environment did not work very well, any more than it mattered in science fiction that the science did not add up: Demo art was visionary in that it speculated about what art might be like someday. That was its particular slot. If I had closed my eyes during some of the talks on the "emergent" art forms of the future, I could imagine a scene from a movie in which the whole planet is enveloped in a gleaming chromium ring, emanating a radioactive cloud of consciousness, a higher consciousness, of course, nothing to do with paying bills, queuing at the doctor's, or feeling hungry. Collectively the art would raise us up to a higher plane. I remember a *Star Trek* episode in which everyone wore togas and wrote poetry, played the lyre, and contemplated abstract sculpture. Down below, the idyllic state was made possible by slaves toiling in underground prisons.

In the mid-1990s some new media evangelists spoke as if they expected the whole of art, from Port Moresby to Krakow, to go virtual and interactive through VR and the Web. Perhaps dissenters, old-style painters included, would be in the slave class working in the underground caves. It would add a new dimension to the art experience. I remember one artist complaining that the paintings in the National Gallery were noninteractive. Nothing happened when you stood in front of them, he said, whereas all sorts of things might be tripped off into motion once you stood in front of his work: voices, an interactive parrot, or perhaps a live webcam shot of a piece of sky from another city. I was too timid and outnumbered to speak, but I did feel this was really missing the point of painting in a big way. It was reducing the whole of the Renaissance, impressionism, whatever, to a form of audience behaviourism where the audience might as well be rats. But it was also quite a stimulating challenge. Painting is repeatedly put on the spot by a more impressive interface—a video installation, a Web piece, a game—though the modified format never strays too far from the conventions it supposedly subverts. You end up in this quiet space taking in something as if it were a painting.

Expecting art to be improved wholesale through electronic engineering was a symptom of the digital euphoria at conference time, which, thankfully, didn't survive the dot-com crash or September 11. It did prompt some wonderful speculation. The Great Leap Forward to Art II to date has not happened, and it probably never will happen, but it was worth letting the idea run riot for a while. And who knows, we just might wake up one day and find that, yes, a truly awesome species of electronic art has got to us in our sleep.

Ghosts

One of the wisest digital artists I know, who certainly believes that a new kind of art can be engineered, is fond of telling me that the trouble with software like Photoshop is that it uses the wrong metaphors. We shouldn't be thinking in terms of cameras, canvases, pencils, brushes, or paints at all. It is all a form of camouflage hiding the real nature of the digital. Ah, I say, but what is the right metaphor? Precisely, he says.

Do we need the ghosts of old media as the formal templates to structure the new digital art? Does it make any sense at all to talk of digital media when it could mean a video, a TV program, a Web site, an Epson print, or some random flashes and sounds triggered by our footsteps? I don't like the term *digital painting,* because it indicates a special subcategory stranded between two worlds, and those of us caught up in it do have a real problem of knowing where we belong. If I use photographs, do I become a photographer? Is what is good about a good painting what is good about a digital painting? I have rarely heard digital artists openly discussing their likes and dislikes, in the way painters do all the time. Nor have I heard anyone praised as a naturally gifted digital artist. If you talk about drawing, people immediately think in terms of good and bad drawing. They know whether they are able to draw, and they recognise the innate ability that runs in a family. Once, it might have seemed incongruous to speak of a talented pianist or a talented photographer. Pianos and cameras were just machines. I mention this because such instruments accumulate very gradually the familiarity that makes them seem natural. This is obvious enough to anyone who has studied an instrument, but how long it will take before digital instruments are recognised in such terms is anybody's guess.

Learning to paint means grasping what the materials can and cannot do, and also finding out what you yourself can and cannot do. Clever painters exploit the restraints of the medium and make their own weaknesses look like strengths. The conventions have evolved for a purpose. In the 1960s there were numerous attempts to "improve" painting. Paintings began to appear in all sort of experimental shapes, with rotating squares and triangles on them, with lights and other optical effects. This has certainly left a legacy—kinetic art is one obvious precursor to later experiments—but the essential format of the painted rectangle has not been dislodged.

Pigments differ from each other not only in hue but in their material properties—some are opaque, some translucent, some grainy, others squidgy. The medium that binds the pigment— oil, acrylic, gum Arabic—also has characteristics. You may have to wait anything from half an hour to a week for each layer to dry. Nor can you put a clear yellow over a blue. Working "wet into wet" is fine, but you have to accept greyed and muddied colour. If you had only known paint as it behaves in paint software, you might find this frustrating, as if the materiality of paint were a real obstacle preventing you from doing what you wanted. A continuing dilemma for developers of paint software must be how much they should simulate the behaviour of existing pigments—allowing for mixed paint to muddy up—or should the software offer "improvements." For the painter it is far from obvious which output to choose—print out the image, project it on the wall, convert it into oil paint, put it on the Web? Few established artists are pointing the way. You can hardly expect a form to "be itself" when there are so few clues about its identity.

I may have been self-taught on the computer, but knowing something about the elements of painting and what I wanted to achieve was a huge help. Without this I would have been more or less rudderless. Sometimes the digital-art community has a habit of speaking of traditional art forms as if these forms are frozen in a time warp, like a 1950s movie, and all the painter thinks of doing is painting the view from the window. In reality, painting has been evolving one way or another since the year dot. It has more than once had to compete with an optical technology—the camera lucida, the camera, film, video—which eventually became part of the native language of painting. Painting shows every sign of persisting for a few years yet. Of much greater importance than its material limitations is how it is shaped and tuned by cultural pressures, including the market, while all the time individual artists move it this way and that. The painter works within a milieu and, even at a subconscious level, navigates by means of feedback. Unless digital painters have some grasp of this, unless they have a mental map of what has been going on since the 1980s, they cannot expect to hold their own. They will be at a loss flipping through an anthology of contemporary painting. They will miss the irony, the in-joke, the cross-reference. Being stuck in the computer lab is no excuse. If you want to be taken seriously as a painter, digital or nondigital, you have to know the territory, know the history, know why "painting" became the bogey of conceptual art, know how neo-expressionist painting held sway, know how "conceptual painting" came to the fore. These are quite superficial categories, but I mention them only to point out that the neutral "canvas" you get when you open a file in the paint program is far from being neutral.

Separate Streams

If you drop in at a newsstand at a major train terminus in London, you can get a rough sense of how the readership of computer and art magazines divides—about thirty to one. Within each sector there are further divisions—five or six computer graphics magazines, perhaps, ranging from do-it-yourself Photoshop tips to the glossier publications that showcase high-end animation software. All these depend to an extent on brand loyalties—PC, Mac, and, sometime back, SGI at the top. The main features are new-product reviews and tips from the experts. If they feature "art," it will be as a demo for new software or as an example of wacky creativity. This is art without context, memory, or history. It is convenient to label the strange and supernatural images "art." For some years *Wired* magazine managed to lead and sustain a cultural dialogue alongside the gadget reviews, but the pattern now seems set. The readership of magazines like *Computer Arts* and *Computer Graphics World* won't have much idea what *Frieze* or *Artforum* are talking about, and vice versa.

The three or five art magazines on the shelves will divide between the hobbyists—with ads for painting holidays and boxed sets of pastels—and the elite magazines with full-page gallery ads, features on emerging artists, profiles of collectors, and sharp-witted reviews. Reading these elite publications, you feel you could soon be on nodding terms with a dozen top curators. The magazines reflect their readers' aspirations, though those same readers will not hesitate to talk dismissively of art-world manoeuvring. The magazines leak art-world gossip, and some feature keyhole photos of private views. They will also keep you abreast of the critical debates, especially on the letters pages. The magazines aimed at amateurs have different priorities. This readership is more interested in technical tips. Artists show step by step how they produce their work. The leisure painting magazines are altogether more practical. They associate art with pleasure rather than intellectual rigour, politics, history, or high fashion. Painting is an escape from the office to the dreamed-of villa in Tuscany. This has not always been the case. It was only with the art boom of the 1980s that the "serious" art press began to feature profiles of collectors photographed on mammoth sofas in front of their hordes. In the 1950s, when *Art News* was the dominant magazine, the "de Kooning paints a picture" feature would have been the lead item. Since that time the centre of gravity has shifted away from the studio, and now it is the critic and the curator in the foreground or, better still, the artist as curator and collector and, of course, celebrity.

I have mentioned the wayward graph of the quality of digital art, the uses and misuses of art in trade shows, and computer magazines. Equally, the understanding of computer graphics in the art community, particularly in galleries, is patchy, sometimes wildly off the mark. A phrase like *computer generated* could mean anything from a page of numbers to an inkjet reproduction of a painting. Even when a novice sits down to draw with a Wacom tablet, there is quite a lot to grasp about even the simplest operation—how to pick a colour from a palette, for example. What is an obvious reflex action for an "expert" is not at all a natural move for the newcomer. But without some firsthand experience of moving paint around the screen this way, digital painting would be quite an enigma. Art critics often start out as artists or as art historians, but studying hundreds of years of painting evolution won't help you with the mysteries of screen and print resolutions. There is quite a gap, a gap between the geeks and the connoisseurs of painting. If the most mind-blowing painting tools ever invented are more often than not wasted in the production of kitsch, this is one possible explanation.

There are how-to guides for the leading paint program Painter—not as many as the numerous spin-offs from Photoshop. These guides supplement the standard manuals and provide useful tips.[20] They assume the "artist" is working in a modest domestic setting rather than in an industrial-scale studio. Pitched at the level of the master class for the amateur, the guides fulfil their brief well enough and can teach you the essentials. The issues of mainstream art are not on the agenda. The examples in the illustrations tend to be the staple of evening class—beaches, sunsets, portraits of loved ones. Duchamp might never have existed, and Warhol's biting sarcasm becomes just another look. These are not heavy-breathing existential texts or discourses on modes of representation. They are not written with competitive art students in mind. One Painter master class I attended had the subheading "Expand Your Creativity," which alluded to "the art of transforming your photographs into beautiful paintings." The art students I know are more likely to be beavering away, turning paintings into unbeautiful photographs. Again, there is this discrepancy between the mind-set of the digital experts and the mind-set of switched-on artists.

Ideally there would be more information, advice, and critical discussion for such students. Practising digital artists do receive requests for good, practical information. If sufficient catalogues, magazines, and paperbacks were already out there, this would not be happening. There are some excellent text-books, such as Anne Morgan Spalter's *Computer in the Visual Arts,* Stephen Wilson's *Information Arts,* the SIGGRAPH Art Show catalogues, ZKM publications, theoretical works by Lev Manovich and Peter Lunenfeld, and surveys by Christiane Paul and Rachel Greene, among others.[21] But what these enquiries are after is not just information. They want the inside story. They want to match their own efforts against the benchmarks. Within the "regular" contemporary art world, there would be magazine articles, interviews, monographs, and biographies of prominent artists.

Informed and critical writing on what has been going on in digital painting is rare, even within excellent sites like Rhi-zome.org. Misconceptions fill the vacuum. One that hovers like a curse over the whole subject is that *digital* means "virtual," something without its feet on the ground, something surreal, something futuristic, something disconnected from the here and now. Another misconception is that any art that has a digital core must be part of the breakaway from more conventional art forms and have little in common with mainstream art. Another assumption is that what is produced this way should openly reveal itself as digital. None of this is necessarily the case. Steven Spielberg could have been speaking of painting when he said that the technology is most powerful when it is invisible.

Within graphic design, there is not so much fuss over the huge changes that have made typography and image editing a hundred times more convenient. If there was a digital revolu-tion, it is complete. As for design principles, they remain more or less the same. The ways paintings are made have been less affected. iMacs became common for gallery receptionists be-fore the machines found their way into studios. There are explanations for this slow uptake: lack of money, technophobia, inappropriate programs at the outset, the failure of colleges to see the relevance for fine art, the absence of a major stimulus like a stunning exhibition. The number of practitioners, professionals in fine art, still has not reached the critical mass at which these preconceptions drop away, and then, possibly, we could see software being designed with these specialists in mind.

Crossing Points

Meanwhile, some social recoding is required every time I cross between the painting world and the digital world. Within the same month, I was exhibiting works both in the John Moores exhibition—which for forty years was the UK's principal painting competition (now eclipsed by the Turner Prize and other competitions)—and in the SIGGRAPH Art Show. The SIGGRAPH has been one of the most consistent digital-art showcases for 2D works. In 2002 it was held in San Antonio, Texas. At the Moores, there was the usual press view that preceded the private view, with critics and TV celebrities, notebooks and microphones posed for quotes. I had not adjusted and felt I was at a computer-art show, where "art" is the poor relation in every respect. So this level of attention given to the actual objects was disorienting. I found myself asked quite sensible questions about how my particular painting had been made, who influenced it, and what it might be about. The implication in the question was that the act of painting involved your whole being and would be imbued with influences, attitudes, and ideas. It was the day job. The "piece" was not a demo or an academic exercise. Unfortunately, being still in SIG-GRAPH mode, I was tongue-tied and defensive and quite unprepared for that kind of interest. At the SIGGRAPH show, the exhibitors had been required to place explanatory panels

81

alongside the finished piece explaining the processes involved in making the work. Some brave exhibitors could even be found alongside their exhibits working on their Macs, showing how it was all done. Until a few years back, every digital show would require the "artist" to cite the software used and to provide some sort of written explanation.

Compared with the Moores exhibition, the SIGGRAPH was like a student show, where you have to explain how you have addressed the issues of the set project. At SIGGRAPH shows, I have never yet encountered a critic at any press view over the last decade or two or ever been asked those searching questions. Nor for that matter have I ever read more than a couple of reviews of the SIGGRAPH shows or found myself rubbing shoulders with celebrities there. What I exhibited at both Moores and SIGGRAPH was similar, almost the same image, but the way it was scrutinised at the Moores, even the way people walked past, or felt they should or shouldn't keep silent and respectful, spoke volumes. I enjoy the ambivalence of the SIGGRAPH Art Gallery, its accessibility, the artists giving their talks, but sometimes it is more like a hotel foyer than a gallery.

All the same, perhaps this is a cause with broader perspectives and we cannot expect exhibitions of digital art to become top-class society events overnight. There have to be several intermediate stages, and perhaps the next stage is simply the dissolution of the category, as digital and nondigital blend together. Also, I should never forget the debt that younger practitioners owe to those artists who, in making a name for themselves, established this computer-art tributary of the mainstream. The branch would not have come into existence at all without their dedication. They have not just been artists; they have been exceptionally determined individuals. They were self-taught and self-reliant. They did not have the critical mass supporting them, the college courses, the magazines, the theoretical literature, the galleries. Without their effort, we would be nowhere at all. So this has to be borne in mind when a critic tears into the unintentional rehashes of abstract styles that were done to death in the 1960s, or when a much younger art-school product who has played around with Flash for a couple of years tells me these pioneers are not "real artists." The debt may soon be forgotten. The next generation may be more "art smart," intolerant of the psychedelic swirls and psychother-apeutic installations that have so often got past the juries.

To become fluent in computer graphics requires patience, intellect, and manual agility. I have never met as many former philosophy students as I have met at computer-art conferences. If you know your symbolic logic, you can program. Nonusers imagine a process that is more or less automatic. In my experi-ence, working digitally is very much hands-on and requires complete absorption. You become just as bonded to your equipment as you are when you go through the studio rituals of preparing a palette and picking a favourite brush. It would take only two or three digital artists to break through and become major art-world figures—with profiles in key art magazines, museum shows, prizes, endorsement from critics, weighty monographs—the works—and the misconceptions and doubts would evaporate. The practitioners themselves, few of whom manage to sell a significant part of their output, often lack con-fidence in their creations' viability as art rather than digital art. Outside the SIGGRAPH circle, most gallery visitors are still as perplexed as ever by computer art. They appreciate that it must be quite clever, but they cannot tell whether it is the work of the artist or the system.

Despite the incredible resources of Google, the glut of magazines, the proliferation of TV channels, and the expansion of galleries, we still tend to notice only what we are primed to notice. The world of computer art was strange to me, but still relatively small, in the 1980s, and it would have seemed even stranger to think that within a decade PhD students would comb through this activity. But specialisation has its drawbacks. Tunnel vision means two specialists see the same territory but see two quite different pictures. A student at Goldsmith's, one of London's leading art schools, was doing a PhD on "painting and virtuality." My ears pricked up. But it turned out to be a study touching only on a theoretical idea of what such painting might be like. The student was puzzled by the phrase *digital art*. What? He was quite unaware that, for a decade, artists—Char Davies and Jeffrey Shaw, in particular—had been making major works with virtual reality.

The doctoral student's lack of awareness is not uncommon. I mention this and other similar instances, not to blame anyone for a lack of universal knowledge, but to underline how specialisation isolates one area of expertise from another. At a 2003 Tate conference on new media, a speaker who was an expert on avant-garde film revealed that she had no idea what a Web site was. In 1998 I gave a talk at the Tate on the painter Patrick Heron, the great colourist, who had a retrospective there. I showed a few slides of digital works made by other artists to suggest where the next generation of colourists might turn up. After the talk I was quizzed again and again by members of the audience who had no idea that images of any kind—let alone colour ones—could be produced on a computer. One of the real masters of digital-effect animation, Chris Landreth, who in 1998 made the wonderful *Bingo* animation, which featured a clown, had never heard of Bruce Nauman, the pioneer video artist who had also made a video about a clown. We all have our black holes of ignorance, but we seem to be going through a period in which it is common for two artists from quite different disciplines to be standing on the same spot without realising it.

The fine-art student can spend as much time in seminars discussing theory as learning actual techniques. Could you learn painting or photography just as a skill? I doubt it. But the sheer number of students makes the old atelier system of one-to-one tuition impracticable. There could well be ten times the number of students that there were thirty years ago, and the staffing and studio space may have hardly increased at all—especially in a leading school located in an inner city. The whole character of a course has had to change. After a few months, the student is as likely to be making a video installation as a still life. To an outsider it might seem sensible to begin with a solid technical grounding, but this begs the question of whether there is actually any common ground. What is the core art discipline? Drawing? Programming? Criticism? Video editing?

Drawing is the most commonly cited candidate, but to say that drawing should play the role doesn't help much, because drawing itself is being reinvented from the ground up, in part because of the impact of new technology. You could advocate learning through practice, working with materials, but again there is such a range of things to practise—painting, photography, video, performance, installation. And within each discipline there are so many subdivisions, so much history. Do you learn how to use a camera, even a digital camera, from studying Cartier-Bresson? If you join a six-week course on Photoshop, what understanding of photography do you gain? The artist who emerges from today's fine-art course may well decide that painting plus some digital printmaking is the right direction, but there will be difficult decisions to make. Does this artist buy the iMac or rent a studio? A secondhand litho press or a high-end inkjet printer? Already, galleries look at the inkjet print as quite normal—not at all my experience fifteen years ago.

The appreciation of the *artist's print* has an unwritten etiquette all its own, with special papers, limited numbered editions, and high levels of craftsmanship. In many cases, the prints are not printed by the artist at all but by specialist printmaking workshops. These prints have long provided a steady income for painters whose major works will sell much less easily. The computer print—it was first called computer output—could have undermined this status. It could cut out the middlemen entirely, the carefully built up "studio print" culture. All you needed to do was press the button. There was no need for a separate plate or a screen for each colour. At the end of the 1980s, I had to overcome some resistance to persuade my gallery to exhibit my carefully produced inkjet prints. Admitting that the prints had some merit as images, other galleries would nevertheless enumerate a list of reasons why the prints didn't qualify as proper prints: The paper was too thin, the colour might fade eventually, they were made by the computer and not the artist, there was no skill, they were graphic design and not art, the texture was inadequate, they must be reproductions and not originals, they might be faked. And so on.

At the beginning of the 1990s, when I was teaching paint programs like Studio 8 to the fine-art students at the Royal College of Art, the Printmaking Department was uneasy. I accepted the professor's challenge to hold an open seminar in which all the (rather small but brightly coloured) inkjet prints the students had made in three weeks were spread all round the room. In terms of expressive freedom, variety, and, most of all, quantity, there was no way the students could have achieved a quarter as much by using the department's own resources of litho, silkscreen, and etching. The staff members clearly wanted to express their doubts, and they argued that this was not proper printmaking. They used the same arguments. The printmaking professor made a point of telling me how artists live and work, and that as a "technical person," I probably would not get the hang of the lifestyle. I obviously wasn't intuitive, impulsive, or capable of the spontaneous, lateral thought processes of the true artist. (On the whole, the printmaking tutors concerned hardly lived up to this image, since they worked most of the time at the college.) Whatever I felt internally, I did not want a confrontation. I let the staff members feel they had made their case and shown that the new upstart printing technology was never going to be an art medium. The students were made to remake their prints conventionally, with the colour dulled and all the vitality taken away because of the laboriousness of traditional processes. (While this was going on, I had the quiet satisfaction not only of selling to the Victoria and Albert Museum the inkjets that my gallery would not show, but of having them on permanent view there for the next fourteen years.) Some of those students went on to become leading digital artists. The Computing Department, however, was closed down in 1993, and I was out of a job.

The status of the computer print remained something of a problem. By the end of the 1990s, the Iris print, specifically the giclee Iris print, became the acceptable standard, with proper "art" paper and saturated pigment rather than dye-based inks, and this guaranteed longevity. (I also have more primitive inkjet prints that look fine after being on my walls for seventeen years.) At the same time that these prints have become acceptable to the collector, the digital art world has turned its back on 2D digital art. The major festivals of ISEA and Ars Electronica ceased exhibiting 2D work of any kind in the 1990s— too traditional.

Artists develop their own individual ways of working. Some wander round the streets with a camera gathering images; others sit at a desk. Still others spend hours tidying up their studios to avoid facing their work. To transpose an idiosyncratic working process into the work flow of a program could be asking too much. You can customise the look and mess up the palettes, but the laptop cannot do everything. A studio is not really a factory, an office, or an information-processing centre. Take the question of time spent on a piece of work. With even the relatively crude systems of the 1980s I could run through several dozen permutations of any given design in a morning, changing the colour, the scale, the thickness of a line, and so on. The quality of the printed output didn't matter; nor did it matter that the paint was clearly electronic and simulated. I was learning so much through experimenting with the different combinations. How could I return to a pattern of working where a gouache study would take two days, an oil painting two or three months, with days spent waiting for each layer to dry?

Typically a painter's studio will have several paintings being worked on simultaneously, often in series, with a family of similar motifs, all at different stages of completion. A pencil drawing may take ten seconds, a large painting two years, but part of a painter's craft is the ability to tell in a glance what needs to be done—perhaps an idea for the next work. Unlike the birthday card designer or the illustrator working on commission, painters must supply their own work plans and set their own criteria. They depend on the continuity, the steady accumulation of knowledge, and distrust the shortcuts that might cheapen the distinctive, personal quality. This is a huge generalisation—there are brilliant painters like Polke, who go out of their way to downgrade their techniques—but bearing in mind that graphic packages have modelled themselves on the commercial artist, it is a distinction that is worth hanging on to for the moment. In the use of studio time, the independent painter has different priorities from those of the graphic designer working to deadlines.

The use of space can be quite different, too. Carrying your work with you in a laptop or in a memory stick is wonderful—no storage or studio rent to pay—but what you can't do is have all your work pinned up on the wall in front of you, so that each morning your eye catches something different. Some studios are chaotic, others are minimalist galleries, but they are much more than functional workshops. They are places for thinking, places where time stands still. The studio wall is like a diagram of how to think laterally, your eye skipping at random. Working on a screen absorbs the attention in a quite different way. It cuts out peripheral vision. You can switch programs, check your e-mail, visit and tweak the Mars lander, but fundamentally you sit in a different space from the space you are manipulating. If I have a painting on the wall, I know that it is four feet across. If I walk away, it gets smaller, and up close, it is huge. I don't need to press the magnifier icon. To make it disappear I just walk out of the room.

Chapter 4 **Gone Fishing**

The Art of Art

I have long been a fan of John Ashbery's poetry, which glides
effortlessly sideways through apparently disconnected thoughts
and conversations and yet somehow makes its own kind of
sense, its own kind of music. I would not call it surrealist or a
collaged form, but it is dreamlike and immaculately phrased.
He gave a public reading in 2003 at the Tate Modern and an-
swered questions from the audience with patient attention. I
am more used to artists giving talks, in those evasive and con-
frontational sessions where you suspect the artists are being
inarticulate to preserve a sense of mystery, a way of seeming

profound, a way of hanging on to their privacy. Perhaps if you have a gallery or a critic speaking on your behalf, there is no need to let anyone else into the studio. Perhaps, quite reasonably, artists prefer their work to speak for itself. Some artists can be generous with their time, seem to have no secrets, and will gladly let visitors wander round their studios. They also enjoy teaching. They like to borrow the younger eyes, and see the work afresh. Either way, when artists step on a public platform, it can sometimes be an ordeal, a thorny session—and will they open up or close down the shutters?

I was struck here by how thoughtful and reflective the discussion was, stimulated as it was by Ashbery's poetry. All the same, he was not at ease answering the "what is your work about?" question, especially when someone was expecting a clear-cut answer that could go straight into the MA research. The question that pressed the right button and put him at ease was the simple one: How do you go about writing these poems? It turned out that he no longer revised and rewrote as much as he had done in the past. He gathered much of his material from overheard conversations in the street, advertisements, daytime TV. This answer did not explain his poetry or why it cast its spell, but it was revealing. The mud of his river, the material he worked into shape, was made of the conversational fragment, the goo of discarded phrases that floated in the air like ambient thought waves: an internal monologue, a traffic report on the radio, a neighbour's small talk, a chat show.

I have limited ambitions as a poet, but I doubt that were I to follow Ashbery's "method" I would come up with anything special. Like the experiences of everyone else in London, it seems, my bus journeys are regularly filled with what you could call "involuntary" poetry from overheard mobile-phone conversations—fragmentary because you only hear one side of the conversation. But that is just the raw material, just as the view from the bus window is raw material. I may have developed an eye for looking at such passing scenery, simply through spending my time photographing, drawing, painting, or just looking. It becomes a habit. But I don't have the necessary ear for recognizing and capturing the telling phrase. I couldn't become a poet overnight anymore than I could become a concert pianist or a pole-vaulter overnight. It would take years of dedication, decades of practice even to become a passable imitator of an Ashbery. Yes, artists of all kinds have methods, their techniques for gathering material and for shaping it, but it would be ludicrous to look just at the assembling technique, as if by following their recipe you could produce your own masterwork.

No software claims it has condensed the secrets of the old masters—or an "instant poetry technique"—into a boxed set of program DVDs, but the term *creativity* does get a lot of use, as if this is a latent state of mind that needs just the right skill set to give it full expression. On your home computer you can "create your own" impressionist painting, symphony, 1970s guitar solo, haiku, or whatever you want. Instead of going out to get your material you can just scan it in or skim it from the Web. You may understand that it is only a simulation, an imitation, but what with culture supplements with free CDs and online museum tours, this difference is getting blurry. This is an obvious point, but one that is passed over when one thinks only in terms of physical versus virtual. It is not a question of a "traditional" technique being supplanted by a digital technique. You don't spend all those years in college just acquiring facility with the brush and a set of how-to formulas. You learn by constant practice, observation, immersion in the entire culture of visual art, past and present. If it is "training," it is closer to training the mind than training in software "skills."

The tutorials that come with Painter software and the how-to articles in magazine and practical books that follow in its wake all tiptoe round this issue. They tell you how to get along with the interface and how to "paint." You follow step by step. Though an accomplished painter might find the advice useful, it is usually pitched for those with modest objectives: Follow these steps, and you will end up with something that could pass for a painting. Part of me wants to be liberal and tolerant and say yes, this is all fine, and the more who find their way to becoming accomplished painters the better. But another part holds back. These methods make it so easy, the images so numbingly bland, that I want to say emphatically that this is not an art form but a kind of substitute, a kind of fake art, a kind of kitsch. It makes the task of raising digital painting to a credible category doubly difficult.

It is also a question of intensity and passion. Nothing in any software package conspires to prevent you from producing significant art of one kind or another, and a completely

Ken Huff, *2005.1*, 2005, variable size up to 60" × 90" (152 × 229 cm), chromogenic print of digital image. (See also Plate 5.)

"untrained" artist could emerge this way. Perhaps an upcoming exhibition of digital paintings will raise the bar for painting in general. I should not imply that you could only make headway with an art or art history degree. Ken Huff is one of the most consistently interesting digital painters around—the software Maya uses one of his pictures on its box—but he studied anthropology. All the same, he knows the field of digital and nondigital art inside out and works as intensely as any "real paint" painter.

Painting with the computer still hovers between being just a technique and being an art form in its own right. There are no artists in this particular niche with the reputation that John Ashbery has as a poet. Harold Cohen is widely respected as one of the seminal figures with Aaron, his programmed alter ego painting system, now creating "realistic" paintings of plants and still lifes. But Cohen attracted a much smaller audience a few months later in the same lecture theatre. I had expected the theatre to be packed. Here was a painter who had represented Britain in the Venice Biennale in 1966 and led computer painting for decades from his base in California. At present, the only people who show up for such talks appear to be a few fellow digital artists and academics specialising in what now seems a historical period. It is not a matter of agreeing or disagreeing with this. It is just the way things are. There is a small fan base. Digital painting can be regarded as a backwater.

Perhaps one explanation is the prejudice that if it's virtual art, it can't be full-on art. The artists must live in flotation tanks. They don't tread the same streets, see the same shows, wash in the same water. They lead this half-life in what used to be called *cyberspace.* They would not be gathering material on the bus; they would be shut in the lab. So it is hard to break down the stereotype. I have had conversations over the years with galleries that have explained why they would not touch

computer art. The reasons included these: (a) It was not produced by real artists; (b) it was insubstantial physically, on thin
paper, or just a flicker on a monitor; and (c) it was inherently of
a low quality. In the past I could sympathise with one or more
of these reasons, but when Iris prints became acceptable in fine-
art-editions prints, on weighty Somerset watercolour paper, the
same prejudices lingered on. Ken Huff, I recall, asked a leading
New York gallery why it said there was no chance of showing
such work, even though it specialised in all kinds of prints and
claimed to represent the most advanced work around. The
gallery's explanation included the suggestion that he might like
to work as a technician for one of its artists and guide the artist
through the process. I have had painter friends make the same
request: They could sit beside me and I could follow their
instructions and make their paintings for them. Somehow, I
wriggled out of doing this, fee or no fee, a little irked that they
did not ask to see what I made myself. Would they have agreed if
I had dropped round at their studio and asked them to paint my
pictures for me? Perhaps they would have, for a fee, but at least
they might have suspected some irony in my request.

The trouble is that if you make too much of the spectacular tricks that can be done with this new paint material—and, if
you are demonstrating to an audience of students, this is hard
to resist—you can leave the impression that this is all you can
do with it, dabbling with effects. You can wow them with kaleidoscopic patterns, splotchy runny watercolour, and instant
homemade animations. But this is trivial, the same visual acrobatics that are used to reveal the must-have chemistry of sham-
poo. It no longer dazzles an audience that has something just as
intricate at home as a screen saver. Someone is bound to say
that it is all great fun, but where is the connection with the
world, with the heart? Or more simply, why should it be connected with art, and if it is art, where in the museums is the

96

evidence that this is anything more than playing around with graphics pretending to be paint? Good questions.

Here and there museums are acquiring computer-based art quite methodically, especially the early groundbreaking work, so some artists will be able to answer this by saying, go to the first floor, second room on the right. But this does not really answer the larger question. How many practising digital artists would put any such work in their top ten works of art of all types and of all time? I would have to distinguish between the spectacular and the ones I can see again and again and never get tired of seeing once more. Given the choice of a third visit to the IMAX cinema or seeing *Double Indemnity* for the umpteenth time, which would I choose? I can see rationally that a new medium can take decades to mature, but during that period, it does make sense to keep in touch with the fundamentals, with what makes art what it is, whether that is timing, narrative, formal elegance, dramatic lighting, control of colour, suspense, surprise, beauty. At the same time, the new medium—or media—may fail to develop along the predicted paths or may jump tracks, and at first only the practitioners involved will appreciate what begins to emerge. It may prove significant that the distinction between a video camera and a still camera is disappearing because digital cameras can capture moving images, and video cameras can capture stills. Phones, videos, and cameras have merged in formats few would have imagined twenty years ago. The number of amateur digital artists is bound to increase. Photographers are investing in large-format inkjet printers and find they can paint directly on the printed canvas if they want. These small changes in consumer products may do no more than eliminate the need for darkrooms or bedroom studios. But one consequence could be a well-informed audience much more capable of understanding exactly what *digital manipulation* means. An audience with a special feel for this might develop, much as an audience for niche forms in poetry, jazz, or video art started out, grew, and eventually went mainstream.

Tools, Models, and Minds

One way to explain the impact that digital painting can have on "real" painting would be the live demonstration. Here and there, Photoshop user groups have staged head-to-head contests with one artist equipped with a Wacom tablet drawing, say, a portrait of someone dressed up as a cowboy, and the other artist poised with easel, palette, canvas—the works. The difficulty with these demonstrations is, again, that they presuppose that by art you mean nothing more demanding than what you might come across in an evening class. They also presuppose that the digital part of the painting exercise would simply recreate the look of "real paint." Not surprisingly, the results could look strikingly similar—at least in reproduction.

Another demonstration might show how several artists, all using digital equipment, might start with the same raw material but go off in quite different directions. I can imagine this arranged as a game show, with a clock ticking and the images projected onto large screens. It would have something in common with a concert in which a jazz quartet was thrown a theme around which they had to improvise. I would like to see the artists play around using the full freedom and power of a paint or 3D system, modifying impossible brushes, moving whole blocks of pattern this way and that, juggling layers, lots of hits and misses. The "painting" would not have to be constrained by either the "realism" of the evening class or the realism of imitated paint. The participants could follow this event by trying out similar processes in a studio, cutting through sheets of drawings, using unlikely materials as brushes, and varying the pace from very slow to very fast. Conceivably, the demonstration could become an art form itself, a fusion of painting and performance art—"celebrity chef" with paint instead of food. Some workshops are already run on this pattern.

A sociologist may one day propose a study of digital artists. What is the effect, the study will ask, of such factors as sitting at a desk all day instead of walking up and down a cold studio floor, of constant checking and dealing with e-mail, "researching" across the Web instead of wandering around town, of hours spent manipulating "objects" that do not exist as true objects. Other professions and activities have become home based and free floating, but will this mean the stereotype of the somewhat alienated, somewhat marginalised artist will need to be revised? Would this eventually have an effect on the character of the art produced? A tendency toward the immaterial, the fantastic, the weightless, the religious even? Or, as a reaction, toward the weighty and textural?

Alan Lee, who illustrated the 1991 hardback *Lord of the Rings* and was one of the concept artists for the movies, recently went digital. After six years of working with the movies, he explained in an interview with the *Guardian* how he really got involved with the digital in postproduction:

> Digital artists were using methods and a language I didn't understand. I moved into the visual effects art department and started working on a computer for the first time. We were taking stills from the movie and replacing the blue screens with designs for the backgrounds. . . . It was a case of throwing myself in at the deep end. I had thought I was a technophobe until I realized that computers had moved a long way towards people like me—especially Macs, which seemed very user friendly.

Q. *Have you carried that on after completing the films?*

A. Yes, I still use my traditional media of charcoal, pencils and watercolours but I've also set myself up with a G5 and Photoshop. Macs still seem more suitable for people who think visually. A lot of people use Corel Painter. . . . With Painter, you can more easily reproduce watercolour effects, but if something is going to look like a watercolour, then it should be one.

Q. *Do you use a tablet?*

A. Yes, I use an A3 size Wacom tablet which I have set up with two screens so I can spread out my material. I wouldn't be able to use a mouse to create my work—it's amazing how easy it is to draw on the tablet without looking at what you're actually drawing. It's also very fast and easy to produce several saved variations of what you're doing.

Q. *Any pros or cons to switching to computer for your illustrating?*

A. It has opened up the scope of what I can do—I've been using it to work out ideas I will finish in watercolour. But I can't think of too many cons—other than a tendency for illustrators working on computers to lose their distinguishing traits. That's why I still draw on paper and then scan it in.[22]

There is quite a gap, as already mentioned, between what a concept artist gets up to in the movie world and what a conceptual artist gets up to in the art world. The sociologist could offer better advice than a critic as to which was more connected, more grounded, and more earthed, even to middle earth. What interested me here was that Alan Lee, like artists of all types, preferred to scan in a physical drawing and associated that physical drawing with his artistic identity. I also noted how this entirely imaginary world required such complete physical solidity. It could not afford to "float."

Is this an absolute truth, that a handmade mark on paper is always going to be more of an autographic mark than one made, say, through a Wacom tablet? I fear this is a philosophical question, because credit-card companies have come to reject the signature as an unreliable "indicator of individuality." It can be faked. A number remains the same number however it is written, typed, punched into a keypad, or spoken. Those of us who now write principally through a keyboard probably find writing their signature a self-conscious process. Travellers from Britain to France were for some years impressed because French petrol stations allowed drivers to punch in their numeric signature and their pin number, and now the same is true in Britain: My identity is now a number rather than a semilegible scrawl.

I also put some faith in the "autographic" mark on paper, while accepting it may be an irrational belief, a residual reflex from my art education. It is one of those breaks in the logic I cannot quite cross, and like the artists who scan watercolours, I often fall short of being 100 percent digital. In my own case I need the feeling of connection that drawing can give, that is, the sensations of manipulating a pencil, brush, or stick and the instant and sometimes unpredictable feedback that prompts the next move—or just as often, holds it back. It could also be the instinct to trust what is solid and resistant, in this case, paint drawn on paper on a concrete floor. Incidentally, I do not mention this as a recommended method, but just as one practical example of how physical and digital can be integrated.

I have a favourite large Japanese round brush and a special stick, and using both of these, one in each hand, I set to work, usually working on six to ten drawings on the floor simultaneously. I often use Plaka paint, which is more tempera than gouache and is bound by casein, and I mix it with water in two or three consistencies from thick to thin. I would first have made several absent-minded doodles in a sketchbook or hit upon some simple formula such as five Xs and six Os as an idea, but often some motif will get repeated from drawing to drawing. On occasion I also arrange large, flattened-out pieces of cardboard from packages on the floor and "draw" across these. Apart from its colour and the texture, cardboard has the advantage of being a cheap material—in reality it is not always so cheap, as it may well have been the packaging for a new computer. So I convince myself that whatever I draw on it, it doesn't matter. There is no cost. I can have the same freedom as I have when drawing on the screen. I can be quite detached and carefree, or if I want, I can be intense and focused. While the paint is still wet I then photograph the drawings—you could say the paintings—taking care to keep them square and free of obtrusive reflections. Alternatively I build temporary reliefs and sculptures out of the drawings, nailing them to the wall for the few minutes of their existence, and photograph them from several angles.

What can often happen when I am working this way in a studio, and what does not happen so spontaneously when I am making a set of drawings through a stylus on a Wacom tablet, is that one drawing will have a direct influence on another. When gazing across the floor or wall of a studio, my eyes can take in the feel of a dozen drawings in an instant, and I can make comparisons and edit them down without taking a breath. I can also look at a drawing as whole, right to its edges, whereas on a monitor or when printed out, a drawing's edges are not so definite. On the monitor the drawing ends where white turns to the black or grey of the background, or where the edge is cropped, and on the print where the paper is cut or where the framed area begins. On paper it is like falling off the edge of the world.

After photographing the drawings, I may feed them into the computer and look through them with my digital eyes. One part of my working routine is to walk around outside the studio with a camera and take photos of whatever strikes me at that moment. I also "draw" on the computer. Even amid other tasks, I find it useful to make even the most cursory drawing. Each strain of drawing and observation can eventually become connected: By regular freeform drawing, my eye is alerted to certain forms I may see on a walk, and so the photos I take have a visual rationale to them. Working with circles, I am alert to circular forms. Although these activities can sometimes seem to be just a game or just exercises that produce no results, the practice keeps me in shape. By having quite a range of hardware—from a wooden stick to a G5—I learn how the tool influences not only the marks I can make, but also the forms I learn to see. And when I do make a find I appreciate my catch.

The Patient Painter

The benefit of having parallel streams of work in photographic, drawing, painting, and digital formats sometimes pays off. Pictures and ideas can arrive without an apparent source or much of a point beyond fulfilling a certain personal quota—a job done, so to speak. The same mixture can work for a slower project, a project that may begin from something seen out of the corner of the eye, something that may take months or years before it can be fully realised in a painting.

Even when the image is "abstract," patient observation is the key to painting. An artist can practise drawing by making patterns rather than drawing a bowl of fruit, and practice can still help in picking out what to photograph, how to look for prompts and motifs among the ordinary objects that surround you. It is worth stressing how misleading some of the common terms like *representational* and *abstract* can be, especially when moved across to classify digital work as being of one type or the other. Abstract painting, for example, is not a term abstract painters themselves are happy using. In the 1920s Malevich, Kandinsky, or Mondrian certainly alluded to an otherworldly abstract realm, a spiritual realm even, but in the years after 1945, that idealistic vision faded away or at least came to seem meaningless. For the abstract expressionists, for Pollock or for de Kooning, the physical existence of the painting was what mattered, and by the 1960s, the concrete fact of the canvas, its shape, size, and colour, its literal in-your-face there-ness, became the whole point. In no way were these latter developments cases of "abstracting" an image from "reality." They were emphasising the reality of the painting, its colour, its surface, its scale.

The "abstract" patterns and images of the early computer art of the 1960s and 1970s are closer to that prewar version, the idealistic *mindscape.* They do not have any obvious connection with the observed world—what you see out your window or what you see when you go shopping. They exist in a separate space, perhaps a mathematical world. This is one reason that, from the outset, computer art looked dated. The postwar abstraction of the New York School of the 1950s was much less preciously "abstract" and remote; it was gutsy and dynamic, and yes, it did—and still does—have this feeling of connection with the street, the play of light on water, the noise of traffic, the softness of flesh. This rich sensuality evokes the visual collage of a city street, with the painting itself conceived as a "real object" engaging with the space of the room it hangs in.

The painter in me is very familiar with this distinction. Academic realists, pop artists, expressionists, postmodern ironists, all seem able to see each other's work without necessarily agreeing with the opposing art ideologies. They don't need a verbal explanation. This is not always the case in a show of digital art, where either a statement or the artist in person has to be on hand to enlighten the viewer. For the painter, whether a portrait painter or a committed minimalist, everything he or she sees is potentially source material, what you might call part of a visual continuum; the artist is liable to look "abstracted," to drop out of a conversation and look at some peculiarity in the reflection on a glass. This continuum stretches back in time, so that in a museum the art of several thousand years ago can be as present, as contemporary as what was painted last week. Painters have frequently been ticked off for being naive in speaking of the innocent, all-absorbing eye in this way, seeing the world as if it were just flat patches of colour like an impressionist painting—or even a film set. What we see, we are told, is "constructed" in one way or another. But "the visual" is the one kind of research where the painter is a true specialist and does not rely on any other profession—apart from perhaps the optician. All evidence here is visual and firsthand. The text is supplementary, a caption to the experience.

But all this looking, as if anything can be turned into a subject or a research project, can get out of hand. Better minds than mine have recognised that preparation, searching around, fiddling with equipment, is not the same thing as delivering the goods. Way before anyone thought about the credentials of digital art, of describing it as research, or calling it "art practice," Sir Joshua Reynolds was arguing that painting was inherently intellectual. As president of the Royal Academy, he delivered his Twelfth Discourse in December 1784:

> In the practice of art, as well as in morals, it is necessary to keep a watchful and jealous eye over ourselves; idleness, assuming the specious disguise of industry, will lull to sleep all suspicion of our want of an active exertion of strength. A provision of endless apparatus, a bustle of infinite enquiry and research, or even the mere mechanical labour of copying, may be employed, to evade and shuffle off real labour— the real labour of thinking.[23]

Today we would call this *displacement activity*. It describes my diversionary tactics down to a T—though in 1784 there was no way you could waste a morning searching the Web for the latest deals on a digital projector. However, it is not always easy to tell when an activity is just playing around or moving an idea along a few inches. In my experience it is well worth playing around with an idea rather than worrying about wasting time. It is all too easy to abandon a project before it gets off the ground just because it looks pointless. One of the great benefits of digital photography is that you don't have to pay for the film, so you don't worry about wasting a photograph on something stupid. To many of us, this is a great liberation, simply by taking that doubt, that inhibition, away.

Joshua Reynolds made another point in that same discourse:

> The daily food and nourishment of the mind of an Artist is found in the great works of his predecessors.[24]

This remains sound advice—rather than reading aesthetics, art theory, research papers, or flicking through online galleries, we should look at actual paintings. Or just look out the window. But to deliver this advice properly, perhaps you need to write a book.

One motive I have had in piecing these thoughts together came from the simple thought of what happens if and when I am run down by a bus. As I have mentioned, I have had several friends who have died in their prime, and it is distressing that each time this happened, their legacy seems to have vanished into thin air. I wish they had had the foresight to condense what they knew into a book, a treatise, a set of "Discourses" in the old sense, or a definitive set of works. I am not singling myself out here as a significant contributor, but rather as a witness, someone who has absorbed what he has seen, listened in on numerous conversations, and made most of the mistakes in the handbook of wrong turns. I am on the fringes of the generation that has straddled the low-tech and the high-tech worlds. One way or another, we found ways of connecting painting and the exploitation of computer graphics. When we were students, there were few clues that electronics and printmaking, or painting and programming, would ever have anything to do with each other. We had to find our own way. Our own solutions. There were no institutions of digital art, few reference books, and few exhibitions.

The painters who learn to think fluently within the languages of Photoshop, Illustrator, or Painter may find they have backed into a new dimension without realising it. There are precedents in different art forms for minor mechanical adjustments in cameras, typewriters, pigment binders, paint tubes, piano actions, that had quite unpredictable consequences. The sustaining pedal on Beethoven's Broadwood piano gave him his "cathedral in the living-room," and a few springs in the keyboard action gave Chopin the possibility of rapid repetition on the same note. It would be quite wrong to say the outpouring of great romantic compositions was brought about by technology, and it would be wrong to expect some equivalent renaissance from the combined efforts of Apple, Microsoft, Adobe, Corel, and whoever else. Yet in many of its aspects the romantic movement—the concept of the individual genius, the origins of what is loosely described as the modern movement—did depend on the very industrial advances that were so often despised and disregarded. Without the steam trains taking them to the countryside, the tubes to make the paint portable, the Kodak to catch the snapshot viewpoint, the impressionists would have found *plein air* painting quite a stressful process.

The routine way of gathering visual data when I was a student was still a sketchbook and a ticket on the Circle Line—the part of the London Underground system that goes round and round so that one ticket can last all day. With a digital camera, a video, and a laptop linked to cricket scores as well as paint programs, life is a little different, though in my own case I still draw a lot. The point of drawing is to make sense of what you are looking at. If you draw your camera, or even look at the drawing in the instructions showing how it works, you get to know it a little better. The trick is to think of old and new technologies as not competing with one another but complementing each other. I see it as still quite reasonable to use painting as a way of understanding the visible world—I hope that does not sound pretentious—but from an oblique angle. Some eight years ago I began, but never completed, a project with BBC News. I was to shadow the process of the acquisition, editing, and presentation of stories, with the idea that I could produce digital pieces that would go on the walls and columns of the new BBC News centre. In explaining the BBC project, I found the most useful analogy was to speculate that if Turner were alive, he would be using computer graphics in painting, and just as he was fascinated with speed and light, he might have been fascinated with the phenomenon of a news bulletin. At 6 or 10 P.M. millions of families receive the same messages in their living rooms and kitchens. The newsreader sits alone in a studio set that is half virtual—the cameras are robotic—like a priest at the altar. It is an extraordinary ritual for an outsider to witness: the cool professionalism of the handful of people in the studio, the millions in their homes. I think of flying over cities at night and looking at the pinpoints of light. Composing a thirty-minute bulletin that condenses everything that happens that day throughout the whole world is an extreme example of rapid research and drastic compression.

Though the project ran aground, I spent quite some time attempting to visualise this scarcely comprehensible process, thinking of the different viewpoints, editing, compressing, simplifying, and how something readily communicable is condensed from the vast complexity of raw information available. Ever since then I have been sensitive to the difficulty of making a definitive statement of what it is I am looking at. I don't mean this in a theoretical way, but as something felt: the actual texture of information, its structure, how much can be digested in a glance. Any news story has to be selected, framed, cropped. Its treatment indicates the editorial point of view, even a neutral, third-person point of view. This may be basic epistemology, but it is something I had neglected, and something left unresolved in discussions on drawing. When we speak of models, we refer to a secure, "out-there" model, the life model, the still life, the landscape, the found material. Even if we talk of a subjective interpretation, we habitually think of this as an alternative to an objective approach. What we do not normally contemplate is how unknowable "out there" can be, even when we measure it. This is by no means a new idea springing from insect-size video cameras. If we follow Ruskin's exercises in *Elements of Drawing* and attempt to draw a tree, we don't just pay attention to the type of leaf, but consider its orientation toward us or away from us, its angle, the weight of the branches. It happens that foliage, like hair, is where 3D programmers like to show off what they can do. From either point of view it is still a shock to realise just how little we really know of each tree in the park.

From the technical sessions I would drop in on at SIGGRAPH conferences, the visualisation of the tree became a 3D rite of passage: getting the leaves to follow the sun, rustle with the wind, reflect some light, be translucent, and hold the dew; having the branches bend with the extra spring growth. The detail and thoroughness of this research, presumably, made possible the luscious foliage scenes of John Lasseter's 1998 movie, *A Bug's Life*. That was certainly following Ruskin's truth-to-nature principle. Before such naturalism was possible, the objects, the characters of 3D animation, had to be closer to the geometric primitives, the "ideal forms" of Plato. The tree replaced the teapot. The teapot, first created by Martin Newell in 1975 in Utah, had been the ultimate "life model" of the early days of 3D.

Newell's personal teapot would become the most famous icon in computer graphics: Many graphics researchers would use it—actually a 3D database from which he measured directly—to show off their latest rendering tricks at conferences. The original teapot itself now resides honorably in the Computer Museum on Moffatt Field, along with the Shoup SuperPaint system.[25]

At SIGGRAPH you can find perceptual psychologists and programmers discussing medieval painting technique, with optical tests to determine how much visual data is required per square inch to model the pull of gravity on fabric. After one of these sessions, I mentioned to a speaker that I had trouble agreeing with some of the observations, and she said, "Oh, but I haven't seen these paintings myself. I am relying on the published research data—that is, other people's observations." In a quite different context I recall an archivist telling me that one of the great problems in his field, medieval documents, was the preponderance of fakes. In the teaching of drawing, some of the phrases that were common a generation ago—like drawing *"the truth," sight size, objective,* and *authentic*—now seem embarrassing unless you are suitably blinkered. There would be no reason not to draw a beech tree, or a teapot, but you would now be in competition with a decent array of quite refined machines. A student pointed out that the only truly individual and authentic mark that any of us can make and that defines and embeds our identity is the thumbprint. Our view of nature has become contaminated, contaminated even by the animatronic simulations of the movies. A child next to me at the Audubon Zoo in New Orleans complained about a perfect living example of an alligator beneath the bridge we were on: "But, Dad, it doesn't look real."

The Amphibian

Reptiles and amphibians can have intricate markings, with each pattern apparently as unique as a thumbprint. These animals provide interesting case studies. If you are drawing one "from life"—assuming your subject stays still—you have somehow to reconcile its overall shape, the way it carries itself, with the visual texture. You have to bear in mind that the patterns are usually not there for decoration but to confuse the eye, the eye of the predator or prey as much as the intrusive artist. Getting this camouflage right and in solid 3D is a tough call.

One of the best reasons for painting is that almost anything you see—rain on a windscreen, a spoon in a bowl—can become a starting point, and you never know where that first tickle of an idea will take you. In the same way, every time you finish a painting or are completely stuck, you can walk around and see something that gives you a clue. One July, I photographed from above one of the frogs in our back garden "pond" (an old kitchen sink). I realised straightaway when I looked at the image on the computer screen that this was more interesting than the paintings I was doing right then. All I could think of doing was drawing over this image in bright reds and blues. This did not work. I shelved the project. In retrospect I can see that the overall form of the frog, the muscles of the patient, crouching predator, was connected with what I was working on in paintings and drawings that were, in conventional terms, "abstract." I had been imposing snapshot images reduced down to two or three colours on a "ground" of painterly stirrings. So

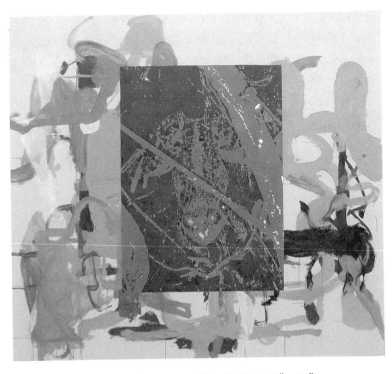

James Faure Walker, *Frog, Greenwood Road*, 2004, 61" × 68"
(155 × 172 cm), oil on canvas. (See also Plate 6.)

my first version of the frog was a digital print, with lower layers
made up of drawings, drawings made both with sticks and with
the wirelike lines you can manipulate in Illustrator.

Some months later I was wondering how I could engineer
the next move on a medium-size, six-foot-square painting that
had been moving along very slowly for a year or so. I had turned
it on its side and been using quite a diverse range of brushes—
old electric toothbrushes, cardboard squeegees—and I was
pleased with its rhythm and colour. But it still lacked the decisive blow. It didn't have much of a point for being the way it
was. I wanted it to look as if it had been done in a flash, fluently,
and without any dithering. It takes quite an effort and some

Original photograph, 2003.

patience to make a painting look effortless. Then I thought of my frog. For the digital piece, I had already edited it down to three colours and worked out several colour permutations. This cream-coloured painting had been digitally processed (simply by photographing it and trying out variations before realising them in actual paint), so it was simple to slip the frog image over the top. I spent a few days worrying about its size and its position on the canvas, but once I had made my mind up, it was a straightforward process.

Straightforward but a labour of love, I should say. One method I use for transferring the digital into the painterly is the stencil. First I need to convert the image into the right form.

113

Frog, Greenwood Road, 2003, 24" × 24" (60 × 60 cm), inkjet print.

Paint programs have filters that can do this in one shot, but I sometimes go the long way round through several processes so that I get to know more about the image. It is often surprising how much can be conveyed in a pattern of irregular shapes, forms that you would never invent or draw directly from observation. The second stage, after printing this out at the right scale, is to cut the stencil. In this case I had four A2 sheets, and the task of cutting them out took a full two weeks. I made this particularly difficult for myself because the skin patterning shifts from being positive to negative, like an Escher design.

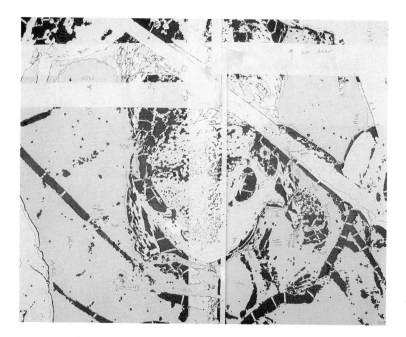

Paper stencil.

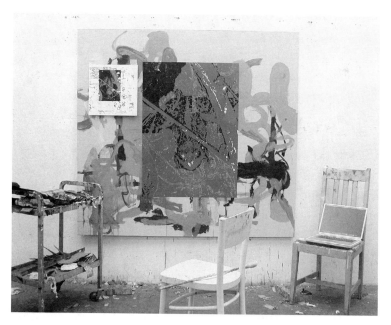

Painting in progress.

Because every positive "island" in a stencil has to be attached to the "continent," this called for a steady hand. I also decided to make the one stencil do the job of two, by incorporating the highlights on the same sheet as the dark accents.

On the painting itself, I had first to reestablish a ground area by sanding away the existing paint, painting in the white rectangle, and then painting the colour that would be the dominant colour of the image. This was a lesson I had learned from previous pictures. As the colour of that layer is crucial to the overall effect, it is wise to make it an underneath colour. With this approach the imposed image must look decisive, not exactly printed liked a silkscreen, but not tampered about or changed. Best to be sure of the colour at this stage. Fixing the stencil to a canvas that is quite large with sufficient precision is a fiddly business, and it is wise to mask out the areas of painting where accidental splashes won't be welcome. This may sound absurd to some people—to work on a painting with splashy marks and then switch over to a completely "precise" mode—but that contrast is what this particular game is all about.

The actual painting through the stencil required considerable concentration. The viscosity of paint has to be just right, or it clogs or runs irritatingly under the paper. In large areas, I needed to use a chalk pencil through the stencil to outline the areas, which then needed careful filling in. I had made a mixture of lamp and ivory black, and made a rough calculation of how long it would take. Even though it was a complex and broken area, I could not stop halfway, or for more than fifteen minutes, as the paint would show a tidemark. I reckoned on about five hours. I made a slow start on a Saturday at 2 P.M., but did not finish till 5 A.M. the next day.

Never again, was my initial response. Since then I have taken advantage of the drop in price of excellent digital projectors and now find it quite possible even in sunlight to copy in paint what is projected on the canvas. This solves one or two problems, but as I have said, I am not sure whether I want all my problems solved. One footnote to this painting was that while doing it I was thinking about a talk I had to do at a conference on whether the practice of art could be counted as research. I took a lot of trouble in the stencil to get the little white bobbles differentiated exactly as they were in the image. I was not after the impressionist blur, nor a photorealist glisten; I just wanted the data, so to speak, left raw. Naturally, in the weeks of cutting the stencil and working out the painting method, my mind had wandered over that strange geography—like flying over Finland. Painting reduced to such mind-numbing tasks can bring you to a state of Zen receptivity. When I finished I noticed that the white bobbles on the frog's "nose" were like a constellation, perhaps the beautiful Pleiades. I make no claims for that as serious research, but it was a case in which a project had started as a glimpse into a pond and ended up thinking about something millions of light-years away.

Why use such a laborious and painstaking process when there are "instant" solutions available? This question goes deep. Why paint? One answer is simply that the absorption in the process, the constant feedback, what some psychologists call being in "thin slicing" mode, where the mind takes in all kinds of peripheral clues subliminally, taps into something that cannot be accessed any other way. The digital is too instant, too perfect, too front-of-the-brain. Possibly. The very imperfectability of a painting process allows for something else to emerge and suggests images and feelings that might pass unnoticed in a streamlined process. Like walking instead of taking a plane. For someone of my generation the studio is still a very special space where time can stand still, where you can exist in a trancelike state, where you absorb rather than search—a state much closer to being stupid than being smart.

Machines and Intellects

There was this story: A New York museum offered a young curator a large travel budget. His brief was simple: Find out what is going on in contemporary art, and report back in a couple of years. His report identified two parallel tracks. One demonstrated the steady growth in painting, sculpture, and installation; the other consisted of art driven by new technology. He predicted that the most interesting place to be was where the two tracks began to converge.

Even in the mid-1990s, it could be tricky to speak of computers and painting in the same breath. They belonged to different worlds, different sides of the brain, different epochs even. The digital world is a world of instant communication, so perfectly engineered we only notice it when it goes wrong. The world of painting is slow, silent, and by comparison agricultural in its timescale. Time is counted in seasons, decades, centuries, or in the entire lifespan of an individual painter. Paint chemistry does not get upgraded every year. For many painters the working day is still set by the hours of daylight much as it was before the invention of electric lighting.

By and large, paintings cannot be turned on and off; they don't flicker or give us news updates. They hang on the wall, sometimes changing the atmosphere of a room, sometimes in a museum corridor. The technology used to produce paintings has not changed in its essentials over the past five hundred years—some might say the past three thousand years. As an art form, it is infused with its own cultural DNA. The need for images that record human presence, or symbols of deities, goes back way beyond antiquity, to a shadowy past. Modernists may have tried to break free of some traditions, but sometimes more ancient ones became reinstated.

The exponential increase in computing speed over the

118

past thirty years is quite a contrast. The application of paint to canvas can be fast or slow, but it always takes time, consumes time: A painting doesn't just happen like a printed-out image; it is a record of human craft, and perhaps some superstition and passion; it can be elusive, ambivalent, playful, ironic. It can capture the present moment in a fashion that no photograph can. The daylight of the impressionists strikes us as relatively recent, yet their "modern" world was a world without cars or neon light. Painting took decades to come to terms with photography. The messiness of paint, the stickiness of oil paint, the translucency of watercolour, seem at odds with the snappy images on TV, the "user-friendly" graphics of the laptop. How can the painter, with one foot in this past, adjust to this digital world? It is a recurring question.

Occasionally some simple remark reminds me that there was a world before e-mail, that it is only in the past decade or so that we have come to take computers for granted. We rely on them for communication, research, shopping, and almost as the dimension through which we think. In my case I also do much of my visual thinking through paint programs. Being smart means being quick. So to think slowly is like being left behind in a conversation—being slow-witted. To work without a thought accelerator is to be left out of the loop altogether.

I was at a MacExpo show in London, worrying about the inevitable upgrade I would soon need and how much it would cost. The new machine would be several thousand times faster than the first computers I used, which were absolute magic in their time. Then I reflected on something else I had to do that day. I was particularly nervous. With some other colleagues, I had helped set up a series of memorial lectures at the Tate Modern for an old friend, Stuart Morgan, who had died the previous year. My friend had become one of the leading art critics of the 1980s and 1990s; Thomas McEvilley called him "the pre-eminent

British art critic for perhaps fifteen years."[26] Unlike an artist who leaves works behind, where they can still exude an influence or catch a young artist's eye, a critic—especially one as lively and sparky as Morgan had been—leaves few traces: old magazine articles, an anthology or two for posterity. In a few years all this could be no more than a few footnotes in an academic article combing over the art talk of the 1980s.

I had to make a short introductory speech, summarising his life and his achievement. It suddenly struck me that we had this collective delusion in the computer world that the quality of our intellectual output depended on performance figures. A G5 would be a whole lot better than a G3. Didn't it follow that the art made through it would be a whole lot better, too? But Stuart had in fact used a seriously out-of-date Mac Classic, which had required expert resuscitation to recover old writings. And incidentally, like the majority of his colleagues, he took little interest in the slowly emerging flickerings of digital art. But what he had achieved—and his influence had been considerable—had been realised without much hi-tech. It was done just by thinking things through: seeing a lot, reflecting, reading, rereading, and writing and rewriting till the thoughts shone through.

So when a friend remarked casually that you couldn't actually expect the computer to do that much, and that Stuart had done what he had done with sheer intellect, it set me thinking. Demonstrating just how much you can do without touching a computer is not the best of topics to suggest at a computer-art conference. In fact, at such a conference in Paris, some visitors would not even think of visiting the Louvre or the Pompidou Centre: How could you be into predigital art . . . it is so noninteractive . . . so yesterday? It would be a betrayal. The whole mission was about demonstrating that the new technology took us through to a completely new art.

This again reminded me of the ambivalence of those of us

caught between these two worlds. We took part in these exhibitions and conferences, but we were also painting in a studio, exhibiting in galleries. Though I had gradually found ways of integrating digital and nondigital techniques and had become fascinated by the tension between old and new tech, the public face of this new art form was of something disconnected from the "traditional." Equally, within the world of galleries, museums, magazines, art schools, studio complexes, and general gossip—the so-called traditional art world—computer art had long been dismissed as second rate, though in the 1990s, through video artists such as Bill Viola and what soon became known as "new media," it was fast becoming cool. All the same, the milieu of a digital-art exhibition was quite different. Most of the viewers would be other artists, and the accompanying labels and catalogues would be full of technical information and somewhat leaden statements. There was critical feedback, but scarcely any proper reviews or commentaries in art magazines.

Blurred Vision

Sonya Rapaport had a long career as a painter before working electronically, often with Web-based pieces. She was one of the artists I got to know through the Inter Society of Electronic Arts. The ISEA, which began its life in Holland in 1988, by the mid-1990s had held its "symposia"—mixtures of exhibitions, concerts, and conferences—in Sydney, Minneapolis, Helsinki, and Montreal. After the 1996 event in Rotterdam, she reviewed the San Francisco Museum of Modern Art's "Electronic Media: 1996 SECA Awards," where one of the winners of the award was the excellent artist Jim Campbell.[27]

> This is the first year that an award in Electronic Media is included and the impact of the cool, elegant venue in which the work of the four electronic winners is displayed is

impressive after returning from the casual installation environment at the World Trade Center in Rotterdam. I didn't realize until later that the electronic art on display in the museum is being swallowed into the screened filter of sophisticated museumship and the work no longer appears to be cradled in the category of electronic art. I don't know if this is good or bad; I had always felt that art is art and there should be no such categorical differentiations. Lacking in the exhibition is the cacophony of experimental mismatches that I have observed and enjoyed at ISEA. Nobody ever had to remind me of their "electronic category". However, sometimes I had to ask myself, "is it art?" Now I am beginning to feel uneasy about the assimilation.[28]

One way of expressing that unease would be to say that there was a more probing and intelligent conversation going on at an ISEA occasion than in a museum, where anything on display is a fait accompli. The excitement for even a half-convinced player at ISEA was that here was an art form still in gestation, unsure of itself, and at that time not as neatly divided and labelled as it is today. A lot of thought was going into this, and many individual pieces of work were engaged in the collective conversation. At the same time, it was easy to slip into the habit of seeing electronic art as one collective movement, with a common objective, an art form that was inherently brainier than traditional art because of its silicon circuitry.

A moment's reflection should have corrected any illusions I had on this issue and reminded me that real accomplishment in any art form—drawing with a pencil or in a 3D program—comes about through quite a combination of factors; the drive, determination, and talents of the artist count for far more than the hardware. That is not saying that hardware, software, the quality of the camera, and so on, play no role. But one has to keep a sense of proportion. Artists always work in some context or another, even a marginalised context. Once we lose sight of these connections, we lose our bearings and lose sight of what we actually mean by calling this activity art in the first place. Certainly, there are acres of artworks that are unremarkable, and many more minor talents than major ones, and these observations must apply in the field of digital art as much as in any other field. What we tend to end up discussing are the exceptions, the sporadic flashes of brilliance.

Nevertheless there are plenty of reasons why digital painting has not set this "mainstream" art world alight. If you are relying on a directly printed "painting," the surface cannot achieve the worked and individually crafted character of the handmade painting. The surface is cold and anonymous, without the grain, the physical resistance, the visual noise we expect from painting. It is essentially an imitation of what it is not, a kind of kitsch. Plenty of digital painting championed on Web sites has the look of "heritage packaging," which you might get on a souvenir pack of soap—a nineteenth-century salon portrait or a faded sepia photograph—with various degrees of kinkiness in the way the images have been adjusted in Photoshop. There are Renaissance portraits where the head of a forgotten courtier is replaced with the head of Elvis. I would not want to dismiss all "painting" in this genre as a cheap trick, but serious connoisseurs of painting won't be won over this easily. I should add that I do admire several artists who work within this "painting nostalgia" mode. Viktor Koen is one (with eerily armoured medieval insect warriors); Horkay Istvan is another (Renaissance beauties in old factories). The Los Angeles Center for Digital Art registers this style as a new direction, noting the work of Hans Bauer:

> One of the major trends among many in digital art is the
> appearance of work that represents a "throw-back" to earlier

historical styles. Spanning multiple cultures and an array of eras, this kind of work has been popping up internationally and shows much promise in the refinement of digital techniques . . . a reversal on the very electronic looking "cybernetic" art seen in the 1990s.[29]

This may be the case, but it would still mean that such digital art would not really encroach on contemporary painting, which has never ceased playing with throwback styles. Scanning reproductions, collaging them with or without a degree of wit, would be neither here nor there. Painters of my generation were conditioned to believe that *looking like* art was not at all the same thing as *being art*, and calling some painter a mere picture-maker was definitely an insult. Our motto was to "make it new and true" or please don't bother.

The trouble here is that the throwback style looks too much like cultural tourism, especially when it has high production values and dresses up a cheap idea—a touch of soft porn, perhaps—in period costume. "Pioneer" digital art may not have had much punch as art, but at least it was scratching about in the dark, looking for answers. For the first artists to get their hands on the equipment, it was an exhilarating adventure. I have met some of these pioneers, and they speak with watery eyes of mortgaging their house to get hold of the first eight-bit paint system, of playing with these blocky pixels till two in the morning, knowing for sure that no other human being had ever gone this way before. Alvy Ray Smith, one of the real inventors of paint systems, has recounted the fascinating story of accidental meetings, improvised solutions, and the incredible dedication that lies behind the smooth interfaces that we now take for granted.[30] I was only at the tail end of this period, when computer graphics was still esoteric, when the inaccessibility of the hardware, the sheer difficulty of operating systems—sometimes without any "undo" facility—made you feel a member of a hardcore elite. In that atmosphere, it would not have seemed such a wild conjecture that, through computer art, the very foundations of visual art could be reinvented.

Almost forty years after its initial formation, the Computer Art Society reconvened in the offices of Systems Simulation on 26 February 2004, with many of its leading spirits present. George Mallen spoke of the importance of ideas, rather than just applications and technologies. He pointed out that the society had become unnecessary by the end of the 1980s because computers had become ubiquitous. At one point a group of us pored over the modest collection of work from the 1960s and 1970s, mostly plotter-drawn geometry, here and there trying to identify the artist. If much of this material were presented today in an exhibition, it would not look like much, a piece of wrapping paper perhaps, but with a date of, say, 1968, the work would be significant. This is the paradox. A piece of this art, possibly of little merit in itself, can be a hot piece of research property, provided it lies neglected in a drawer for forty years.

Tricks of the Eye

In 2001, I curated an exhibition called "Silent Motion," which brought together the work of ten digital artists, and these works were set alongside the photo-sequences of Eadweard Muybridge.[31] I had begun working as a research fellow at Kingston University in Surrey the previous year, and when asked to put together an exhibition on an art and science theme, I soon realised it would need to be centred on Muybridge. He was born in Kingston in 1830 and died there in 1904, though all his significant work was done in the United States.

I was well aware of the parallels between the gradual emergence of cinema from optical experiments, tricks of the eye, and scientific enquiry and the emergence of digital art from the computer labs. Muybridge is one of the essential pioneers in the "technology artist" canon. But I wanted to draw something much more specific out of the comparison. I knew of several fellow artists who were interested in building sequences of still images, or in giving visual form to something as complex as a city or the movement of refugees. It did not matter that they were not inspired or even particularly aware of Muybridge's *Animal Locomotion* studies, because there would be the germ of a connection between the patterns of figures in motion and the repetitive sequences in the digital works, which ranged from prints, projected video, and slides to Web sites.

I had my own reasons for wanting to arrange this juxtaposition. First, one of the earliest lectures I went to when I began my foundation year at St Martins School of Art in 1966 was by the head of what was then called complementary studies and would now be called art history or art theory. The head was Aaron Scharf, who two years later would publish his seminal *Art and Photography*. Scharf's talk had been my introduction to Muybridge. Scharf had been a potter, and—it was rumoured—during the Second World War as a US bomber navigator, he had deliberately messed up the bombing of Ravenna. The second reason had to do with the new features on the digital camera I had bought a couple of years earlier. Although these features are now commonplace, I found that, after years of using a relatively primitive digital camera that could only take eight photos before it was full, the new "almost video" features were marvellous. Without any elaborate shutter settings, or Muybridge's rows of cameras and trip wires, the amateur could easily create a sequence of still images by pointing the camera out of a bus. In short, I soon found myself making complex visual collages out of these sequences, and this brought back to me the Muybridge sequences.

When you are arranging an exhibition like this, there are
so many details to look after, from arranging framing, to where
visiting artists can stay, that it is hard to stand back and see how
well it works. It was relatively modest as an exhibition, moving
to just one London gallery after being at the Stanley Picker
Gallery, a decent-sized gallery, but still essentially a university
gallery. We produced a respectable catalogue and had one or
two features in magazines, but there were no reviews and it did
not make much of a wave. The mild reception was not so surprising, given the setting of the gallery and the lack of local
interest both in digital art and in Muybridge—three years later
a conference on Muybridge in Kingston commemorating his
centenary had to be cancelled because of the lack of subscribers.
On the other hand, somehow we managed to bring all but one
of the overseas artists together for a seminar at the exhibition,
and the high level of that discussion was worth all the effort.

Muybridge is a curious touchstone to use, because each
generation finds something quite different in his images. The
minimal-artist Sol Le Witt collected these prints, clearly identifying with their serial format, their "scientific" objectivity;
Francis Bacon used some of the wrestling and contorted figures
as the basis of his near-psychotic painterly studies. *Eadweard
Muybridge, Zoopraxographer,* a film by Thom Andersen made
in 1974 and narrated by Dean Stockwell, is remarkable simply
because it is a film essay about film, and being grainy and
imperfect, it looks dated to our eyes, which are so used to the
cleaned-up, digital recreations of Muybridge's sequences. I saw
this film as part of a small Muybridge festival at Kingston
Museum. By coincidence I had seen a few days earlier a performance by the Forkbeard Fantasy group at the Hackney Empire,
a bizarre piece of music hall, nostalgia, and optical trickery
called "shooting Shakespeare." It began and ended with projections of re-animated sequences of Muybridge, used to evoke the

lost world of 1900s cutthroat theatrical management, when the silver screen threatened to put the theatre out of business. The action consisted of the convoluted plot of *The Tempest* mixed up with an attempt to shoot a silent version of the play, with startling shifts between live and filmed action.

One small success of the "Silent Motion" exhibition was that it did focus on Muybridge as a possible godfather for the digital artist, and some three years later I found myself chairing a discussion featuring one of the participating artists, Andrew Carnie. He had put on a solo exhibition, "Slices and Snapshots," that took the analogy with Muybridge further. He had set up installations that were essentially slide-show narratives told through stark images of the body. Two or three slide projectors would throw medical images of nerves, bones, cross-sections of the body, onto translucent screens, hung one in front of the other. These images were manipulated and morphed into lyrical drawings of trees or organic patterns. He had been working in collaboration with the neurologist Richard Wingate and had become fascinated by the patterns made by the growing cells of a chick's optical nerves. Again, there were the photo sequences of Muybridge hanging alongside these contemporary "technological" works. The discussion, inevitably, ranged across the subjects of Muybridge, art and technology, the wonders of science, and the compromises and limitations of mixing these ingredients together.

The following day, I went to see the newly opened exhibition at the Hayward Gallery: "Eyes, Lies and Illusions" featured magic lanterns and every species of optical trickery going right back to the seventeenth century. This was both good timing and bad timing. Good timing, because it provided an opportunity to pursue this theme. Here again was a roomful of Muybridge images. Bad timing, because it happened to be half term, and the exhibition was packed full with delighted, frustrated, and

128

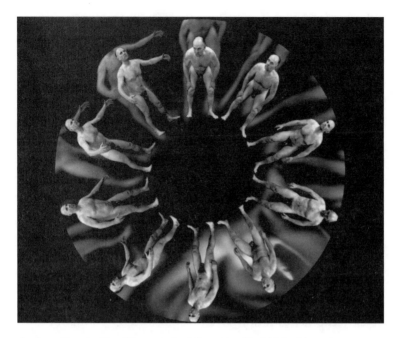

Andrew Carnie, *Eye: Through the Mirror Darkly,* 2004, video piece.

screaming children and their tired parents and grandparents. I also felt a twinge of guilt, because I had not taken my own children here, though as teenagers they prefer to go on their own. In fact, being amid so many children was a blessing. I had had a previous encounter with a mass array of magic lanterns in one of the most unlikely museums I have ever come across, in San Antonio, Texas: The Magic Lantern Castle Museum. It was in the outskirts on the bleak Austin Highway, a one-story mock castle that had been a pizza parlour but was now a private museum. The excursion had been arranged at SIGGRAPH 2002 by Erkki Huhtamo, who in addition to being a leading writer on the history of art technology is a magic-lantern collector. Erkki had been competing with Jack Judson, the owner of the museum, on eBay over rare magic lanterns. I went with a group

129

of magic-lantern fanatics, which is another way of saying I went with a bunch of digital artists who between them could have put on quite an interesting exhibition themselves: Yoichiro Kawaguchi, Rejane Spitz, Patrick Lichty, Perry Hoberman, and Rodney Berry. Jack Judson and his wife welcomed us with great hospitality and put on a proper magic-lantern show, using the authentic, and highly volatile, original limelight. The magic lantern was "the father of motion pictures, and the grandfather of television." We were entranced, like children, and although the colour wheels, sunsets, little melodramas, and tales of the perils of drink were pathetically inept compared with any current feature film, we could easily imagine ourselves swept back to the 1880s.

Real children might have been more critical, as I found at the Hayward. Each optical trick or magic-lantern effect was quickly checked out and given a "that's clever" nod, but anything without a trick got a frown and a "what's supposed to happen?" There was a small dark room, with curtains at either end to keep out the light, with a small pinhole in one wall facing the rest of the gallery. It was a simple camera obscura, and if you looked carefully, you would see on the wall an upside-down image of the people outside moving around. Children came in impatiently, looking round for a gadget and seeing what they thought was a peephole, looked through it. Disappointed, they rushed out, leaving the curtain open and thereby wiping out the image with the light. The "picture" was never as strong as some camera obscura setups, but the social interaction, the frown of the one or two people patiently waiting for their eyes to readjust, the stream of impatient children, was one of my favourite moments in the whole exhibition.

Riding home on the top of the 76 bus though the City of London—if you get a front seat at the top of this bus, it is one of the best rides in town—I began reflecting on why I had found the whole exhibition unsatisfying. It was not an exhibition of art, but a display of optical devices. That was one reason. The projectors, with brass plates, cogs, levers, and mahogany mounts, are beautiful objects, like steam engines, but I prefer coming across them a few at a time. Second, the effects only work with historical perspective, and it is weird to be celebrating the mechanics without being truly swept away by the "visual magic." The effects, to work, have to involve a suspension of disbelief. No one would put on an exhibition of contemporary film cameras, editing suites, and rows of computers used in producing today's movies and expect to get the same experience as a cinema experience.

I had been surprised at how far back the magic lantern went and how the magic of illusion, the peep show, was part and parcel of the travelling fair. Huge treatises on optical machines and other optical effects were published in the seventeenth century. So though we conventionally think of the combination of art and technology as something that grew from the nineteenth century, and that photography was the first real challenge, the story goes back much further. At the same time, there is a clear distinction to be drawn between the optical trick, the illusion, the cleverness shown for its own sake, and the substance of art itself—though they can overlap. One difference is that many of these optical illusions only work if the viewer is strictly controlled, and conditioned—this requirement is also a limitation in digital-art installations, especially when the space is dark and behind curtains and you have to wear special glasses. The stereoscope was a common nineteenth-century toy, like cardboard binoculars with a double photo, one photo taken a couple of inches to the side of the other. Or, there could be a fixed box showing a nocturnal scene, say, of a mansion ablaze, backlit by a candle, inviting you to peer through two nicely polished brass eyepieces. Naturally, you bend down to look through.

In doing so, your peripheral vision is cut away, and your side-to-side movement is similarly curtailed. You are submitting to the machine. Even when you enter a dark space, where all but the presented image is hidden, you are submitting and your vision is directed in more senses than one. This is also true of the image on the monitor—it is cut off at the edges; it inhabits a separate space.

The view from the bus was—of course—more spectacular than anything in the exhibition, though this would also be a tribute to the exhibition. I have felt much the same after sitting though two hours of a program of the finest computer 3D animation. I recall the computer graphics pioneer Jim Blinn saying something similar: There's the *wow!* you say when seeing the animation, but there's a deeper *wow!* when you walk outside. Painting has always competed against the real world, both through the illusion of its window and through being a mere object on the wall: not a machine or an optical device, but something that you can stop in front of, glance at, or walk past.

Sometimes I forget that great leaps in thought have been made in art without mechanical aids. Dependent on cameras and laptops for gathering images, communicating, and painting, I convince myself that the next project needs some new piece of equipment I cannot afford. But let me pause a moment. Would I or anyone else in a similar position really be better off if I vowed never again to use any high-tech aids? A large-scale painting, say, twenty feet across and ten feet high and in an enclosed room or hall, and suitably vivid and graphic in its images, perhaps entirely "abstract," even geometric, could be a refreshing change in an exhibition of video installations in dark spaces. You could move around in front of such a painting; you could find details here and there, ignore it if you wanted. It wouldn't make a noise and it wouldn't need plugs and minders. You would not have to sit down and wait for the beginning to wind round so you saw the full sequence. Even a very large painting like this would be something you could catch in a glimpse.

Another option would be to make a painting small enough to fit in your pocket; it would probably need to be printed or embossed. It would have little "unique object" value. On buses passengers enjoy caressing their cell phones and iPods, and perhaps one future role for the painter could be the portable, wearable painting that somehow remains distinct from jewellery. A painting as an accessory? A low-tech worry bead? Thinking of what could possibly lie in store for the painter two hundred years hence is a nice game to play, and though the answer could be something that we would not now recognise as an art form at all, the concept of the painting may prove more durable than the concept of digital art or new media. Like poetry or music, it does not depend on a handful of gadgets with built-in obsolescence—gadgets, as Bruce Sterling put it at the Montreal ISEA conference—with the life span of a hamster.

Chapter 5 **Slack Water**

Gold Standard

There is natural and there is natural. The first gallery I showed with was run by a remarkable woman, Vera Russell, who had an imperious streak (she was from an aristocratic Russian family, whose prerevolutionary estates counted Rothko among the tenants).[32] She commanded that the artists "look natural" while they were being photographed. Once you have that idea in your mind, it is something you simply cannot contrive. Similarly, natural media in paint programs are not natural, real time is not real, and—of course—one wonders whether the art that is

James Faure Walker, *Baroque Thoughts for a Rainy Day,* 2005, 24" × 32" (61 × 81 cm), inkjet print. (See also Plate 15.)

fed through the system is art or "real art." Just to be preoccupied with the question is probably a killer.

The jump from using conventional paints—watercolour, acrylic, oils—to using colour on the computer screen, with the "painting" printed out on an inkjet printer, is quite a drastic one. When I began, there was no suggestion of any future pathway between the noisy computer graphics of video games and the chic gallery spaces of contemporary painting. It seemed impossible that a printer would ever be marketed specifically for fine-art use, with guarantees that the prints wouldn't fade. Yet now there are not only numerous print bureaus producing "giclee" inkjet prints in limited editions—I use one regularly— but whole ranges of specialised, pigment-based printers. One is sitting beside me as I write. My regular art store has been selling inkjet printing paper for some time, and just as the shelf space taken up by digital cameras is now four times that of old cameras—60 percent of Londoners now have digital cameras— I wonder how this will play out.

Coming from painting culture and stepping into the visual cacophony, the garish colour of computer graphics was to step into seriously bad taste. Yes, there had been a cult of "bad painting" and vile garishness in painting in the 1970s too, but the difference then was that the artists knew very well what scores they were settling. Bad art can be rich in irony, or it can be just plain dumb. In the computer trade show, it was the latter. Matisse was just a trade name for another bespoke hardware "paint" system, a system that would run into trouble with Quantel about patent infringement. This was a visual culture, but one that disoriented the spectator with power, with spectacle, with trickery. It was the funfair. It was not a poetry reading. In terms of optical seduction or subtle innuendo, painting had no chance at all.

From the 1960s to the 1990s, the whole idea of computer art was—to painters—like a bad smell. You pretended not to notice. This is something that is omitted from exhibition catalogues. Yes, there were exhibitions—concrete poetry, holograms, telepresence, virtual reality, Web installations—but by and large, they were noticed and then forgotten. No impact. As a practitioner, you would always instinctively want to defend this art form, whatever doubts you had about its quality, as art, so there was one question that you would consider heresy to ask: Is it actually art at all? It is the kind of direct question that digital artists loathe. I have seen a panel of leading practitioners paralyzed with frustration—or fury. You might think it is an unsophisticated question, and some of my colleagues will roll their eyes and walk away if they are asked it. They'll say the question is just naive and a waste of time. I am not so sure. In computer shows, the art show has to be called "art" and cordoned off. This differentiates its exhibits from the scientific visualisations and commercial demos elsewhere. In galleries, it takes some effort to think of anything that has not been brought in as art—ever since Duchamp's *Fountain,* the upturned urinal of 1917—and some cynics would say that if an exhibit looks like art, then it is more than likely a deliberate parody, or just plain nonart.

The question could wound or prove lethal. If all this activity could be shown not to be art at all but something else, then we might feel a little deflated. The high-class giclee prints elegantly placed on gallery walls could be considered merely computer output, the product of graphic effects, the playing around with mathematics, or programming tricks. At best they would be just plain old printmaking, part of that history, a technical footnote, harmless wall decor. All the experiments with virtual reality and interactive systems would be just that: experiments, research leading nowhere, promises that came to nothing. Without this "art" premium attached—like a designer label—digital art would be so much tat, and a string of associated enterprises would collapse: galleries, university departments, research institutes, conferences, collections, official histories. Quite a few of us would be out of a job. The subject would not merit a serious book. It would be like discovering that what you thought was real science was fake science, or that the astrology section had infiltrated the astronomy section. There is more at stake than a simple quarrel about definitions. It comes back to the question: Is digital art as good as other art?

The panel members may well counter the question by alluding to the art world's ignorance and general phoniness, and perhaps subliminally invoke the plight of other avant-garde movements and new technologies that had a rough ride before being admitted into the fold. They will mention the noble idealism of the lone pioneers who laid the foundations

138

back in the 1950s and 1960s. That was hard science. We may be shown foggy reproductions of patterns on oscilloscopes; fragments of repeating triangles someone managed to program a few years later in the laboratory; or the art and technology experiments of Rauschenberg and John Cage, or the first algorists who programmed their own drawings and seeded what was to follow. Computer art emerged as something distinct, with its own pledges and with a pedigree that goes back to the science labs rather than the art history anthologies. The panel members would talk of an art form, a relatively new art form that has not yet bedded down into the hierarchies of the more mature forms. They will mention photography, video. They won't mention other groups waiting out in the lobby like impatient circus performers: textile artists, glass artists, printmakers, potters, folk artists. These tribes also have their agendas and recruit critics and academics. Nor will the panel explain why it is so desirable to be recognised by an art world whose values it clearly despises. In fact, art magazines routinely carry a letter or two after a major survey show panning the survey, complaining that "the art establishment" has deliberately excluded this or that category, be it portrait painting, photography, or performance art.

The question "Is it art?" might not have been hostile, but might have been asked out of genuine curiosity. The viewer might want some help in identifying the right criteria to know whether something is art or not—how do you tell good digital art from bad digital art? Is there a feedback loop, a tasting system, a milieu of experts who give the nod? Is it based on sheer technical accomplishment, or on one level of artistry against another? Is the first demonstration of a new technique or interactive process always going to be the most admirable? Is digital art a genuine movement or a blip as the mainstream begins to colonise the new technology? Should a person know about contemporary art, art history, or computers and the story of computer graphics?

If—and, I hope, when—this phenomenon settles its identity problems and becomes appreciated and enjoyed in its own right, these anxieties will disappear. What it needs is a broader fan base, a clientele, a crowd that hangs around simply because they like what they see. One of life's pleasures is watching an old and familiar film on TV, that *Double Indemnity* perhaps, and you can be in tears, laughing, completely caught up in the action. You don't worry about whether it is a film or not, and you don't need to know the history of film in great detail or that much about filmmaking technique, or the ground rules, or even the name of the director.

Bricks and Definitions

In the mid-1960s, I switched from studying painting to studying sculpture at St Martins. The sculpture department was far more go-ahead, with an international focus bearing down on it, with fierce crits, with artists like Anthony Caro, William Tucker, Gilbert and George, and Richard Long. In that milieu, to make something that looked like art was a small sin. The idea was always to go back to first principles: How was this "thing" going to exist, stand up, absorb or reflect light, move, vanish? It had to have its own "integrity" as an object. Sculpture had lost its heroic connotations, its monumental postures, its self-indulgent textures, its pseudo-poetic ambiguities, its swelling organic forms— what came to be called "homeless biomorphs." In Britain, sculpture was to be everything that Henry Moore wasn't. It had to come down off the pedestal and onto the floor. It wasn't going to be carved or modelled but industrially assembled. It was to be open, honest—no hidden volumes, no allusions to ancient Greece. Throwback styles were definitely off the agenda.

I have noticed—I mention this in passing—that the "sculptures" made by 3D prototyping shown in recent SIGGRAPH art shows need their pedestals to identify them as sculptures rather than as random demos. They have the look of miniaturised bronze abstracts of the 1950s. If they are a step anywhere in terms of art, they are a step backward, back into an amateurish understanding of the possibilities of sculpture. Two-dimensional digital work similarly depends on the framed image to differentiate it as art, and titles hinting at classical myths or hidden "personal" depth are not uncommon. At the biennales, these "artistic" prompts would look quite out of place. If such an "Art Show" were to be tacked on to a biennale, the crowds ambling through would chuckle to themselves, chuckle that such modest "techno art" was presented as cutting-edge. A while back, that way of presenting art, shrouded in mystery and evocative titles, was ridiculed out of existence. Painting, most notoriously through Jasper Johns, Frank Stella, and Andy Warhol, broke free of the rectangular frame and metaphysical "nonsense"—that is, the symbols, the expressive gesturing, the soul-searching. "What you see is what you get" was part of the stripe painter's vocabulary: The paint on the canvas was the paint straight from the can, and what you saw on the canvas was all there was. There were no hidden metaphysical extras; no imagery, subject matter, content, illusion, mystic infusion, fancy brushwork, emoting. The key word was *presence.* Presence was real. Illusion was unreal. Simple as that.

The campaign against "the poetic image" was soon overtaken by what came to be known as minimal art, and then by conceptual art. These sought to purge the "artwork" of anything other than presence and its literal bricklike existence. Students were poring over Wittgenstein's *Tractatus,* and *Artforum* was written in a deadpan, autistic voice that reported the "artwork" as though it was reporting the weather. Artworks were phenomena. In art schools it became a game to see who could come up with an artwork that went the furthest from "looking like art." At the first college I taught at—Coventry, the home of the Art and Language group—there had been some controversy. The atmosphere had been thumbs down for students making paintings, but thumbs up for the student keeping chickens in the studios. The group may have been right. The clichés of "humanist" painting—the artist as a visionary tuned into the spiritual, myth, interior life—were giving way to the hard-edge, plain-speaking, descriptive, behaviourist, and literal building blocks of a new and uncontaminated language.

By the mid-1990s, a loose-knit community of digital artists came together at Ars Electronica, SIGGRAPH, ISEA, and many more local festivals. This milieu was a heterogeneous mix ranging from sociologists to composers. It was also more international and internationally minded than other artists' gatherings. But what did it mean here to be an artist? Art was a hazy concept, not a list of in or out galleries, and this audience was not clued up with biennale gossip and postmodern painting theory. The big idea everyone seemed to share was the prospect of building a new kind of art from this electronic material— from the mud of the digital river. It was convenient to assume that the existing art world was asleep and unaware of the digital revolution. It was just a matter of time before the old gave way to the new. In the event, no one else wanted to go along with this plan; at least most nonelectronic artists do not appear to have been affected in any way by this "electronic art" as art, and now that they have their own digital cameras and laptops, they take for granted the fact that images can be produced, processed, and sent across the Web. It has become routine for artists to work digitally, to slip a CD of images into the portfolio, to update their Web site, to run off inkjet prints of scanned paintings. No one can count himself or herself among the elite

142

just because of a faster processor. So does it still make sense to have digital art shows?

It is a difficult question to answer. Certainly, the focus has softened and the intense debates that took place in the 1990s have given way to the recognised subgenres of new media. All the same, digital-art still presents a distinct viewpoint. This can be both a plus and a minus. Exhibitions of digital prints vary enormously in quality, but you can usually be sure to find something—for example, "spiritual" geometric abstractions, pop art collages, surrealistic photomontages—redolent of the 1950s or 1960s. These works represent not so much a throwback style, which implies a knowing reference, but an embarrassing ignorance and indifference to the art form's history. Only the flattened-out inkjet printing betrays it as contemporary work. This lack of awareness can be can be refreshing, and the plus is that you may come across some naive but fresh twist on a hackneyed motif. But these are now just styles, and dead styles at that. It is frustrating to see ingenious graphic devices employed to make clones of dead ideas. Only occasionally do you have the sense that someone is visiting a motif for the first time. Above all I miss the intelligent cross-referencing, the tact and restraint, or the outrageous excess you might expect from more clued-up exhibitors.

I am of two minds about these exhibitions of "prints." I have taken part in many of them as an exhibitor. I wish the aesthetics involved were not skin deep. But I am also glad that these exhibitions are so open to all comers, are so international and culturally diverse, that you do not get a completely edited and repressively "curated" exhibition. Considering the chaos that streams through the desktop—atrocities, porn, sports, spam—it would be appalling if all that artists made of such river mud were a few deft white-on-white inflections. There is such a visual flood and such wonderful ways of making something from it, that it would be ludicrous to filter all the life away in a few variations tuned in to the current art-world fads. Thankfully, a younger generation of curators goes out of its way to recreate the visual jumble of a high street in the gallery space, and the aesthetic of visual surfing is challenging designer minimalism.

I also have misgivings about being roped in as a printmaker or roped into a category in which the computer plus printer is seen as a way of updating printmaking. Perhaps I am splitting hairs if I insist that I am a painter, maybe a digital painter, and that when exhibiting a print, I am exhibiting a painting. But it is a matter of emphasis. I usually have connected works that are self-evidently paintings, whether or not I have used some form of transference from digital file to canvas—a painted-in projected image, or a paper stencil that has been printed and cut through. One analogy would be to think of a musician in a recording studio, perhaps a jazz pianist who was then and there improvising something for the first time. It would be inappropriate to call the pianist a CD maker. Listening to the CD at home, a person would find no contradiction in hearing it as a "live" recording. I like to think of a digital painting in these terms—perhaps this is a potential not fully realised as yet—as something that is both a record and that "lives" when you look at it.

I would not normally pay much attention to the small print of a competition—be it for painting, printmaking, or digital art—but sometimes you find some clause that betrays an entire attitude about how an art form is perceived and defined. In the mid-1990s and earlier, the term *digital manipulation* was associated with deceit, with faked photographs. In the application form for a major art competition called East, held in Norwich, you had to tick a box on the form if your slide, a 35 mm slide of course, had been so treated. I took this to imply that you might be cheating. There is also now a prestigious annual drawing competition called the Jerwood Drawing Prize. The character of the show depends on the jury. One year, if you looked at the works selected from a huge submission for the show, you might think drawing is all about experiment, digital drawing, and unmentionable body fluids, and you would think this is really the happening area in contemporary art. The following year, you can have a jury that sympathises with a traditional idea of figurative drawing. It selects a quite different version, exclusively pencil or charcoal on paper, where the model might have been Lucien Freud, and the date anywhere between 1950 and 1980. This time it would be the experimental drawings that were outside the canon; they would be nondrawings. If you had only seen this exhibition, you might well think drawing was timeless, independent of fashion, honest, boring, and in a backwater, with no connection whatever to digital art.

Definitions matter. Not only do they determine how one type of art is seen, but they determine whether it gets seen at all. Here it depends on what the jury thinks a drawing is. In one catalogue, a conservative jury wrote that drawing was primarily something made directly, as with pencil on paper. Prints were not drawings. This excluded most digital entries. There are also painting competitions that define painting in such a way that a digital painting would be out of the running. (To be fair, I recall exhibiting a framed painting, a work on paper that was quite splashy and informal, alongside iris prints in a digital gallery and getting strange looks. What is that? An accident with a printer?)

It has been quite an advantage to have been part of the mainstream painting world, to have been listening in on so many conversations about what are and are not the building blocks, the basic terms that define the art form. At one time, *fundamental painting* meant a plain, one-colour painting, a Brice Marden of 1974. Then, within a decade, the essence of painting became a soulful outpouring, the expressionism of

Beckman recycled into the large-scale German neo-expression-ists, the paint-on-crockery extravagant images of Schnabel. By the 1990s, Gerhard Richter's cool and detached renderings of photographs, or torn abstractions, became the dominant model, and the painter was once again an intellectual rather than an urban magician. I don't think of these changes as shifts of fashion, and at any one time, there are several different con-stellations of influence at work, constellations that can be as far apart as conceptual art and society portraiture. But painting is constant only insofar as it is constantly being remoulded, and a new generation, a new committee, is picking out a different look from the heap. Any individual painter has to find a way of existing, surviving, and thriving amid these ebbs and flows. Being rejected from competitions or galleries or knowing the whims of collectors can certainly be dispiriting, but at least it is a context, an ecosystem where the art is under pressure. There is feedback, and exhibiting means something. In comparison, the digital show, especially in what is lamely described as 2D work, has been languishing in slack water.

It would be great if these questions did not need to be asked. No one would worry about whether digital art was art, or whether it counted as drawing, painting, or print or should be slotted into some special, digital section. You could say that if you have to ask, you don't get it. Digital art would have become a genuine subculture, the equivalent of jazz: hard to define, but instantly recognizable, an attitude, a way of life. At present digi-tal art consists of a mishmash of art forms using new instru-ments. Up to now it has rushed to adopt each technology that comes along, and the new technology—not a special look or taste—marks it out as different. It feels like familiar art pro-cessed through unfamiliar formats.

Differentiation is a problem. Some digital shows have a category for software art, but they don't run this as a commercial competition, where the latest version of Flash or Adobe Illustrator would be in contention. There is an implicit convention that art means noncommercial work. The "artists" in software art are usually not the pros but art-trained hackers who have written some ingenious program, or played with the concept of the database, often no more than a detail or plug-in if looked at in broader terms. Similarly, a show of digital prints has to be kept distinct from graphic design, commercial posters, and photos. More than once, I have seen some commercial graphics that outclassed what was being called art.

This is not a problem that crops up in regular art exhibitions. The gallery space is a powerful framing device. "Computer art"—as it used to be termed—has often been shown in temporary "galleries" that are really the foyers of computer shows, without any history of being art places. To show that the exhibits are art rather than random demos, curators have always had to put up signs explaining that this is a gallery, and this is art. In a sense, every exhibit has to strain to be seen this way. If an installer leaves a hammer on a table in these shows, there is no danger of its being mistaken for an installation. So, again, as a critic you enter a time warp and have to look at much of this work as though nothing much has happened in art since 1950.

To speak of the difference between art at a computer show and art in the art world means risking giving offence. Some digital artists just don't want the heat of that comparison, and for the others who spend their lives in galleries, in studios, or simply teaching in art schools, it is as irritating to have to repeat the ground rules. You either know whether it is an installation or not. Objects of all kinds—string on the floor, a projected image, pictures on the wall, straw—have a confidence in their identity, whether at Tate Modern or in a fringe warehouse. When you enter "the space," you enter a contract to contemplate whatever is there. The object may be a horse or a sound, but the artist can play with its identity because there is never really any doubt that this is an art context. No art-world in-crowd needs a huge sign saying *art gallery*. In fact, the more important, or self-important, huge, and minimal the space inside, the tinier the sign outside. (This trend was well under way when the massive first Saatchi Gallery had a sign outside no bigger than an apartment number.) Some types of digital art, particularly interactive forms, could be more at home in science parks and conference sideshows. Perhaps there really are distinctive forms yet to be discovered. Just as there is more to jazz than the technology of the saxophone, there has to be more to all this than the simple trick of making artlike visuals through new and wonderful technology. Aren't there here and there special flavours, optical rhythms, something like an electronic zeitgeist? The kaleidoscopic energy of computer graphics is so dynamic that it would be surprising if nothing like that emerged.

Indecisive Taste

Some have described the mind-popping visual excess as the psychedelic baroque, alluding to the tendency to use twenty special-effect filters when just one might hit the spot. When this is said in dismissive tones, then all digital art is lumped together as an ill-conceived barrage of visual noise. The use of digital tools or computer display systems for making art is rejected out of hand. Traditionalists allude to the coldness of the medium, the lack of soul, the lack of human feeling. They regard the entire phenomenon as a symptom of a society alienated by TV and video games, a society that has got into the habit of confusing the virtual with the real. I first started painting through the computer in the mid-1980s, but I still find the process an amazing leap into the unknown. The power of the modern paint program—especially the hidden and less obvious devices—is formidable and grows more sophisticated year by year. And this is not even taking 3D, animation, virtual reality, video, or the Web into consideration. I am still coming to terms with what one could call the aesthetic aftershock. If it is now possible to create significant art this way—this is a big *if*, I admit—then what does that mean for "traditional" art? Have the conventions of the painted picture been turned on their head? Do you still have to learn to draw, study art history, mingle with the art world? Or can anyone with the right software and a little know-how conjure up the digital masterpiece hinted at in the manual?

My instinct says this cannot be so. But then I wonder whether that instinct, formed from my education in a nondigital age, should always be trusted. Like a musician schooled in the prejazz age, perhaps I just won't be able to get the swing, the rhythm, of an art that emerges from this complex mix. I will stand right in front of it and not see it. Something like an acquired and inbuilt sense of "good painting" will prevent me from pushing colour combinations or extreme imagery over the edge. On the other hand, without learning how to draw, how to compose, how to work fluently, I would not know the edge was there.

I have mentioned SIGGRAPH, the major computer-graphics event of the calendar, several times, and its substantial exhibitions of digital art, as one of the key events in the intersections between computer science, art, entertainment, and commerce. In 2003, when the conference was held in San Diego, there was an especially ambitious exhibition curated by Mike Wright. It displayed over three hundred exhibits, with many leading artists, veterans, and newcomers represented. I had four pieces in the show, and I was curious to gauge some of the response. I also knew that there were at least three survey books in the pipeline, and curators going round the exhibition with notebooks and stickers to pick out their favourite pieces. This was the most thorough and well-curated exhibition by far, and collectors prowled everywhere. I went round the show with some care, knowing that if I wanted to figure out what was happening, there would be no better opportunity for years.

I soon twigged that the talent scouts, the new media historians patrolling the show, were keeping their thoughts to themselves. Apart from a few guarded asides, there were no clues as to who was in and who was out. The more competitive exhibitors—these included me, ready with CDs of images and old catalogues—were having to finesse the correct etiquette: not too pushy, keeping to a more or less cool visibility. My second realisation was that each team was cherry-picking quite different works. One group of scouts would lock onto what they thought of as pioneer work, another onto a visual effect that to my eyes was a cliché, another onto technical virtuosity, and another onto what was good in its own right "as art." Others would stroll round knowingly with the seen-it-all indifference of a stroll through a New York gallery. Reading the feedback was complicated. My third insight was that I was just as much at sea, and just as incompetent a judge, as anyone else.

There was a large print, quite a beautiful image that seemed to be of an airliner's cockpit at night, and on my first few rounds it was certainly on my checklist. It was what I would call a straight piece—not gimmicky or flashy, not depending on one or another of the clichés of computer art, and not sloppily "nice" in the way of much conventional middle-brow art. When I checked in the catalogue, which is, I admit, a kind of insurance, to see that the artist had sufficient credentials to go into my pantheon, I found this was a local artist, a member of the Photoshop users' group. How did that affect my view? Was I turning out to be just another art snob?

My inability to be a decisive—or incisive—critic was a dent in my confidence. My painter's ego would claim that you could more or less tell how good anything was just by looking at it, letting it work on you. Here my knowledge of filters and tricks of the trade was confusing my response. In addition, I had spent ten years in the 1970s writing criticism as a sideline to painting. Here was an issue I just could not crack. Perhaps I was just too close, too caught up in the overlap between the digital and the painterly worlds. I mean this in the technical sense of developing a bilingual working process, one that allows the creative kick of computer graphics to coexist with the physical presence of the painting on a wall, but also a process in the deeper sense of combining the "fix it" pragmatism of technology with the stubborn resistance of art to be rational. In other words, I find it difficult to accept that in terms of solving problems, the Mac, however fast, is not much help. So I should watch out in case I grow dependent on a silver box. In fact, I may spend several months avoiding the use of a printer of any type, so that I have to develop some other means of expressing images that may or may not come together on the computer. Pressing that *print* button can seem too easy, too much like closing down, finishing off. At other periods, I may play with the difference in look between the hand and the digitally painted mark, making one look like the other, and depend heavily on the printed output. Somewhat to my surprise, I have found the approach of improvising between the physical and the digital is sustainable; at least it launches one idea after another. But do I become a more enlightened critic? No.

I have become more sceptical. Much of the speculation about digital art assumes that we are all moving along some track, working our way out of "traditional" media into some improved and higher form of art. The improvement in performance of the hardware is so dramatic, there just has to be a parallel improvement in the performance of the art. Few writers on the subject have suggested that—in art terms—we might not be

151

moving forward at all. This is now a false division, as so many traditional, even academic, artists use computers. I sometimes wonder whether it is my digital self that is lagging behind. I am seldom knocked out by a digital piece, but often by a contemporary painting, and that has less to do with the medium itself than with the creative effort of the artist. If the influence of the digital on the mainstream turns out to be so much less than was predicted in the 1990s, then we would have to think again about specifically digital exhibitions, about prizing pioneer work done in the 1960s or 1970s. We would have to let go of this idea of the digital as the Big Solution. The solutions—such as pressing that *print* button—came at a cost. Any art form has to get beyond technique and cliché. It needs a survival instinct, sustaining roots, real development, and a purpose beyond its own vanity. And an audience.

Special Knowledge

Glance at the promotional slogans at a trade fair, and you might think that painting "skills" have been absorbed into software. The distinction between professional and amateur no longer applies. Training is supposedly unnecessary. Anyone can be creative. After half an hour with the manual, and half an hour of experiment, you can "make" a painting on your desktop. You can achieve an impressive result without any angst and without any of the bother of preparing canvas, paints, and brushes and clearing up the mess afterward. I should try to keep an open mind on this, for in theory the most impressive paintings of five or fifty years' time could be produced by artists who never knew the smell of turpentine and whose only experience of brushes and palette was as icons on the interface. Our interface, our icons, probably would not make much sense to them. All the same, the concept of a painting, whatever the material—real or virtual, wet or dry—will probably survive intact.

The fact that leading painters and other practitioners have not "gone digital" but have picked and mixed—using a digital camera, a scanner, a printer, or Photoshop manipulation here and there—is of some significance. To speak of contemporary art as a whole is misleading. There is such a diversity of format, philosophy, culture, and levels of achievement. *Pluralism* is a convenient term, but it covers over many irreconcilable interests. In an art school where twenty students were studying painting or sculpture forty years ago, there may now be four hundred, and the subject will be "fine art" without any particular medium specified: Performance, video, installation, and photography will be going on alongside painting and perhaps alongside a digital section, too. Whatever hang-ups "digital" artists may have about their ranking, painting has its status problems, too. Nevertheless—and to return to my dilemma over making that choice at the SIGGRAPH Art Show—I find scarcely any digital art that comes close to the level of wit, intelligence, and economy of painters such as Neo Rauch, Tuymans, or the godfathers of current painting, Richter, Polke, or Hockney. One simple difference is that the painters would have undertaken an apprenticeship lasting decades and have absorbed not just software and technical know-how but the accumulated learning of centuries of painting, of debates about realism, about modernism, about the validity or otherwise of painting itself. It is disappointing to have to admit this failing of the digital, and it does puzzle me. Surely, with the extraordinary extra firepower, shouldn't digital art by now be competing more effectively? The alternative and—for a painter—reassuring view is that here is evidence that painting is such a human phenomenon that it cannot be "got at" and transposed into software.

Specialists may not have the broadest of horizons. At one extreme, you have the computer scientist who thinks of impressionism as a cool brush-mark effect, and at the other, the art connoisseur who imagines that computer art is generated by a robot. The first two generations of digital artists have been for the most part self-taught, and for all the expertise they have in one area, they have huge holes in some other area. Not that the methods used in an art-school computer lab to teach Photoshop to painting students—the sessions are sometimes called *inductions*—would have been much help. Once the computer is segregated from the studio and labelled *information technology,* the organic connection is lost. It would be like going to a separate building to learn "water-based paint technology" instead of picking up a tube of acrylic. I have watched as the computers acquired for fine-art students gradually became the brainless workhorses for video editing. They are perceived as presentation units rather than as creative instruments in their own right, and when it comes to the final "degree show," no piece of hardware is more sought after than the digital projector.

Suppose for a moment that a generation of art students as fluent in computer graphics as in art history emerged from colleges. True experts. What kind of painting—or other format—would they gravitate toward? Would they see painting as too technologically backward? In colleges as much as in museums, special rooms and annexes have been set aside for "screen-based" work, with elegantly glazed galleries full of natural light blacked out and converted to lightless art cinemas. On that evidence, the planners don't see painting as the dominant art form of the future.

One of my addictions—aside from painting with the computer—is cheese. Spending my holidays camping in France and having a truly obsessive cheese-shop nearby in London, I learned how to appreciate the key forms, tastes, nuances. I am no expert and would be useless in a blind tasting. I do enjoy the sense of a conspiracy of the cognoscenti, the categories, the regulations, the details of place-names and the precision of *affinage* timing. It may not be a culture that I will ever understand comprehensively, but I am impressed that it exists. I respect it. It is also there to give pleasure. One cheese guidebook is actually written by a Japanese duo who are even more censorious about improper cheese techniques than any French expert I have come across. They dismiss processed cheese as simply not cheese at all.

Computer graphics may provide the painter with the most mind-blowing paints ever, yet by and large what has been produced through this synthetic process is as disappointing as processed cheese. It doesn't feel—or taste—authentic. And that remains the case, even when you have tried to rationalise away your preconceptions. It has fallen way short of what was expected by the optimists of ten or twenty years ago. Fallen short, I should say, as art. An Epson print on real canvas, a giant video projection of a morphing kaleidoscope, a picture that talks back to you? Big deal.

So, awkward questions remain. What are the limitations, and what are the real gains? How far can paint software be integrated with conventional studio practices? Could a gallery-goer get something extra and special from a piece of expert digital art? Does digital art have to look technological or be about digital things? Why have no influential writers on contemporary art looked seriously at these issues?

Where paint software really comes into its own is in free-form improvisation. This little-understood aspect is neglected in the instruction manuals. I despair when I come across the tips for using the software, or for drawing, that make no mention at all of the liberating potential of play, of just messing around, with different combinations of brushes and effects.

Again, the ability to know enough to play around with new techniques is part of the insider knowledge that cannot be dropped into the software like a plug-in. Nor can it be taught through a correspondence course. Here is the opportunity to extend the existing conventions of drawing—drawing as much as painting—where the combination of pressure-sensitive drawing tablet and software comes into its own as a new instrument. These new methods could be to drawing what the saxophone was to jazz.

Writers and musicians speak of following a thread, a line, an association of ideas where one motif leads to another. Paul Klee wrote of "taking a line for a walk." Drawing with a line, especially a line where the pen never leaves the paper, is such a common activity that we take it for granted, like thinking aloud, like doodling in the margin while speaking on the phone. It is a form that is both formless, in that we are not actually writing, and form finding, in that we rarely just make marks; we form shapes, faces, objects.

Traditionally, painters have developed their ideas informally in sketchbooks or in charcoal on canvas, roughing out forms, eradicating, redrawing. In offices, the ballpoint pen or gel pen is ideal, because it doesn't need to be refilled or sharpened. Normally, we would not stop to think of any connection between the viscosity of the ink and the resistance of the paper and how that would affect what we were in the habit of drawing. When transposing this informal drawing process onto the "canvas" on the monitor, we find that the physical qualities of the tools can be customised in hundreds of ways. We have choices to make. In fact, the work, the creative effort, in improvising can be as much in devising these conditions as in the execution.

Some painters draw compulsively, as a way into their work, perhaps repeating the same forms over and over. The materials—pencil or ink and paper—cost little compared with the cost and time involved in preparing canvases or working with photos. Drawing can be a throwaway art form. Pared down to a single wandering line or a few silhouettes, it is where an emerging motif is most naked. Instead of spending hours on one piece, some painters will work on twelve pieces in rapid succession and then spend some time looking to see which is the one to take further in a subsequent work. This is where the physical studio is unlike the desktop studio. Physical drawings "talk" to each other. Too much refinement in one set of drawings leads to bolder treatment in the next batch. The only way this can work on the desktop is if you miniaturise a group of drawings and scan across them. On the other hand, there are ways of drawing with the electronic tablet, and ways of using a camera, that cannot be achieved in the studio. On several occasions, especially after being preoccupied with a certain kind of serpentine line that must be drawn in a single swooping motion, I have found myself drawing the same line with a camera. I set the camera to a night setting and photograph the lights in the park, shifting the camera about. Loaded into the paint program, the image inverted into negative, the trails of light become elegant, fine lines.

One of the more eccentric features that has been in Painter for some years is called the *image hose.* On the face of it, it is a gimmick allowing you to paint with tiny images of leaves, stones, mushrooms, koi fish, faces, so that you can manufacture instant foliage, flowers, crowd scenes. It is quite easy to program this feature and make your own set of images, which can be sprayed out through your brush, or "hose." It is a classic case of a feature ahead of its time—or at least ahead of the natural media ethos of the program. It does not imitate an existing paint technique, but gives the user a glimpse of the hidden power behind the friendly icons. Using this feature freely would

PAINTING THE DIGITAL RIVER

mean working outside the safe boundaries of the formulaic exercises of the manual—still life, cartoon face, landscape, surreal collage. Unless you go for something that is just freaky, it is a challenge to turn it into a useful "brush."

One approach is to work in reverse. The first "drawing" will be the source for developing twenty small square motifs, which will stream out of the hose. In practice, I find it pays to keep to a strict regimen, using just one or two line types, and half a dozen colours. Once loaded into the hose-brush as a "nozzle," the spray can be fine-tuned. It can be made to behave so that it is almost uncontrollable. This is something a painter may well work hard to achieve and value, trying to overcome brush movements that are overfamiliar, exploiting and improvising the accident—allowing the paint to spill and splatter. A knife may rip from one layer to another. Runny paint may be left to "find its own way." Working with a complex digital brush with its own inbuilt and unpredictable behaviour also prompts the user to improvise, to go with the flow. Each drawing may well need its own special brush, and the character of the drawing can be predetermined by the way it is programmed to behave.

This is interesting, because for normal purposes the draughtsman focuses entirely on where a line goes, what shapes it describes. Here the focus initially is on the design of the brush. On the other hand, this is consistent with the traditional rituals of painting with a brush in China, with calligraphy, where the feel and balance of the brush, the precise quality and dilution of the ink, are critical. While I remain an eternal novice as a calligrapher, I do have a favourite Chinese brush I use for drawing, and I have noticed that I get better results when I let my thoughts run loose. I concentrate on the feel of the brush, let the line play, and only think of the form or image afterward. This is something I have picked up from improvising with these peculiar digital brushes. I have also made physical versions of

158

some of these brushes and found again that whole paintings can be structured around the way a given brush behaves—a single special brush for each picture. This is only possible if you have begun to develop some fluency in both digital and physical formats. I suspect you can only learn to make a line "dance"—as they say in China—through hours and hours of practice with brush and paper. The Painter program offers you a set of calligraphic brushes, but without learning the art, you are just using pretend brushes. Buying a pair of skates is not the same as learning to skate. Calligraphy, one of the most refined and "live" ways of drawing, can only be learned through constant practice.

This poses a dilemma, both for the students wondering how to combine new and old methods and for the teachers and professors wondering how painting or drawing should be taught. What would be the difference between a contemporary drawing class, where getting to grips with the image hose might be on the agenda, and a life drawing class of forty years ago? Students studying drawing today need to be, so to speak, multi-skilled. They need experience in drawing from observation and through improvisation; they need to learn drawing with a pencil, with a brush, and through a range of 2D and 3D software. They should be able to make an informed choice in whatever method they take up. Even if they end up specialising in straightforward figure drawing, finding out about how the "bendy wire" of a vector program like Illustrator works can only be an advantage. It is an alternative way of shaping a drawing, refining precise curves. In the life class, much of the drawing process used to consist of making minor corrections with erasers scraping away at "wrong" marks, eyes screwed up and pencils extended to estimate proportions. It was a useful discipline, perhaps, but it was not the art of calligraphy, which, incidentally, is a far more ancient art. It was a cold and mechanical technique for reproducing what you saw. Why emulate a camera?

159

Prints and Originals

If someone suggested replacing drawing with cameras, or installing rows of Macs in the painting studios, then any round-table discussion I might envisage would lose its pretence of being a civilised debate. While looking round an art school in Atlanta in 1996, I did come across a door with "Life Drawing Studio" boldly printed across it, and yes, inside there were rows and rows of computers. There was no smell of paint anywhere. Five years later, I am told, those studios were reclaimed. Life drawing had returned.

The reassessment of drawing is only one piece of the evidence that points to a period of coexistence. Pencils, laptop, and digital camera will continue to fill the same backpack. Each tool has its role. In time, no single tool will seem more traditional than any other. At some point in history, a drawing tutor probably objected to a student's using a compass for making a circle, but one of my favourite Greek vases in the British Museum, by the Berlin Painter, has a clear compass point mark at the centre of Achilles' shield, and this was drawn in 490 B.C.[33] If the round-table debate is to get anywhere, it has to speak about technical questions and art objectives in the same breath. It is as pointless to reject all mechanical aids as it is pointless to base an art form on using just one set of equipment.

I wonder too what would be gained by such a seminar on the future of technology in art, as if there really were a choice. Would an art form without any technological aids be possible? Meanwhile, the shops in the high street, businesses, individuals, are finding their practical solutions. Painters may hesitate, but they recognise a bargain and they buy the printers that can produce flawless images. Yes, you have to keep in mind what kind of artist you plan to be. Is that wonderful image quality really necessary, or a luxury, a status symbol? And what of the studio rent? Do you need to keep some money back for paints and canvas? Should you be able to function with equipment that is five years out of date? The phrase *practising artist* is often used in academic circles, as though you could still be an artist and not actually practice or produce anything. In reality, being an artist means dealing with a string of practical questions—leaking roofs, packing works for exhibition, getting materials, and, if the digital plays a large role, keeping an eye on the next upgrade. The nagging and unanswerable question is whether your output would really be better if you get a set of better boxes.

While wondering about this, I receive three e-mails within a few hours of each other. One scares me because it reminds me of how little I know, and how even stopping to philosophise by the banks of this imaginary river, I miss so much that is flowing by. I feel left behind. The e-mail message is an exhibition announcement for "The Analogue Surface: Painting in the Digital Age." The show is near where I live, down the road in Shoreditch, London. I first go to the Web to check through the five artists in the show. I have only heard of two of them. The paintings look good online; at least they are vividly graphic, images of exotic birds, of flowers simplified into symmetrical patterns. I check through related galleries—some are entirely online galleries—and find quite a genre developing of flora and fauna, a genre that is digitally processed in some way and made available as an edition in an inkjet print or as a painting on canvas. I cannot decide whether this phenomenon is too glib, too much of a shortcut method, or whether it is the straightforward answer to how to take advantage of the digital world and still come up with a painting. The answer? Cut out the existential scruples, the harking back to the ancient lore of painting, and just copy the image out on canvas. Forget calligraphy, painterly nuance, the adventures of Picasso. Be a box. Paint like an inkjet printer. Transcribe the "found" image line by line.

161

When I visit the actual exhibition, I realise in a microsecond the difference between the painting "on screen" and the painting on the wall. This work doesn't look half as good. It looks designed on the screen and then, yes, transcribed onto canvas. As objects, as surfaces, the paintings are so-so. An experienced painter could see instantly where the handling is inept. What interests me most is the label beside the canvas of simplified tulips by Lis Fields: "hand-brushed oil on canvas." I have never heard that expression before. Does it mean they were actually painted and not inkjetted on the canvas? Does it guarantee that the artist painted them? Why should this matter? I pick up a press release:

> This is an exhibition of paintings which were made by hand yet have distinct digital qualities. All of the artists produce exacting work with smooth surfaces and precise edges. Their paintings share a concern for particular ambiguities of surface, whereby it is not immediately clear what one is looking at or how it was made. In contrast to a digital era preoccupation with surface and instant gratification, these paintings, made slowly with extraordinary technical skills, manifest complexities and subtleties.[34]

The thought crosses my mind that combining slick graphics and painting via the computer screen is one big mistake. On this evidence, and if this is a glimpse of a future where paintings are applauded just for being skilfully executed with "precise edges," this is an art form in a nosedive. Eventually it could be a tourist market—"hand-brushed oil paintings." In the ideological battles of the 1960s and 1970s between "authentic" existential painting and clinically analytic "conceptual" art, the "gestural mark" was always potentially numinous, a loaded gesture and not just the trace of a moving brush. Rauschenberg made a drawing by erasing—with de Kooning's amused consent—a de Kooning drawing. The anonymity of photorealism, a method of painting without visible brushstrokes—the artists often used spray paint or an airbrush—had an ironic twist. Warhol's silk-screened canvases, which belatedly I now admire enormously, were not only sloppily made and mis-registered, but in many cases not made by him in person. Sol Le Witt, one of the originators of conceptual art, made large-scale wall drawings on gallery walls—rows of faint 10H parallel lines—but all he did was write down the instruction, the program. In effect this was an algorithm:

> When an artist uses a conceptual form of art, it means that all of the planning and decisions are made beforehand and the execution is a perfunctory affair. The idea becomes the machine that makes the art.[35]

So the draughtsmen who actually "drew" the lines were just machines, as expressionless as the desktop printer. The lines were hand-drawn, but not by the artist's hand. (I was one of those draughtsmen back in 1969, and with the fee, I bought a piece of technology then ubiquitous but now extinct: a manual typewriter.) So after this brief reverie, I reflect on how attentively painters have played around with the way the surface is touched, marked, abused, and printed and how this game never ends. I look again at what are the all-too-familiar "mysterious" digital images—symmetries, textural close-ups, filterings, offbeat colourings, logo geometry—and I think of a door being slammed shut. Painting is not an art form because it shows off someone's skill. I don't go to the theatre just to be impressed that the actors have learned their lines and can act. I hope there is a little more at stake in an art form than that.

By coincidence the second e-mail is from a US company

whose magazine, *SellArtSmart,* invites me to join up as one of its artists who supply artworks for its eager clientele. This is more than an online gallery. It is a complete service, an art consultancy. If as an artist you are one of the lucky few whom the client chooses, you could be into the big time, as the magazine enthusiastically explains:

> Editions. Never done one? Here's one way: select a work you think will be popular. Or create a new one (possibly based on one that has been well-received, but may no longer be in your possession). Then contact a local printer (search Google for a "printer" within your state) and discuss options. Some printers are moving to "print on demand" technology that allows you to minimise your upfront costs and inventory.
>
> Here's how you save money—you only pay to list the edition once, no matter how many of that edition you sell! When a copy sells, simply send us one from your inventory or (if using print-on-demand) contact your printer to produce one.
>
> Here's how you make more—sometimes a designer is looking for a number of identical pieces, for example to put one in each room of a hotel, hospital, or nursing facility. They may purchase hundreds of that one piece, at a time. Sounds interesting?[36]

This is another way of taking commercial advantage of the digital process—a way that has nothing whatever to do with the painful growth of computer art. Bear in mind that some of the key artists in that world have never sold a single piece. This call is not aimed at digital artists at all, but is openly recommending selling reproductions of a painting as an "edition."

The third e-mail comes soon after and is also about printing, or rather, printmaking. In attitude, this is the polar opposite, the studio print.

There is no better way to experience contemporary art practice than to see the output from an innovative, creative print
studio. The Print Studio, Cambridge, Ltd is a collaborative
printmaking enterprise run by Kip Gresham. It is truly
experimental in its outlook, more laboratory than factory
and embraces the best of both the new and old technologies.[37]

On the Web site, the studio takes a stab at the question all
such studios have to answer:

> What is an Original Print? A tricky question. There have
> been many attempts to arrive at a finite definition, none of
> which has been very useful. Artists often approach the mak-
> ing of prints in an experimental manner and (rightly) resist
> an imposed restriction. Our working definition is that the
> image has been made through and for printing and that it
> has involved the artist directly in all stages of the image for-
> mation. The requirement is that the image could not be
> formed in any other way and that it realizes the artist's vision
> for the piece. The artist is in the driving seat. It is not a repro-
> duction of a pre-existing image. It stands alone, there is no
> point of reference.

The prints here are by established artists and—I suppose—
would cost more than the repro editions, though the inkjets by
artists connected with the "Digital Age" show are by no means
cheap. I cannot take a superior position on this. I have had
works on several online gallery sites and have sold prints this
way, limiting the edition. This may seem an arbitrary convention, just a number in the corner. In practice, it has been expensive and time-consuming to produce the necessary quality of
inkjet, so it is not as if the prints come streaming out of a
machine like photocopies. However, I note that the print studio

that speaks of new and old technologies has little evidence in its Web site of any inkjets at all.

These questions are clearly in the air.[38] Here is another message, this time from the Royal Academy, inviting submissions for its annual Summer Show:

> This year's theme will be the multiple image or object. This broad theme will cover printmaking in all its manifestations and also include other forms of multiples and works created using mechanical/technological intervention; it is anticipated that this will spread across all categories of entry.[39]

The looming question is what happens when the distinction between print and painting becomes even more blurred than it is now. There must be plenty of other artists wondering how to find a balance between their old and new technologies. Is it enough to produce a large-scale inkjet print? What is gained by making it into an "original" by copying it out in paint?

Better Boxes

I cannot answer these questions except by trying out each alternative. For a period, yes, I will become the box, an output device that processes the digital image onto the canvas, through stencils, through copying, through transcribing a projected image. Then I will have a blitz working on a project that is entirely digital from start to finish and notice that the qualities that I thought at the time were truly painterly in the painting were nothing like what I thought they were. Meanwhile, the hardware is evolving, and I have to make some difficult decisions about an upgrade. Do I need a better box?

There are any number of excuses for upgrading, but professionals who depend on photography, printing, or digital manipulation of one kind or another don't have a choice. Or rather, if they stand still, they are choosing to be left behind. Regardless of any other quality the images may have as images, prints from the obsolete printer tend to look fuzzy—cruder, weaker, thinner. Higher-resolution images, put simply, look better. You can fiddle around with older equipment, but it is an unequal struggle. At one point, with an inkjet printer I nursed through several technical crises, I had to work around the fact that its blue nozzle was blocked for good. I had already spent quite a sum replacing nozzles, but this time I found that a new printer would cost considerably less than the one nozzle. That cheaper new printer would produce far better prints. I know I am being manipulated by the immaculately tailored images of the new boxes, and I know I am just one among thousands of other consumers in the queue, and I know that a "serious" painter might be worrying about higher things than image resolution. But then worrying about the fine grain of a shadow's texture is quite a serious subject. Perhaps. There is an inverted snobbery among painters—I plead guilty—a snobbery that prefers the low tech to the high tech, but only when you have the luxury of having the choice.

So, rough equals authentic. Smooth and perfect means shallow and suburban. The crudely cut woodblock prints of die Brucke, the expressionists of a hundred years ago (some of whom had studied law and were thoroughly middle-class), yearned to be simpler peasants in a medieval world, where people spoke from the heart, and art was bonded with Nature. Likewise, "rough pixels" reject the soapy-salon look and expose the primitive soul of, well, the high tech of ten years ago. Patrick Lichty has made some wonderful videos in his *8 Bits or Less* series, all jerky and in grey-scale, filmed from his Casio Wrist Camera Watch, with a commentary explaining that it's great to be eight-bit. I would not want to be eight-bit all the time, though, and have never yet gone backward to a lower-resolution monitor, printer, or camera or to the really slow early Apple II and thought, yes, this is the real thing. I can feel nostalgia for such dead technology, now in display cases in London's Science Museum, but I have to accept that the upgrade is as much part of the painter's life as anyone else's. Alarm bells start ringing in my ears when I find students casually presenting prints far superior to what my six-year-old inkjet can achieve. Just thinking of the difficulties of operating those first DOS systems I used twenty years ago, the flickering screens that mashed my eyesight, is enough to stop my wobbling. If I want to do things, and do them well, I need to upgrade.

Every three to four years, I go through upgrade anxiety. It is an exciting moment when—and if—everything starts up afresh, but much faster. I find myself again in a new landscape without familiar landmarks, or perhaps it would be better to say that I am in the same landscape but can now see twice as far. The new camera shows up five times the detail of what was there before. It is like a new set of eyes. Not only can I photograph or video in the dark, but I can look at houses lit by street lights at night and see precisely how the lighting moulds their forms. The extra resolution is a mixed blessing, because when I look at a piece of work that I had painstakingly assembled at the lower resolution of my previous setup, I find to my horror that its colour has gone sour, there is far too much unnecessary detail, and all I can see are the blemishes. It is as if I had been working with half-closed eyes and now that I open them the illusion is shattered. The file I have moved by FireWire from the old system to the new may be identical, but I had presumed that the file was a fixed entity. Now I realise that it will only work, say, with one printer. This runs against all my instincts as a painter. When I work the paint into a certain texture—perhaps by scraping cardboard across it—I know that what I see is what I get. If I move the painting from one room to another, or take it overseas to an exhibition, it won't look completely different. Yet move the file a few feet, and it has been altered just enough to start me worrying.

Confusion has its creative payoffs. Testing a new camera or printer opens your mind. Knowing that you can now photograph great detail at night, or a bird in a tree a hundred feet away, makes a difference. In previous years, I conditioned myself to avoid colour ranges and gradations that I knew to be hazardous when sent through the inkjet printer. Turquoise always seemed to move toward purple. I emphasised the graphic and tonal at the expense of subtleties I knew were quite impossible to produce. When I began, it was an advantage to be an abstract painter, especially a painter specialising in squares and circles. Unfortunately, I preferred much looser forms, indistinct blends, watery colour. Now, more and more of the quieter aspects of painting are viable. Painters were attracted to the low-resolution photograph because it looked broken down into blocks as if it were painted. Now photographers themselves have large-format Epson printers in the space that used to be the darkroom. They are printing the photos onto canvas and realising that these pieces could be "paintings." Some are tentatively working on the surface with paint. Ten years ago, I got into some trouble giving a talk to professional photographers about the merits of digital over chemical photography. I even spent a day as a would-be fashion photographer at the London College of Fashion to make the point—of course, my camera was ridiculously crude by today's standards. The photographers said it would never catch on.

Digital artists of all types have to adjust to the shifting ground. Some get round the problem by having an idea that is sufficiently forceful to make issues of resolution and presentation irrelevant. A 20-kilobyte JPEG, a massive TIFF file, it is all the same. A fine-grained image is not necessarily better than a low-grained one, but our eyes do get used to what they see as normal.

I overheard an artist earnestly explaining a set of paintings to a potential client at an art fair. There were eight almost identical paintings of the same still life, just slight changes of viewpoint. He was explaining that he had carefully transcribed the image in paint from images taken from an "ordinary" digital camera, meaning the images were nothing special. His point was that this way he could show the limitations of the painted image—this has been one of the more popular painting methods in art schools, in the shadow of Gerhard Richter and Luc Tuymans, the post-modern "deconstruction" of representation, as they would put it. What fascinated me was not the row of paintings, but the assumption that the digital images could be considered mid- or even low-tech. *Low-tech* is such a relative term, such a shifting standard. He was right, of course, and there are competitions for cell-phone photos that come up with images a good deal better than the highest technology of the early 1990s. The graininess of an image is perceived against some semiconscious template of a nongrainy image in our mind. There must come a point where we no longer trust our eyes to do the job.

London's National Gallery is introducing special booths where viewers can look at close-ups of selected paintings. John Cupitt, of the gallery's scientific department, said viewing images on the screen was as close to looking at the real thing as the technology allowed.

> The 100 megapixel camera is calibrated against international colour standards, as are the screen. . . . We have a pretty precise mathematical pipe joining the two together. So what you see on the screen is very close to how the painting actually looks. You are seeing it as it is, not how it appears on a photograph.[40]

This is all very enterprising. I have been to a conference on computers in art history where this process is explained in

Plate 1

James Faure Walker
Pigeons Kyoto, 2002
29" × 43" (74 × 109 cm)
Giclee iris print

Plate 2

James Faure Walker
Ideas and Music: Curiosity, 2002
68" × 92" (173 × 234 cm)
Oil on canvas

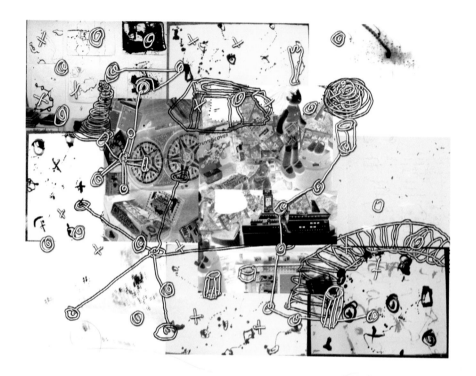

Plate 3

James Faure Walker
A Song for Upper Street, 2004
26" × 33" (66 × 83 cm)
Inkjet print

Plate 4

Henry Jamyn Brooks
Private View of the Old Masters Exhibition, Royal Academy, 1888, 1889
23" × 42" (60 × 106 cm)
Oil on canvas
Copyright National Portrait Gallery, London

Plate 5

Ken Huff
2005.1
Variable size up to 60" × 90" (152 × 229 cm)
Chromogenic print of digital image

Plate 6

James Faure Walker
Frog, Greenwood Road, 2004
61" × 68" (155 × 172 cm)
Oil on canvas

Plate 7

Neo Rauch
Unschuld, 2001
117" × 77" (298 × 200 cm)
Oil on paper

Plate 8

Roman Verostko

Pearl Park Scripture—I, 2004

20" × 30" (52 × 76 cm)

Algorithmic pen and ink drawing with gold-leaf enhancement

Text: Nonrational glyphs

Format: 224 characters, 8 characters per line, 14 lines per column, 2 columns

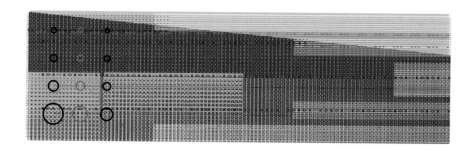

Plate 9

Mark Wilson
VB3T134, 2004
24" × 72" (61 × 183 cm)
Archival inkjet print
Edition of 5 on Somerset rag paper

Plate 10

Stephan Lochner (1410–1451)
The Martyrdom of the Apostles (The St. Lawrence Altarpiece)
47" × 71" (120 × 180 cm)
Tempera and oil on walnut
Frankfurt, Städelsches Kunstinstitut

Plate 11

Jan Gossaert
The Adoration of the Kings, 1510
70" × 64" (177 × 162 cm)
Copyright National Gallery

Plate 12

Cynthia Beth Rubin
View from the Women's Window, 2005
Variable dimensions
Inkjet print

Plate 13

Anna Ursyn
Horsing Around, Flying High, 1996
12" × 24" (30 × 61 cm)
Photo-silkscreen, photolithograph

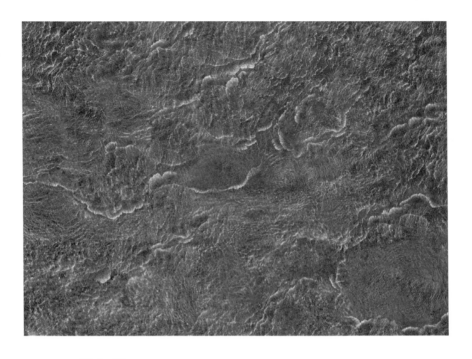

Plate 14

Shelagh Wakely
Five Seconds—Lamu, 1999
34" × 48" (87 × 122 cm)
Inkjet print

Plate 15

James Faure Walker
Baroque Thoughts for a Rainy Day, 2005
24" × 32" (61 × 81 cm)
Inkjet print

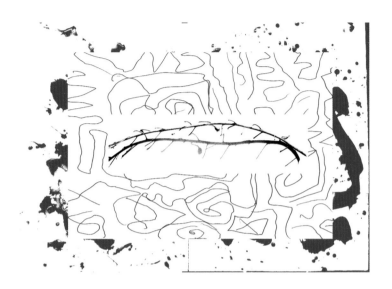

Plate 16

James Faure Walker
Found, Drawn, Painted, 2005
27" × 36" (69 × 92 cm)
Inkjet print

detail. In the Louvre, the cameras scan the backs, tops, and sides of each painting like patients going through a scan. I wonder what the philosophers, particularly aestheticians, make of this. Is the object (what is) to be distinguished from the impression we get from it (how it appears)? Is the worth of a work of art measurable, weighable, calculable down to the last photon? A painted canvas, then, could be a real object, but a digital image would only be as real as its resolution. If the camera were to inspect an image with a resolution lower than its own, then that picture would evaporate. It would not really be "there." It would be a mirage of pixels.

There is a paradox in that throughout the nineteenth and twentieth centuries, the tendency in painting was from smooth grained to rougher grained. Ingres portraits took the soft-brushed gradations of flesh tones and fabric to the ultimate "high resolution" of continuous gradation, and his paintings have the flawless grace of an image reflected in a mirror. Yes, at least 100 megapixels. But move on to the rival school of Delacroix; Courbet in the Louvre; the Musée d'Orsay and Manet, Monet, Seurat, and Cézanne; and then Picasso, Pollock, de Kooning, and perhaps Dubuffet and Tapies, and the resolution gets cruder and cruder. This is hardly textbook art history, but it would not take a genius to work out that painters have been just as interested in the way our eyes and our minds work as they have in anything else. The one thing painters have not believed in is this supremely correct, perfect image of what is "out there."

Doing Without the Explanation

Some things don't crop up in regular—that is, not specifically digital—art shows but do crop up in digital shows. One example is the catalogue artist's statement, with an obligatory how-it-was-done technical paragraph. On the face of it, this is useful information, but such a statement would be out of place in an ordinary art show and as relevant as knowing which brand of ink Dickens preferred. Nowadays, technical information is the legacy of an earlier phase, when computer art really was computer art, when both software and hardware were custom-built and part of the presentation. The story of the process involved in weaving the tangle of lines together might be as interesting as the image itself. Nowadays, if you say, "I used Photoshop," you are not saying very much. It would be like exhibiting a drawing and saying, "By the way, I used a 2B pencil."

The statement can help out in other ways, however. There may be nothing special to put into this technical section, but the actual work on show—an immersive, interactive sound piece, for example—may need some explanation. This is another difference, because in a normal gallery context, the viewers should be able to come to the exhibit and get it more or less in a glimpse, that is to say, come to it unprimed. If they are in the know and read the previews and go to galleries regularly, they can pick up the cues subliminally, and most of what might go in the statement can be left unsaid. They see it, they like it, they don't like it, they shrug, they look at it again, they leave. Enough said. A week, a month later, they can read a review and reflect on what they missed. Digital art is not like that. It is rarely reviewed or commented on with the cold eye of the critic. Most of what is written is gently supportive and uncritical. After all, it is written by the artists.

So, digital art exists in this limbo land where you cannot predict whether a viewer has been reading *Computer Graphics World* or *Artforum,* or neither. But the viewer won't have read both. In an ideal world, the exhibits would be self-evident and a curator could orchestrate the exhibition to bring out similarities and differences. It could be interesting to know who was influencing whom, what kind of art these practitioners looked at, what their preferred context was. Were they freelance artists or academics? No one works in a vacuum, though it can look that way when the work is shown in the nonspaces of conferences and science parks. Critics, generally, need a context, and they don't use separate score sheets for technical performance and artistic quality. One exception is ice skating. There the judges come up with points for artistic effect after they have marked athletic performance. But digital exhibits should be an art context, not sport or pure research. Staying one step ahead by using top-of-the range hardware should not come into the reckoning. You should be able to come up with the goods by using the same cameras, paints, pencils, and furnishing that everyone else uses. You should be free to use photocopiers, Palm Pilots, Amigas; you could even get away with a performance piece using a landline phone. But if the performance went through an analogue exchange, I suppose it would no longer be digital, strictly speaking.

Without a definite context, the statements have to sketch in the missing framework. The "piece" becomes something other than a row of wired-up processors in a dark space, or something hanging on the wall. It becomes a cultural investigation into, let's see, simultaneity. In the mid-1990s, an exchange of real-time video across thousands of miles—"here is the sky outside my window . . . now show me the sky outside yours"— was serious stuff, enough for at least a paragraph of art jargon about "telepresence." But that was then. If I do something now with my camera-phone, or just send a JPEG, I would be pushing my luck.

Technical statements are not required elsewhere. In photography shows, you do not need to know the make of camera. Sculptors do not have to list the tools and materials used, and painters don't have to specify brushes, pigments, and the weight of canvas. It would be liberating if work made through everyday hardware could be seen in its own right. Worthy explanations are symptoms of an inferiority complex, the nagging feeling that without the prompts, this stuff would not be seen as art. It would not be enjoyed. Even the jokes have to be spelled out. The artist's statement is a throwback, like a scene in a 1950s movie with the artist in a beret explaining to his pipe-smoking café friends the meaning of his existential abstracts. The critic Peter Schjeldahl spoke of the "abomination of artists' statements." No one asks a critic or writer to paint a picture of the meaning of what they are saying.[41]

One excuse for the artist's statement could be that within the computer industry, the point of digital art is to play with the new interactive product before it finds a settled role in the consumer world. Software designers would not be bothered about critics writing it off as science park kitsch. For the industry, it is blue-sky thinking done on the cheap. From the mid-1990s on, a handful of leading artists were spirited off to research labs in Japan or the US West Coast and offered whatever resources they needed, but this never seems to mean their work gets any better as art. Quite the reverse. At computer art shows, the best-funded projects were often the most tedious, and among seasoned followers of the overelaborate installation, the one with four projectors or thirty dancers, there used to be a knowing sigh, followed by the (probably unfairly cynical) comment: Canadian. (The sci-art installation that laboriously follows the specifications of the grant application is just as likely to be British.) But economy of means—economy in every sense—would win the contest: the sound-piece that was no more than a lemon and a speaker.

At some point, the nonspecialist artist will have caught up with the digital specialist, if only because the nonspecialist's integrated TV, media player, wireless broadband, mobile phone, and camera will not be lagging a generation or two behind. Twenty years ago, an artist needed corporate sponsorship or academic kudos to gain access to "avant-garde" equipment that is now only fit for landfills. The term *new media* will have to change to *commonplace media*. Digital artists' studios or labs will look much the same as ordinary studios. They already do. The distinction between a photo-silkscreen and an inkjet print already looks insignificant.

All this leads back to the basic roundtable question: What, if anything, makes digital art distinctive as art? As a category, it is now so broad and amorphous that it includes tweaked photos, quirky databases, video installations, animations, games, prints, paintings, Web art, sound-art, VJs, and "smart" clothing.[42] In no sense is this now a list of avant-garde technology. Every art student going to college has some hands-on experience, even if it is just PlayStation, bidding on eBay, filling the iPod, or text-messaging. It is something of an exaggeration—this was in a recent gallery announcement—to call artists who used Epson printers instead of litho presses "visionaries."

The distinctions do matter to an older generation. Before the 1980s—some would say before the 1960s—any artist wanting to find out how to use the computer would have had to battle with systems that were never designed to work for anything connected with art. The only way forward was to teach yourself, become self-sufficient, and connect up with like-minded souls. You could only get so far. You were flying blind. Your knowledge of the basic terminology of computer graphics could be patchy, and you soon got stuck in your rut. Equally, if you were well grounded in computer science but light on art, you fell head first into the cliché.

Would a student with the ambition to be an artist look at current digital art and say that this is the future? If the student has to specialise, the choice may be influenced by the layout of studio space as much as by the scarcity of top-rank artists who are exclusively digital. Sitting all day in a dimly lit computer lab is not as appealing as the free-form activity of a sculpture studio. Ideally, students should be able to switch between the two and not be confined to daylight or monitor light. This is where definitions are more than semantic games. Painting, for example, would not normally be included in digital media, or vice versa, so that the choice becomes an either-or. The choices for the students must be tricky, and it would not be much consolation to learn that the professors devising the courses are often as uncertain as the students are.

On the odd occasion, an artist has had a work accepted for a digital exhibition but has had the statement rejected. The explanation is inadequate, the technical process missed out. The maker of the piece is pressed to say what a piece of work is "about." There has to be a subject, an alibi, an excuse, a reason, for this thing to exist. If you are an artist, you are supposed to have something you want to communicate. But maybe you don't. It is not that you have nothing to say, or that you want to say nothing. It is that you cannot identify with that way of thinking. Many well-known artists—nondigital ones—have deep misgivings about the very idea of statements, technical or philosophical. You would not expect a jazz musician to give you a text to read before you could listen. Consequently, there is a case for abandoning this stereotype where art is seen as something wafting through the computer after being implanted there by the "artist." It is not the way art normally works except in mundane student projects: Here's the project brief; here's the technical stuff. It makes an exhibition into an apologetic exercise—this is what I meant to do and here, um, is what I did. Statements spoil the pleasure of the fresh encounter. They claim more than can be delivered. You decipher the image according to the description, and not the other way round. As long as this model persists, no one will get round to thinking up software that fits the way artists work.

Chapter 6 **Letting the Paint Know About Art**

Demos and Egos

There was a time when paint software was such a novelty that it looked spectacular whatever you did with it. Audiences at trade shows gasped at the silky airbrush of the Quantel Paintbox, even at a colour printer. It didn't matter what the image was, but the fact that you could scan and print a colour photo was amazing, magic. As has happened over and over again, the spectacular becomes the mundane once it is absorbed into the everyday. Soon it becomes invisible. The laptop I am using to write this exceeds the power of the giants of the trade show of fifteen years ago. No one thinks twice about digital cameras, camera phones, printers, or e-mail. Even exotic technology—haptic feedback systems, the 3D mouse (through which you feel resistance and texture), motion-capture suits, and 3D printing—is moving into the consumer market. What was the exclusive province of the lab professional becomes that of the amateur.

I was window-shopping round the commercial exhibits at the 2004 SIGGRAPH when I came across a demonstration that really was newsworthy. There is nothing unusual in seeing motion-capture demonstrations with dancers in wired-up diving suits animating virtual puppets or virtual insects or virtual movie stars. What is unusual is seeing the stars themselves creating their own alter egos. Here was Dick Van Dyke on the LightWave stage demonstrating his homemade virtual self. It turned out he had the full gear: motion capture, cameras, software. In his later years, he has become an expert 3D animator, and here he was, the real-life engaging personality, introducing his surrogate self—and alongside this virtual tap-dancing self, he did allow himself two blondes to dance on either side. I enquired about prices and realised that while the simpler motion-capture suits plus 3D systems could be bought for less than the cost of a family car, it was not inconceivable that the package would eventually become no more luxurious a consumer item than a colour printer. And who in 1990 expected the quality of digital photos to improve so rapidly, and the cost of prints to fall?

Most of the recent "spectacular" exhibits have been in 3D and video editing, but behind the scenes, the extra processing power has plenty of other spin-offs. It comes in handy for enhancing the capabilities of 2D manipulation of the still image. The 2D paint program has expanded and increased its speed exponentially, like everything else. It has been driven not by the virtuosity of calligraphic action painters, but by video

178

games. The demand for high-speed 3D rendering has meant faster and faster graphics processing units and video cards, and high-speed 2D is a by-product. I have seen research projects into such features as full 3D impasto, the "paint" dragging and mixing with precisely the same viscosity as "real" oil paint. I am always tempted to ask why. Why bother simulating something that is just fine left as it is? But every time, I have been proved wrong and find myself hooked on the new feature. It may seem a banal idea, but try it and see. Just listening to the specialised vocabulary of a technical paper on paint makes me appreciate how much the painter takes for granted: voxelising on the 3D grid, subsurface scattering, diffuse reflectance, compositing nonlinearly, surface extracting, viscoplastic simulating . . . the advection algorithm. The painter has put a dab of paint on the canvas and smeared it. The programmer notes "the brush has moved to a new location." Scrape that palette knife through the gooey greens and reds, and the physics is unfathomable.

Yes, paint simulation has evolved, but so has digital art in general, and so have our expectations. Digital paint now comes with multiple varieties of impasto. It can be sticky or runny. We can simulate woodcut. But what happens once the entire cata-logue of art materials is simulated, once it is exhausted? Should the simulation go further and incorporate the smell of turps, the sound of squelching paint, the feel of paint on your fingers? Where else? Should we go for impossible, gravity-defying, physics-defying paint? Or do we need an entirely different metaphor?

Not surprisingly, the small increments that do boost 2D paint performance don't create much of a stir around the com-mercial exhibits when there is so much simulated hair, water spray, and fairy/butterfly hybrids fluttering about with the vacant look of Vogue models. These days, magic has to be beau-tiful and coyly groomed in 3D. Don't expect glamour in two dimensions. You are as likely to come across a booth promoting Corel Painter at an art materials show aimed at senior citizens. It may be overstating the case to say 2D software has reached a plateau and no more needs to be done. Painter, along with Adobe Photoshop and Illustrator, offers annual upgrades with significant enhancements and ever-greater complexity, sometimes artfully hidden. The barrier to further progress must be the market, the users who already have quite enough to contend with. Bigger would not mean better. The customers remain loyal to the system they know, quite aware that they are unlikely ever to use more than a fraction of what it offers. Learning to find their way round each upgrade is trouble enough, especially if they have to switch between several other newly upgraded programs. Bear in mind too that the "bilingual" artist—fluent in both physical and digital paint—has also to deal with all the practicalities of a day-to-day studio, not to mention the creation of the actual work.

Fine artists, as they are sometimes called, may not have the deadlines and commissions of graphic artists. They won't be seduced by software that claims it accelerates "workflow." But they don't work in complete isolation. One part of their workload consists of keeping in touch. They need to keep in touch with exhibitions, journals, their community. They may well have days set aside for teaching or for other part-time work that helps pay the studio rent. They have priorities to organise, and chasing the latest software is unlikely to be number one on the list. The quality of their work depends on a lot more than the quality of the software, the dpi (dots per inch) of their printer, or the quality of the projector if they work with light. Unless they are to cross over and become exclusively digital artists, they are never going to thrash the software to its limits. They will be magpies, taking bits and pieces where they can. Equally, someone specialising in the more demanding complexities of 3D and animation won't have the time or inclination to keep in touch with all the comings and going of the art world. It's asking a lot to be truly bilingual, a real expert in both realms, both of which are constantly changing. Perhaps it is asking too much. The thought sometimes occurs to me that the software could be remodelled to wrap around this lifestyle. At present there must be hundreds, even thousands, of such artists who instinctively feel put off, because 2D software doesn't seem designed for the way they work.

At one digital art exhibition overseas, I was chatting with two fellow exhibitors from Britain. They said that of course there is not much that is really art round here. Unlike the rest of us in that show, they were not techno people; they were artists, they said. They would pick and mix from the packages and throw a spanner in the works, and make the software do "what it wasn't supposed to do." With a painful flinch of recognition, I realised this is just the sort of thing I would have felt, but, I hope, kept to myself, some years back. This was before I learned that being or not being an artist was beside the point; you were only as good as the work you did. I have heard the same disdain for technological expertise too many times to mention, always with the same assumption that "artists," not scientists, are the ones with the real insights, the ones capable of creative think-ing. (I also like this conspiracy theory that some bureau attached to Photoshop headquarters monitors the globe, check-ing that the user is working according to the preferred work-flow. Do not break our rules! Art is forbidden! This product is for graphics professionals only!) In this case I did have the pres-ence of mind to ask politely which New York or London gallery represented these "artists." None at present, they said. This was something they were still working on. When I checked out exactly how these artists had "subverted" the Photoshop pro-grammers, I found a tame use of collage, but quite smart images. Good work, perhaps, but not out of place on the next Adobe calendar.

Still lingering in the air was that question of how far—if at all—the software determines how you work. Does it really trap you inside an invisible square of the permissible? An earlier generation absolutely insisted that if you didn't write your own software, you could not harness the creative potential of all that computational power. You would never produce anything that was truly your own work. This was an intimidating argument for those of us who were not much good or even interested in programming. Buying a ready-made package like Deluxe Paint showed how unserious we were. Eventually, these voices died down, outnumbered and obliterated as computing became ubiquitous. I have also witnessed the argument being shot down not by Photoshop users but by programmers. They point out that "artists" grappling with software are as naive and limited as programmers trying to paint. Painters don't have the skill set, the right kind of imagination, for the job. It requires a very special kind of detachment, a combination of mathematics and art.

Not Judging the User

I had long wanted to talk with Mark Zimmer, the programmer behind the Painter program, which when it appeared in 1991 represented a quantum leap. Till then the way paint behaved in painting programs was nothing like paint. It had no body or fluidity, no resistance to surface texture. The brushes were just circles or squares in a range of sizes like drill bits. Quantel was the queen of upmarket computer painting for some years, with the smoothest airbrush, but the application had drawbacks. The software was fused with the hardware, it cost more than a Rolls Royce (or two), and my only access was as a very occasional demonstrator on an older machine, teaching at the Royal College of Art. From its first appearance, Painter was something quite different. Its manuals were like sketchbooks or funky recipe books. More important still, when it claimed to provide the artist with "natural media," this was broadly what it did. *Intuitive* and *creative* were words that fitted the experience. It was also affordable. This was the software that built the bridge between the painter and the computer and perhaps between the expert and the nonexpert. Not everyone would admit this straightaway. Some of us had spent months getting the hang of far more difficult programs, which were like impossible geometry kits in which you had to be truly ingenious to manufacture a watercolour translucency. We felt we were the initiates. We were in no hurry to give up our trade secrets and admit that digital painting could be this easy.

Over almost fifteen years of upgrades of Painter's software, I had noticed that certain oddball features that had been in the palettes from the outset remained there. In its first versions, Painter had a fill feature for designing tartans (Mark's first wife was a weaver), and soon it acquired mosaics and the weird brush described in an earlier chapter. Called the image hose, this brush could spray out a succession of miniature images. The rumours I picked up turned out to be true. There was a garage, the "wet lab," where the software designers experimented with whatever material they were focussing on, chalk or acrylic, or perhaps they would throw a sponge at the wall and see how the splodge spread and dribbled. The software evolved so that you not only had watercolour seeping down in washes, staining and bleeding into neighbouring colours, but could control the wind direction, the direction of the running paint. There were also quirky functions that went beyond what real-life materials could do—you could paint with liquid metal. All this was too good to be true, but to my mind, the whole approach was flawed. It treated painting more as a craft than an art. With a little of the arrogance of those British artists, I set out to find out why the program had not been more art oriented.

I eventually ran into Mark Zimmer on the commercial floor of that 2004 SIGGRAPH show. He had cut his ties with Painter some years back—after eleven years, he had wanted to move on—and was working at Apple on Core Image, a program to be embedded in the new Tiger operating system. He was demonstrating a preview of this on the Apple stand. When he spoke with me about the genesis of the program, the choices he had to make, I began to realise how the art world's sense of itself doesn't really mesh with the software world. In a telling phrase, Mark said he wanted to create "a medium that didn't judge the user." It was not just natural media for its own sake. The idea was to engage a constituency of "painters" who would otherwise be left out. This wasn't only altruism. It made business sense. It opened up the field to many more people. If you didn't like the hoards of sub-Dali paintings that turned up in Painter User Group competitions, fair enough, but this is what you get if you make art—the doing, not just the consuming— more democratic. He pointed out that they had looked in some depth at the behaviour of artists' materials, understanding precisely what happened when the pigment was dragged over a resistant surface. Supplying the tools was one thing; what you did with them was another.

All the same, I asked why there was so little reference to contemporary art. The program was more for commercial illustrators. He pointed out that his colleague John Derry's favourite artist was Rauschenberg.[43] If such a program had been custom-built around Rauschenberg's array of techniques, it would have been unapproachable. The interface would have been unfamiliar and would have confused the hobbyists. It

184

would hardly have been as practicable. I think of ways that the program designers could tinker with the brushes, and the way they are presented, but I also wonder whether my concept of a paint program in tune with a more advanced idea of painting is just self-serving indulgence. If it was ever to work, it would need to be built from scratch, and increasingly that looks improbable. In 1990, I was aware of more than a dozen paint programs and tried most of them. Now I only use three. I could probably survive with one. As to the question of how this high-brow paint program might differ from what is already available, one answer would be that it might start with dividing the menu topics and tools according to the way an art student might be introduced to fine art. There would be more acknowledgment of video and photography as parallel art forms to painting, and there would be a more workable interface for "time-based" media than the "fun" animation flipbooks. The program could also offer a device that made an image grow and behave in a truly unexpected manner. Yet this would just scratch the surface of the concept. Undoubtedly, the programs have evolved the way they have for good reasons.

What I might be asking for is a return to a pre-1990s period of raw programming and unfriendly interfaces, where the actual "creating" process was obstructed at every point. Painting that way was really the solving of one problem after another, all the time pretending that the chunky pixels added up to a "real" painting. It needed some imagination. When the visual metaphors of paint, brush, paper, canvas, became fleshed out in Painter's interface, that was a major advance. Yet the current monopolies are not ideal. It is as if in the early 1990s, 2D graphics was divided up into separate franchises, which now look permanent—simulated photo processing, simulated paint, simulated technical drawing. Everyone from design professional to hobbyist has a comfort zone in this otherwise incomprehensible universe. The specialised skills remain more or less intact and as they were before they were transposed into each program. There is stalemate, a lack of direction. The user becomes locked into one interface, one language, one orthodoxy. It is easy to forget that the whole concept of a paint program is an invention, a simulation, a cluster of conventions. Any one program could have been conceived quite differently.

Reinventing the Palette

Photoshop is the equivalent of the 747: a brilliant, functional artefact with an odd shape, excessive and overdesigned, too complex for any single human mind to comprehend. The airplane does its job well, so there is no pressing need to invent an alternative, even though the fuselage has a silhouette from a different epoch. Along with the other leading programs, Photoshop bears the imprint of dated templates. Some basic graphic principles remain glaringly naive and out of step with the parallel worlds they simulate. If you had to work out what painting was, and all you had to go by was 2D software and its concepts of paint and canvas, you would miss 80 percent of the point. You would have no idea at all of what contemporary painting is all about, or why it is thriving, why people have so much to say about it. You would think painting was simply illustration in colour, image processing with a pasty look, the start point either a scanned image or a blank canvas, always rectangular. You would think that the idea is to make a "realistic" image, giving the source image an "artistic" treatment. In other words, you make the key decisions—what to "paint" and what treatment or style to give it—outside the actual process.

You may sign up for an evening class to learn how to draw or how to paint, but it really is a misconception to think that, say, oil painting is a skill that you can acquire, and then pick this

186

or that option of what style you work in. It is not that simple. You learn as you go along, but the skills you pick up do not necessarily come along in discrete packages, and what matters most of all is how far you learn to look at what you do with a practised critical eye. *Palette* happens to mean the range of colour choices laid out in lumps of pigment, and also—appropriately— the user's taste buds. Developing a palette, in that sense, is not something you can buy off the shelf. It doesn't come with the software.

When studying painting at an art school, you learn how to attend to the process, to make the process the painting; you don't necessarily need a subject, a model, or source material. You choose gouache, pastels, acrylic, and spray for their feel, not just to get this or that "look." A previous generation of paint programs was better adapted to the nonrepresentational painter, who could manipulate complex geometry and patterns at will— Kai's Power Tools were the ultimate gift for this. Consequently, those kaleidoscopic patterns could be seen as a closer and more direct method of "working the software" than manipulating the illusion of a set of oil paints. The geometrical repertoire of pentagons, radiating lines, symmetries, is no longer on the menu— too 8-bit, too infantile. In Deluxe Paint, you could even paint with a spinning brush.

For many of us brought up in art schools with life-drawing regimes and plaster casts of Greek sculpture gathering dust, it is easy to think that the tools of our trade are timeless. Painting will always consist of canvas, brush, paint. Transposed into an electronic format, the model of surface and mark remains there, fixed, though nothing is actually marking, scratching, covering, or impacting in any way on a "canvas." But 2D programs will not stay this way forever, and painting itself could shift sideways—whether or not that phrase *hand-brushed* catches on. In the short term, some software hybrids, that is, programs that recombine features from currently unrelated types of software, may provide the impetus for change. They will need to be thinned right down to be usable, usable with a lighter touch. A new program could join the family the way SketchUp has managed to bring spontaneous drawing and 3D together, by rethinking the objectives and slimming the interface. So far it has been about shrink-wrapping the studio into the box, or turning the painter into a factory robot trained to brush skilfully "by hand," but the task of the programmer and the painter could overlap. What we understand by the term *painting* could shift even more, and at the same time the interface through which the painter manipulates the image—the palette and its controls—could become a little more responsive and intelligent, attuned more to the way an artist thinks.

For the present, progress is stalled because of the kind of painting—or painter—that software teams take as their model. This painter is quite a tame customer who has never done more than one or two quick museum tours and flipped through a coffee-table book without reading any of the text. Contemporary art might as well have been happening on the moon. Anyone who goes through the tutorials or who browses the typical how-to books will recognise the repertoire of the neighbourhood art club. The basics of cubism, abstraction, surrealism—let alone conceptual art, postmodernism, or new media art—have not been brought into the argument. There is no argument. It is all smiles. It is chocolate-box realism, fluffy pets and romantic sunsets, here and there some wacky surrealism and psychedelic abstraction. A program that is brilliant at simulating "real wet paint" is groaningly ignorant of what contemporary art has to offer. Again, this observation does depend on your point of view, and if your field is special effects in the movies, you will have a different conception of A-list artists from those who feature in museum retrospectives. I have put this point to the more recent developers of Painter, and on one occasion was told that, yes, they do cover abstract art. But the example they showed me was just another spacecraft, with admittedly quite an abstract design. I was also told that they had included a simulated dripped-paint feature, like "Jack the Dripper." I could see that I was getting nowhere.

Is the alternative feasible? Well, there could be thousands of alternatives, and obviously we get the software we deserve, or that we are persuaded to buy. A totalitarian regime might build in a different range of filters. So would monks. Martians or microscopic life forms would use something rather different again. But what if we could rearrange the priorities in a paint program just a little? As most painters have a limited budget and do not already have a suite of high-end 3D programs to dip into, it would be useful to have some proper 3D capability, just as bitmap programs have some basic vector or animation routes. It might be asking for trouble if an elite panel of painters was assembled and they presented the software people with a wish list—as if with a few deft modifications the interface would be ready for a Gerhard Richter. The selection of such a panel would be critical—should it include digital artists?

One fundamental distinction in sculpture used to be between modelling—adding lumps of clay to an armature, building up the body from torso and limbs—and carving—starting with a block and finding the form inside. Collage and the "constructed" sculpture of cubism, the Duchamp "ready-mades," happenings, the installations of Beuys, all served to transform the definitions of what sculpture was and how it could be made. Paint software is ideal for collage, for building up textures, for any additive process. You just add layer upon layer upon layer. Where it does not cope so well, or rather, where the set of controls is less encouraging, is with editing, the subtracting process: refining, finding the right form through

189

elimination. It is "natural" just to keep adding, to keep processing and piling effect upon effect. This is not the best way to work with real paint; at least it is one trap the novice tends to fall into. The more you work the paint, especially if the paint layer beneath is not properly dried, the deader the surface becomes; the colour turns to mud. With most paints, you have to wait an hour or so between layers—days with oil paint. This is inconvenient, but a useful restraint. It gives you time to reflect and study what you have done. Experienced painters know when to leave well alone.

Should the software reproduce the individual characteristics of each type of paint? The subtlety of a painted surface is one thing; the mercurial qualities possible through manipulated "paint" on the screen is another. Provided the distinction between pigment colour and electronic colour is acknowledged, I see no problem in taking the simulation as far as possible. The real question is what you make of that difference. Reproducing the screen image on canvas without making anything of the tension between the two is—to my mind—missing the point. It is not just scale, material quality, or the way the image is lit or not lit, but the whole ethos of painting being lifted out of its context. It cheapens an art form to pretend otherwise.

You could say that imitation and then true-to-life simulation are necessary evolutionary stages. Mark Zimmer showed that the exacting study of the interaction of paints, brushes, and surfaces gave the software something to grip onto. At the same time, making a distinct behaviour for diffuse watercolour or smudgy oil paint does seem unnecessary when the restraints of the physical context don't exist. To say the least, it all runs against common sense. Virtual oil paint and watercolour can be used at will on the same picture, delicate watercolour over oil, but this would be impossible with "real" painting. Oil paint can be applied to a vertical surface because it is viscous enough to adhere. It has body, can be modelled and blended. For example, a heavily worked greenish surface can be scraped and sanded after three or four days, so it retains not only its roughened forms but a certain residual viscosity. A combination of pink and grey could be brushed over this sticky ground, sometimes mixing, sometimes dragging. The painter does this standing up, and can walk to and fro looking at the surface from different distances, different angles. The colouration, the texture, the modelling of forms can be improvised through pressure and the arm muscle expressed through the brush. The sensation is sculptural—the paint is working against the sticky resistance. Each pigment has its own character—even when the colour is outwardly identical. Some greens are translucent and ring sharp; others—such as oxide of chromium—are so opaque they are like muffled bells.

With watercolour, the paint is usually far too thin and runny to apply to a vertical surface, so you either paint flat on a table, on a gently sloped desk, or on the floor. The colour of the paper is crucial. Usually being white, the paper effectively acts as the light source, since all the colour laid onto it is in effect blocking out the light, though blues and yellows are suffused with its light. The scale will be much smaller, too, and the touch of the brush much lighter. The experience is intimate, private, enclosed, like writing a letter. I am not suggesting that any of this is news or that software should somehow incorporate these extra refinements. I am asking that instead of developing substitutes for real paint, software developers might get more inside the mind of the painting process or at least acknowledge that these differences count for something. When an upgrade speaks of improved functionality or the new printer boasts of enviable quality, this bears little relation to what the painter might want—unless all he or she wanted was to knock off cheaper reproductions. For the most part, artists improve simply through practice, often by only small increments, and often by pursuing a course that would be professional suicide within a design office. Sometimes, studio routines are numbingly repetitive, having no observable goal. Much of the time, painting is dull, monotonous. But without the slowed-down meditative phases, where nothing much seems to happen, a painter could lose touch with the source of the creative impulse. Faster throughput, automating the boring parts of the process, flattening out all the variety in pigment structure in favour of uniformity, might eliminate those "vacant" periods when the subconscious gets to work.

So if simulation and efficiency were not the goals, what other modifications to the interface would come as a real help? The first that I think of would be a sketch pad that was just that. The program should allow the user to sketch at a truly informal level, like the most casual marginal jottings—perhaps by having a different level of "page" always open. Second, the user should be able to generate an initial arbitrary form, perhaps just a "ground" of splodges that could be worked against. Many artists begin this way rather than with a completely blank canvas. It should not be difficult to figure out a set of variables that each user could customise. Third, it would be useful to draw with brushes that were truly cumbersome, as if they were six or ten feet long. It should be possible for any tool to be modified to an extreme version of itself. If the list of what used to be called "goodies" could extend to hardware, it would be great to have more output devices designed to bridge the gap between electronic and physical media—a stencil cutter or a paint sprayer, or even a "hand-painting" brush apparatus. Just for experimental purposes, of course.

What of the autonomy of digital paint? What if there were much less emphasis on imitation and simulation? What is so great about paint, anyway? Couldn't we have something else and give it another name? There are a string of problems about how a purely electronic form of painting could hold its own without a "traditional" model and counterpart. For a start, electronic work would lose its identity as art. It would be lost amid far slicker advertising displays, streams of video. A digital painter could end up turning out screen savers and Web page backgrounds, or supplying fictional paintings for unscrupulous Web galleries. At present, digital painting has little status as an art in its own right and is seen—rightly or wrongly—as symptomatic of a lazy culture where "art" exists in the moronic vacuum of trendy effects and flavours. Just flip the channel, change the filter. Graphic-design software doesn't suffer from this problem, because it has been properly designed from first principles and built up around discriminating and demanding professionals. It benefits from proper feedback, and there is no longer any hesitation in using computers in layout or graphics generally. At the fine-art end, we are still confused. But the next generation of programs may do the trick. The irony is that paint software really is liberating, but painters generally have been too bound up in their own inhibitions to notice that their doors are open.

Novelty Paint

The paint program can now do so much more than spool out psychedelic geometry, sci-fi blobs, surrealist montage, or fabricate the look of real paint. In broad terms, the software could develop further along two divergent paths. It could continue to match "natural" art materials, or it could provide tools and a control panel for a visual language that moves away from its customary standard-painting model. This might seem a choice between "superrealistic" illustration—of fantasy worlds and science fiction—and some kind of psychedelic abstract art. My hope is that this won't happen, and that gradually the influence of the broader painting community will take effect. On all sides, artists are speaking of the overlap between computer art and mainstream art, for example:

> Computer art is by nature evolutionary, relying on rapid changes in technology and software for the substance of its creative work. With so many traditional disciplines integrating digital technologies, the lines between traditional works of art and new media works continue to blur.[44]

From its first stirrings and certainly from my own first acquaintance with the paint program, the fine-art potential of digital was far from clear. Computer art and all the effects and weird geometry would never gain a foothold in fine-art painting. I recall the experience of Joan Truckenbrod, since 1981 a professor in the Art and Technology Department at the School of the Art Institute of Chicago. From the 1970s onward, she has always managed to retain a painterly feel. Whenever she met a certain painter from the Fine Art Department in the elevator, he would shake his head and say, you will never make art with that stuff. For much of the wired 1990s, digital artists were charged up with the promise of a separate and quite new art form; they predicted that "new media" would take over from old media. Books and newspapers would disappear. We would have "smart" paper, and art would be something that happened exclusively online. It might be piped right into your brain. The influential Roy Ascott said there would no longer be any need to look at art. In a small book on aesthetics, Wittgenstein mischievously argued that if art were essentially a means for achieving aesthetic feeling, perhaps this feeling could be administered through an injection. Now we could bypass the injection; we would put on a head-mounted display.

I still hear of projects where the aesthetic experience is to be delivered to the obedient spectator, provided the spectator agrees to wander passively through a carefully orchestrated virtual environment. These sound like academic theme parks, as though they have been dreamed up to attract art and science funding. The ones I have experienced have never engaged me quite as intended, but I may be a resistant subject. I cannot help making comparisons with the fairground flight simulator, IMAX space adventures, a heart-rending Verdi opera, or even a good thriller. There is more than one kind of immersion, more than one way of being taken out of yourself. Nor can I accept that an art or an aesthetic experience is something that needs to be delivered that way. I can plug into experience of that sort just as easily walking across the park. My conditioning as a painter makes it difficult to think of a separation between the delivering medium and the message—in painting, sculpture, installation, drawing, video, they are one and the same. The surface texture of a painting or the graininess of a video is part of whatever message or experience may be on offer. An art medium is not like TV. An aesthetic experience isn't like a news bulletin. I only mention this because at one point, any compromise between traditional and new media was out of the question. The preferred future was one where we would all be singing and dancing in virtual environments, where art would have been universally dematerialised into code. That vision has now been postponed—one more future to put on the shelf and label "nice try." Incidentally, one of the many reasons that virtual reality never caught on and didn't sweep all old art forms aside was that people generally fell in love with small and relatively low-tech gadgets, from Tamagotchi pets, cell phones, and digital cameras to iPods. People were happy to leave art more or less as it was and to spend their travelling time text messaging.

Slipping the paint program into the PC does not yet mean

that you can give up the studio space. The epoch of demateri-alised paint has not arrived and may well never arrive. Working on the screen is a liberating experience for the painter, but it is not a complete solution or a surrogate for the real thing. A painting studio has its own smells, sounds, spaces, and shifting light. A computer room has a constant hum and is lit low, apart from the glow of the monitors. The atmosphere of a studio, not just the timeworn feel of some spaces, but the ethos of the stu-dio, the idea of a special place, cannot be recreated by mood music or desktop postcards from the museum.

Just as they adapted to photography, painters can adapt to the computer without being completely taken over by gadget fever. Subtle changes are taking place—the "hand-brushed oil on canvas" label—which means that we may no longer take some aspects for granted. Is this an assisted, a printed, a directly painted image? One hundred and fifty years ago, the sharp detail of the photograph opened people's eyes. It showed ani-mals in motion, the slaughter of the battlefield, vast faraway landscapes, and close-ups of insects, plants, and bacteria. It was photography that reawakened the appreciation of the exquisite light in Vermeer. Now, on the same screen that I use to paint, I can switch over to look at a landscape softened by the methane rain of Titan.

Painters in many colleges are still schooled in technical processes that go back through centuries of practice. Students begin by drawing from observation, from a still life, from a model posed a few feet in front of them. Many of the landscape paintings they refer to were made long before the invention of the steam engine. When experimenting with paint software, painters, naturally enough, use the bristle brushes, layers, filters, collage, as if they were using the same physical processes. So the electronic processes are forgotten, irrelevant, and the painters can carry on as if they were using an oil painting set. Without that interface, the "paint" would be just flashy video effects, unintelligible as a painting medium. Would digital painters be better off if they got "inside" the technology, took old keyboards apart, soldered burglar sensors to each character terminal, and arranged for a set of patterns to be triggered by the spectator's footsteps? There is nothing wrong with accepting the pretence that this is real paint. They can scan a painting—the same technology that scans the surface of planets and moons—and make subtle adjustments in Photoshop and print out an "archival" inkjet reproduction. That may not be particularly imaginative, but I cannot see that basing a set of pictures on, say, a newly programmable "painting machine" that flicks paint over a canvas on the floor and is controlled remotely through a webcam is any better, any more advanced, any more significantly digital.

All of this has to be absorbed patiently, until it is second nature. While digital art is exotic, a novelty, and expected to be distinct, even superior to nondigital art, this remains hard to achieve. Apart from anything else, the digital artists are always chasing upgrades, running to stay in the same place. We don't care so much whether a novel has been written in Microsoft Word, or in which version of Word, but a painting or digital piece that has been run through ten-year-old hardware will have a certain look. There might be subtleties of layering, which took considerable ingenuity and artistry to master in 1995, but which become routine and ready-made filter effects in 2005. By 2015, the advanced look of 2005 will have faded away.

This would not be so true in painting—looks and styles come and go, but the fundamentals of the technique remain constant. There are sectarian divisions in painting, of course. These can sometimes be interpreted roughly as conservative versus advanced, and the more traditionally minded would prefer the digital trickery kept well away, or at least kept subordinate. But it is misleading to speak of one or another tendency as being more advanced—for years, being advanced has been taken to mean going "beyond" painting. Sticking with painting, in any guise, digital or physical, is seen by some critics as the nonadvanced option. All the same, when it comes to making full use of the repertoire of the paint program, there is widest scope in what is loosely called postmodern, or conceptual painting, or abstract painting. But if artists are seduced by eye candy alone, all the weird and wonderful effects, then the category will be dismissed as novelty art. Integrating the repertoire into the existing grammar of abstract painting is particularly difficult because abstract painting has itself been in the doldrums.

The veteran abstract painter James Adley expressed this well in a letter responding to the point that abstract painting has become something of a secondary genre, with few artists doing anything adventurous, and most simply recycling old glories:

> I find I reluctantly agree with its new status (bottom of the totem pole) yet I still believe it has the most potential for painting in the future. Technology has souped it up but at the same time eviscerated it. The most "interesting" (!) work is the most spectacular technically and materially but is largely vacuous. The rush "forward" as in everything leaves acres of unexplored territory, which immediately becomes seen as irrelevant—and yes, a lot of it is. But in that area, I believe, is the best hope for a truly advanced ("cutting edge"!) art. Novelty and extreme process are OK but are overdone and mostly backfire.[45]

If such values—belief in what used to be referred to as modernism—are to persist and thrive, then painters have to understand what they are up against. Otherwise it will be a walkover. In a courtroom drama, the digital artists would have all the good lines. Progress, history, would be on their side. They would be the revolutionaries at odds with the ancien régime, confronting repressive laws that say a painting must be a static object on the wall. Look, they would say, at this fabulous gift of the electronic machine—it can do so much more, it can make our minds dance, it can dream for us. It should have laws and rights of its own, its own language. To dress it up in the period costume of the artist's studio, or the photographic lab, is to suppress its nature. An authentic art made through the computer cannot be based on the imitation of another art medium. That should be the Law.

But hold on. This might have been the case a few years back, but now the territories between old and new, digital and nondigital, have become mixed up. Yes, there continue to be technophobic painters and tech-mad digital artists, but the digital purists no longer have so many devotees. It is not a question of whether to use the scanner, the printer, Adobe Creative Suite, or Apple's Final Cut Pro. The question now is how to use them—perhaps I should say, how to use them thoughtfully.

How Painters Think

If I had to convince a group of digital-art students that the model of painting in paint software is small-minded, a caricature of the real thing, no more than a recipe for making a pseudopainting, I might begin by taking them through the work of Gerhard Richter. He must be the most influential painter of the 1990s. He is also an artist, I admit, whom I took a long time to appreciate. I first thought the 1960s pop paintings were inept, and the hard-edge abstract paintings like colour charts pointless, but he has been an elusive presence in painting for a long time and is impossible to pin down. He has moved

199

between photorealism, rectilinear abstraction, and gestural abstraction with apparent indifference. His ambivalence about difficult subject matter has often troubled critics.

It would be hard to summarise Richter's ethos in a few sentences or try to explain why he is so admired, but what strikes me forcibly is that all through his career, he has felt that the territory of painting was barren, that the project of making significant paintings was more or less impossible. This conviction actually liberated him—though freedom isn't the first thing you would think of, since his work is made in such a deadpan manner. It sounds like quite a contradiction. Sometimes the subject matter is hot—the Baader-Meinhof terrorist group who committed suicide in the 1970s. At other times there appears to be no subject at all, just a few mechanically produced striations of paint. Critics have seen this as mocking the seriousness of painting, as being detached, politically uncommitted, remorselessly passive. Others have seen the ambivalence as moving beyond the previous polarisations of minimal versus maximal, abstract versus figurative, modernist versus postmodernist.

He grew up in East Germany, and in his formative years was connected with the neo–Dadaist Fluxus group, whose performances and apparent nihilism proved to be the melting pot of a whole generation, with Joseph Beuys at the centre. I went round a massive Fluxus exhibition in Kassel in 2003 expecting nothing but photos of Dadaist events, but to my surprise, I came out realising I had seen a fantastic exhibition of drawings. Most were diagrams, jokes, cartoons. Beuys's drawings are often no more than a few scrawls, but he is one of the great draughtsmen of the postwar period.

Little of this would be remotely relevant to a student group learning paint software. (I imagine a seminar group with hands going up. They have only ever looked at digital art; they have read the statements and take it all literally. How could painting be impossible? Is the system down? How could a drawing that was a couple of lines on paper be worth bothering about? If it were processing some interesting raw data that would give you a handle . . . oh, I see, that's OK, it's tracking a bat's brainwaves . . .) I was intrigued to find a Richter landscape reproduced in a book on digital painting, but not surprised to find that the piece was being used as an example of "straight" landscape technique. To understand Richter's paintings and other painters of comparable influence—Polke, Tuymans—you really enter a debate. Without that awareness, the irony of the "I am a machine" touch will pass you by. It would be a pity to miss it.

In a penetrating interview, Richter speaks of living in a consumer society that has lost its beliefs:

> Our time looks as if we finally got over all of the nonsense, got rid of our need for a larger scheme, forgot history, rejected art, and rejected our fathers so that everything will be free and animalistic, techno-animalistic. I don't believe in any of that. That's just a movement.[46]

If his paintings look mechanical, inexpressive, that is itself a statement—and it's this melancholy coldness that seems so candid.

> I feel very close to this idea of seeing the pain and the loss in the work. I can't paint as well as Vermeer—we have lost this beautiful culture, all the utopias are shattered, everything goes down the drain, the wonderful time of painting is over.
>
> Unfortunately I am not a virtuoso at all. I have some taste. I have an eye for bad things. But in terms of making things I am not a virtuoso, and that has always been my flaw. Today, there is almost nobody (or only a few bad examples) who has

the virtuosity to draw something. I depend on the photograph and mindlessly copy what I see. I am clumsy in that regard, even though I seem very skilful. But I do have the ability to judge whether something is good or bad.[47]

If I were halfway to convincing my audience of this intellectual, or at least poetic, dimension, I would turn to a much younger artist, a recent recipient of the prestigious Van Gogh prize: Neo Rauch, who also happens to be from East Germany, from Leipzig. I would show them a painting called *Unschuld* (Innocence). Rauch's paintings have the air of illustrations from a 1950s comic or handiwork manual, but the figures, mostly stereotyped workers or scientists preoccupied in technical tasks in factories or labs, are placed in toylike landscapes, with the scale out of kilter. His pieces are beautifully constructed and openly painterly and play with compositional frames—hands pointing out of the picture, flattened clouds, overzealous geometry. Writers have pointed to the sarcasm and disillusionment, but I would hope these students would simply note how complex the effect of this depicted world could be. I also suspect that the paintings have been influenced by the fluent manipulations of digital collage. Here it reenters painting language with a flourish.

Painters—not just pop artists—have long been fascinated by the plain-speaking banality of commercial art while retaining the aloofness of the introspective artist. You only have to think of Magritte's impassive bowler-hatted commuter. At times the artist is clearly engrossed in reflecting on the process of painting—by exposing the process or, as here, hinting that the painter shares with the alchemist the goal of transforming base matter into something wondrous. Similar offbeat realists were grouped together in the "Dear Painter" show at the Pompidou, Paris, featuring realist painting after Picabia. This was a provocative exhibition and, incidentally, as cutting-edge as any

202

Neo Rauch, *Unschuld*, 2001, 117″ × 77″ (298 × 200 cm), oil on paper.
(See also Plate 7.)

digital show, and yet it was only one slice through contemporary painting. Many other slices could be made, and painting itself is now a subdivision of contemporary art. Digital art is still the baby. But what differentiates such "new" but more or less traditional painting from the work that crops up in digital shows is not just the technique. It is the sophistication, the critical awareness, the awareness of the power of images.

Testing the Art as Art

One of my favourite quotes from a critic is "Time sorts it out for the squares." This was Clement Greenberg's answer to a question—posed by a young painter—about how we ultimately determine the value of works of art.[48] There certainly isn't any critical system or court of law that could intervene and legislate on the rightful value of digital art. The only convincing answer will come through the gradual process of seeing which art eventually holds its own. The medium involved will probably prove to be of less consequence than we might now think. (Greenberg, apparently, looked at digital art but complained that it hurt his eyes.) Certainly, there are strikingly original artists who work with nothing more than pencil and paper, and there are thunderingly boring artists who use the ultimate in up-to-the-minute technology. The issue is not the competing offerings of new and old media, but that the issue is there at all. These are questions that did not exist for previous generations.

Current programs enable images to be formed and transformed at a speed that would have been unthinkable fifty years ago. It would have been visual magic—and I am not even mentioning 3D programs. The euphoria would have been tempered by worries about the next step. An art made by intelligent robots? What would "computer-generated" art be like? My first encounter was the Cybernetic Serendipity exhibition at the

Institute of Contemporary Art in 1968. What was on show was both fascinating and repellent, like a mad professor's toy shop.

The digital painter can be forgiven for wondering whether this subject actually exists at all. Where are the reference points for any discussion? I leaf through one anthology called *Digital Painting*. It is full of commercial illustration, dragons, and fantasy space cruisers, and I feel no connection. I search through site after site on the Internet, where aspiring artists discuss the merits of physical versus digital, and again I sense only fragments of a conversation. I go round exhibitions of emerging painters who are all too aware of paint software and what it does, and that again would be a different conversation. There is the software itself, the pragmatism, the commercial ecology between users and producers. Even further away from the action are the academics, the theorists. And then there is painting itself, so rich in biographies, histories, critical viewpoints, that one would be hard-pressed to view it as a dying culture.

Let me state the problem: Suppose I produce a digital picture that I am pleased with. How do I work out whether it is any good? Whose feedback can I trust? A gallery opinion, an artist, a critic? I have been in the reverse situation when enthusiasts show me the work they have been doing. It is difficult when what you see is technically accomplished but lacks anything striking or individual. I will say my response is subjective, and anyone who is asked to express instant judgment is put on the spot and liable to be inhibited about what to say. I would express it with—I hope—some tact. When I am the one being judged, I notice that critics, whether digitally expert or painting expert, are quite reticent. They tread carefully, not just so as not to offend, but because this is a minefield. They do not want to make a fool of themselves by going for something that turns out to be astonishingly naive, slick, facile, or a rehash of another artist they don't know of. In practice we muddle through, gritting our teeth when—as has happened—a collector of digital art reveals complete ignorance of regular art (Kandinsky? Who?). Is there a pool of shared knowledge, a common currency, a court of aesthetic consensus? No.

It is not just that different sectors will have different ideas of where the quality lies. They use different maps. Though now much diminished from the period when it was just about the dominant influence controlling British art, the Arts Council still distributes funds to artists and artists' organisations. Its real power is nothing compared with the influence of the Saatchi Collection, the Tate Modern, or one of the international galleries. Nevertheless, the council has carried through an interesting policy, or justification, for its funding strategy. Its scouts see their role as identifying the areas of art that are currently at the edge; it will on occasion contribute small packets of seeding money so that these experimental activities have a chance to put down roots. Once they start growing, they will be left to survive on their own. It sounds fine, but how does the council decide, especially in the confused landscape of digital art, where this frontier lies? And once a frontier kind of art gets the council's official stamp of approval, can the art form still claim to be out there on its own? One difficulty is that the frontiers in computer graphics are real enough to get patents. Innovations can come onto the market within a couple of years. What an arts organisation means by "cutting edge" is something else. There must be several different edges.

Thinking Paint Program

I'm trying to find somebody that can work out concurrently the evolution of tools and how you use them.
I have been waiting for that for decades.
—Doug Engelbart, inventor of the mouse

On some days, I move between conversational modes with the arbitrariness of flipping between channels, and yet in each mode I am focusing on digital painting. After attending an academic conference on the emerging history of computer art, where many of those attending have been put up in hotels, courtesy of their universities, I am e-mailing a friend who for seven years ran the first digital gallery in London. Due to the rising property market and the sheer competitiveness of Hoxton Square, where this gallery had moved in 2002, the gallery has become the victim of a capricious New York gallery that first sought to take over its space, then pulled out leaving a financial mess. My friend now has no gallery, incurs huge debts, and despite all his expertise and experience, he is both jobless and homeless. Digital art looks like one thing when you have a regular university salary and pore over old plotter drawings, and like something rather different when you have to survive by selling it. I then receive an e-mail telling me I can now view some online video tutorials because I recently upgraded my Painter software. This too has a personal connection, because I met the team that produces these videos—as well as the Painter manuals—at the launch of Corel's Painter IX in Los Angeles. The mind-set I need for following these tutorials is quite different from the one I need to follow academic papers or to think about financial survival. Paint programs may exist in a vacuumed virtual space, but human lives do spin around them.

It is just the same with how you make use of a tutorial. Someone who already knows the program will scan it with a critical eye. An experienced painter intimidated by the interface will follow it step by step. A nonpainter who had never seen a watercolour set and thought Winsor and Newton was a law firm would be looking for tips about making a "good" painting. A researcher into the growing adaptation of technology to painting, and of painting to technology, would note each refinement in the convergence of real and simulated paint. One tutorial, by John Derry, one of the other originators of the software, guides you through "digital watercolour." "Watercolour" has been a feature of the program for some years, including blends, running colour, and the wind controls, but "digital watercolour" is actually a friendlier version. The demo shows how you can use a photo of a still life of some peppers, corn, and aubergines as a clone and paint so that "Painter does the work," sampling the colour from the image. In other words, you don't have to get the right colour or the right position, scale, or composition. All you need to do is make the actual brushstrokes, tinting here and there, adding highlights and editing with an eraser. The watercolour controls allow you to determine such factors as the degree that the edges of the dried colour areas are silted with a crisp rim. You can even rework the painting to make it look unfinished.

Having long worked in "real" watercolour, I find that the purist in me does wince. We are asked to look at the work of "real" watercolourists for such tricks as leaving gaps of white paper showing through to define edges. We are being steered toward the cosiest examples—harbour scenes, portraits of pets. Contemporary painters use watercolour, or should I say, water-based paints, but with more energy and with a far broader range. Most painters—loft artists perhaps—would only stray into "pretty picture" mode as a form of parody. For decades, painters from Sam Francis to Joseph Beuys have liberated watercolour from the "blotchy cottage" look. It can be used in gritty, explosive, sour, delicate, rigid, or anarchic formats, and on scales from the microscopic to the gigantic. The technical discipline of landscape, such as achieving an even, gradating, translucent wash and adding detail without being able to subtract, are worth learning. But the basic techniques should not limit what you do. For example, instead of tilting the paper on a gentle slope to allow evenly drying washes, you can lay the paper flat on the floor and allow the distribution of accented pools of colour to find their own form. Instead of a soft, sable watercolour brush, you can use the end of a stick or a piece of cut cardboard, or you can splash or drip the paint from the side, or "print" one drawing over another. These more radical techniques have long been part of the watercolourist's repertoire. Turner used rags and knives and anything else on hand to get what he wanted.

Here the thinking does not stray out of the basic "let's make a nice picture of something." You arrange a bowl of fruit on a table, sit down with a sketch pad, and draw what you see. Painter offers several "cheats," which assume you can simply photograph the fruit from the preferred angle in appropriate light and then either manipulate the photo to make it look like a watercolour or paint over the image as if on tracing paper. You can clone the image onto a separate "canvas," where it magically reappears when you paint over the surface. So far so good. Instead of depending on your trained reflexes to measure, draw, and resolve a convincing image on the paper, these tasks—or skills—are taken out of your hands and completed by the software. Of course, if you felt these skills formed the essence of your painting, you might find this unsettling. Yes, you have a rival, and it doesn't get tired or moody. It is a robot.

Could a tutorial aim a little higher? It does not take much imagination to think up what a chapter on "make your own abstract paintings" might be like, but it would be quite a struggle to make it any less superficial. Creating interesting patterns or cutting and pasting photos to assemble "designs" could be outlined as exercises, but would that take you anywhere? The best way to learn about painting, even abstract painting, must still be to use the real materials in parallel with the simulated ones, and to keep in touch with that larger conversation. It is better to begin with questions than solutions. The simulated oil paint printed onto special canvas should never be allowed to be the last word in "integration solutions."

For four years I taught an MA course entitled "Drawing as Process" at Kingston University. One project that I gave the students sounds simple enough: Present two groups of drawings, one low tech, the other high tech. Students come up with both the obvious and the unexpected: drawings made by fingers in sand, with feathers, with 3D programs, with tyre marks; drawings made by snails; fingerprints; and quite a variety of software. One of the simplest examples was a plastic shuttlecock photographed in sharp morning sunlight, so that its shadow produced a perfect circle looking more solid than its "real" 3D form; it was "drawn" as a shadow. Part of the point of the exercise was to show just how difficult it is to define what is or is not high and low tech. You can always say that the human eye and brain are faster and more sophisticated than "a mere computer," so that mechanically made marks can be considered primitive. Some students will argue forcefully that artists using higher technology should use it for what "it does best" and not use it to simulate existing tools. The problem is that the paint program is an example of what it does do best, and that without the model of the artist's studio—the "drawers" of paints, the brushes, and the palettes—such complex visual manipulation would not be usable in the first place.

Working day to day in the simulated office—with electronic files, folders, mail, windows, and bins—we get along. We can stand back and reflect on how different this office is from the one of fifty years ago, though sometimes everything digitally filed has to be duplicated in those irritating box files. Sometimes it is the more recent desktop fixtures that acquire the aura of strangeness. At the dry-cleaners an assistant rushes to answer the landline phone, but gets tangled up in the coils of the cord. He smiles in apology. I think of his clumsiness. It shows how the non-mobile-phone is now the anomaly. It is identified with cold calling, just as regular mail is identified with junk mail. Until they are superseded, such fixtures are taken for granted. They are invisible, like the mouse, the screen, the page.

Zen Paint

In 2000 I was driving from London to Frankfurt with my exhibition (framed giclee iris prints) in the back of the car, and my German gallerist, Wolfgang Lieser, beside me helping with the map reading. He was concerned that my new pictures were predominantly photographic, digital photos collaged into patterns, and the lack of hand drawing and painting might be off-putting to the potential clients. I pointed out that within a program, manipulating layers and colour curves is as hands-on as drawing with a pencil, but I knew what he meant and I knew I was splitting hairs. We talked on. He suggested I get my larger digital images printed on canvas; something I still resist because I feel canvas is appropriate for paint, not for inkjet printing. I found myself saying—with complete nonchalance as if it were the most obvious thing in the world—that just because an image was on canvas, this didn't make it a painting. He asked why that was, and I was dismayed to find I didn't have an answer.

There should be a way of answering, if only by pointing, for example, at Seurat's *Grand Jatte* and its organisation of vertical forms, the trumpeter breaking the stillness. The delights of this picture have little to do with it being merely paint on canvas. It is about visual intelligence; every part of the picture is like a cell of activity that responds to another part. All the same, if I were attempting to explain to a class of seven-year-olds why I adore this picture, I would have difficulty answering a question like "Did he make it on a computer?" The truth is that even in distant art history, there are many examples of images that have the feel of digital images. This is a paradox. The more I try to explain how paintings achieve their effect, the closer I get to thinking in the language and grammar of computer graphics. I think of pixels, vector forms, repeated parcels of memorised routines, layers, filters, colour correction. There must have been a similar feeling of revelation when painters looked at seventeenth-century Dutch painting with eyes attuned to photography.

One overlooked consequence of having the software to massage information out of unpromising images is the historical dimension. Digital art has an unfortunate tendency to see itself as a *Star Trek* production, the trip to the future where you get a glimpse of the mock-ups of tomorrow's art forms. It can also open links with the past.

Chapter 7 **Strange Plants**

New Planet

The digital-art community encompasses all sorts of groups, three generations at least, spread over five continents, each with twenty distinct ideas about what digital art should be. Along with its enthusiasm for computers, for hardware that could be useful to artists, this community has been, for the most part, optimistic, dreaming of art uncontaminated by the cynicism, doubts, and darkened soul of "mainstream" art. In its formative years, the community was full of goodwill, lacking the competitive bitchiness of the real art world, but it has also been short on criticism, realism, and pessimism. Apart from echoes here and there of the utopian talk of the Bauhaus and the crankier ideas of spiritualised abstraction, its ideology has come from somewhere else. If significant art has emerged, it is art with only a limited self-consciousness, and perhaps no subconscious at all. In comparison, Cézanne, Picasso, Pollock, Warhol, and Beuys were introspective individualists crippled with self-doubt. Not surprisingly, digital art has not attracted much psychological probing. There may not be much under the surface. The digital-art community reenacts the blind confidence of 1960s counterculture, with immersive light shows and mind-bending "experiences." But this is to generalise too far—there are "dark side" artists, too, like the magnificent Stelarc, Graham Harwood, or Victor Koen. What has thrived is the idea—you might call it a naive faith—that digital could invent everything, including art, from scratch. Of course, digital art—digital painting—will be a whole lot better than before, a massive upgrade. Looking only at the technical possibilities of paint software, it is not difficult to jump to this conclusion. Computer graphics should be painter heaven. "When I started," said the pioneering artist Yoichiro Kawaguchi, "I wanted to go to another planet." Certainly, a new chapter seemed to open in the history of painting just when some critics thought the book might be closing. Painting doesn't give way to conceptual art or video installation . . . it goes digital!

Sometimes I wonder what a major exhibition on painting and the computer would be like. Already I notice that the convergence of traditional and digital media has become a topic for panel discussions at contemporary museums. In a few years, a curator will have sufficient hindsight to pick and choose with some safety. Will digital painting be a category that means anything? Would it be possible to identify an extra something that can be traced back to the technology? I expect definitions will continue to be thrown around and will cause some head scratching. Were an exhibition to have limitless resources, then one whole section would need to cover video games, movie special effects, animation, advertising, TV graphics, fantasy illustration, Web design, scientific visualisation, medical imaging, military targeting—the whole spectrum of digital images. Even a limited selection could get across the extent to which all this infects the way we live, and the painter is no more immune than anyone else. The curator will have to come clean as to whether all this is presented as art in its own right, or as the background against which "real" art emerges. This won't be easy.

The Corel company presented the Painter IX upgrade by showcasing the work of top "fine artists" such as Ryan Church. The works were closer to commercial illustration than to what the loft painter would identify as fine art, let alone cutting-edge art. I have been at demonstrations and master classes when these artists have performed, and realised how little I know of the subculture in which they excel. Digital painting of this type is a niche art form, with select "masters" appearing in lavish anthologies. It is quite possible to be a big name in one context and quite unknown in another. Their work doesn't feature in SIGGRAPH art shows, electronic-art festivals, or art-world survey shows and is never mentioned in the academic studies of "computer art." It is as if this body of work doesn't exist, or is too embarrassing.

It would be hard to know what the core of such an exhibition should be. It could be a group of conventional painters who have one way or another absorbed the digital impact. It could be a group of purists—so-called algorithmic artists, for example—who have made images directly through programming. It could be artists who have gone beyond the static image, but who still operate as if they were painting—through multi-screen projections of animations. If the exhibition were to have a few rooms of historical background, then this section could either emphasise the development of cameras, magic lanterns, cinema, TV, and computers, or track the origins in exclusively art terms, looking at the constructivists' preoccupation with systems, and the surrealists' cultivation of the dream. An alternative approach would be to go much further back and show how close in thinking the painters of the Renaissance were. They also measured, analysed, and theorised the space and lighting of the depicted space. I cannot help looking at Holbein's great *Ambassadors* in London's National Gallery without thinking of its 3D armature, the meticulous rendering of surface texture, the frozen stillness, as if it were conceived in a 3D modelling program.

If this exhibition were ever to happen, it could work only if it could somehow contain all the diversity and contradictions in one whole. Perhaps as an exhibition, it would never work. It would spread out too thinly in every direction. And suppose it were to ask the question Has art really got itself a new planet, with new landscapes, new fauna and flora? Would the answer be yes, not yet, or no way?

Departure-Lounge Moments

I often go round galleries, drifting from one item to the next, making a fast exit if I feel I am wasting my time, and occasionally I find I have been standing in front of some little masterpiece for minutes on end—a 1918 Paul Klee, with stars and boat forms—and have been fantasizing about buying it. These six-by-four-inch pieces of paper stained with watercolour would cost a lot more than the average house. Lots of families go window-shopping like this, and it's an easygoing way of browsing through art, and here and there you pick up a postcard, a reasonably priced print. Obviously, you can pick and choose from what is on show, and when you compare notes with friends, you accept some variability in response. Sometimes a first impression switches round to its opposite. It is a spontaneous and relaxing way of spending the occasional Saturday morning.

As with any art form, you find yourself making random comparisons across decades, or centuries—and when you visit someone's apartment, you can read his or her personality by the pictures on the wall or the books on the shelves. This is one way, perhaps quite a modest way, that paintings have an effect. I have to keep this experience in mind when I am listening to a keynote speech at a conference on digital art. None of the speakers ever seem to come out and say how great this or that piece they have seen is. Yes, the technology may be fantastic, and its promises and ideas are exciting, too, but part of me holds back when I am told that "new media" art as a total phenomenon is significant. How do they know? I have seen too many digital shows that have been dismal, where the advanced technology was no help at all. Increasingly, I would like to see that explained. Are we allowed to walk out because it strikes us as terrible art? There is excellent digital art, of course, but like any other good art, it stands out and doesn't need excuses.

My argument goes back to the big bang. If you accept that digital art had no existence before the invention of the computer, that the whole story goes back to Turing, then outside that, it is just darkness. Or rather, there is no outside, no before; all the manifestations of digital art start with this big bang; the diversity, the whole evolution came about as a result of the explosion, the waves of aftershocks, the perturbations and irregularities forming the clumps of different formats and operating systems that we know today. If you reject this theory and point to the debt—enormous—that every supposedly purely digital art form owes to its parent form in systems art, performance, installation, and painting, then it all looks very different. For example, it is no easy matter to pinpoint exactly where or when modernism began; as with Renaissance art, the edges are soft. Reading an anthology on digital art, I can feel badgered. The book doesn't start with cave painting, or cubism even, but with the origins of computing, the reaching into the future. It is an Old Testament journey: Numbers begat the program, which begat 2D, which begat 3D, which begat VR, and Web art was everywhere.

I was having these thoughts over a coffee in the Gatwick departure lounge on the way to a digital-art conference. I began wondering how on earth any of the theorising around digital art ever gets put to a real-world test. If you took some of the wilder promises literally, if you soaked up the talk of digital art's working on the world like a mind-altering drug, then you would expect to see changes happening all around you. How could it intersect with this crowded world of travellers? The queues for croissants and cappuccinos, the anxious looks at the departure times, the passports, the papers, the last-minute calls home on the cell phone, the checking through the hand luggage, the duty-free shop, the lost pills, the hotel details, the last trip to the toilets, and so on. Was it possible to extract any trace of an art phenomenon going on here? Would anyone notice its absence? No. Here was a more or less public space—you could say the same for shopping malls—where all that talk of "the artist" and "cultural critique" would sound, well, bizarre. Nothing would be as significant as those flight details on the monitor. If art—digital or otherwise—was changing the world, its impact was so soft that no one would notice. It was softer even than a neutrino bombardment.

It wasn't that I yearned for a modest gallery alongside the Sock Shop, a few booths of interactive art, the visual equivalent of Brian Eno's ambient *Music for Airports*, or a shot of intellectual sermonising from a top-rank researcher. I just wished I could accept a more realistic mission statement. The expectation that an art experience could be upgraded by new technology, that a broadband connection between an art event in Tokyo and Amsterdam would add even a flicker of a new dimension, is true only if you buy into the illusion. Take these travellers. They are preoccupied with information about flights, safety, and messages to relatives and friends. That is, they are using the monitors and cell phones, not blinking with admiration at these devices' innovative interfaces, but using them. What relevance, what use, could art be in these circumstances? Well, you could have some impressionist masterpieces as screen savers, or you could have an exhibition catalogue on your lap, but this hardly adds up to what would be expected of the "artist" who comments searingly on society. But I didn't feel disconnected from this travel anxiety—even the artist has to go through security now and then. At best I could take photos (inconspicuously, in case of surveillance problems) and try out my artist-as-spy persona, the outsider. But why would these photos be interesting? It could lead to something— I never know—for example, a whole series on queuing for coffee.

Some have described the post-2000 period as the nonexpert phase of digital art. So, in theory, anyone can do what I might be doing in the lounge, just as anyone can draw an apple or write a sonnet. A few years before this, I would be asked by staff at an art school to teach the staff how to send an e-mail. A colleague recalls having a whole class set aside on how to use the mouse. Now I hear colleagues saying it is absurd to teach Photoshop, as anyone can learn it. The gadgets, the programs, are no longer impenetrable, and the art made through them can no longer count on being exotic just because it is from the virtual territory of cyberspace. It has to make its own case.

Postcard from a Researcher

One of the real growth areas in art schools in the UK and elsewhere has been research. Art projects become presented as research projects. Many of these projects have a whiff of science in them, and most mention digital technology. This is unsurprising. The conferences that sprang up in the 1980s and 1990s all had a purpose. Everyone seemed to want to engage. Perhaps this new art form with all its offshoots could be made to happen through collective will.

Some artists are born researchers and spend their time hunting out subject matter or poring over a technical problem. Some become researchers by accident. They come across a subject that is inaccessible from within their own patch. They scratch around to find out more. Once in research mode, they can carry on as a matter of habit. In my case, it was computer graphics itself, a subject with a crisscross of connections in every direction. Few topics raise as many questions. It could be that we feel insecure, that our lack of real understanding of computer science will betray us as naive idiots. No one is sure of the roots, the framework within which bearings should be taken. It is as if a suite of rooms has filled up with strangers, and none of them know how they got there or what is supposed to happen next. Some look for answers in the minutiae of programming code, some look into utopian futurescapes, and others speak of art as "spiritual" in tones long gone out of fashion.

My first hint of the subject came through typesetting. I was both editor and designer of *Artscribe* magazine. In the 1970s, typesetting began to be automated, with large photosetting machines, though there were still many laborious hours spent with Letraset and Cow Gum, with resizing photos, and in endless cycles of proofreading. None of that leaves me with any nostalgia for the pre-Quark days. I recall an excited conversation sometime around 1977, over the pulsating litho presses that printed our magazine, with Steve Schwarz, our printer at Expression Printers. There were rumours of what had been invented in Japan and would turn out to be the inkjet printer that we now take for granted. At that time, it seemed that the machine would have an industrial role. For the first few years, the only way to find out about a possible "painting machine" was to wander round trade fairs. These were not art exhibitions, but the visual displays had the richness of the craziest baroque, with searing limes and pinks. The shows were contests between competing businesses all talking about processing power, resolution, what you see is what you get, throughput, user-friendliness, learning curves, real time.

I watched the demos and had a go where I could. I would pester the salespeople for brochures and samples, but these reps were not geared up to deal with anything or anyone smaller than a production company. They were thinking in hundreds of thousands of dollars. What "art" there was would be facile and geometric and stuck onto the walls no one else wanted. The concept of the fine-art print did not exist; nor did I see how this techno world could connect with the sophisticated art chatter of my colleagues. Some colleagues had become proper critics, had moved on from magazines to work in TV, to curate shows or to work for newspapers. All these worlds—critics, studios, computers, business, media—were far apart. We had no chic iMacs, e-mail, JPEGS, or ubiquitous computing to weave it all together. Unless they were already sponsored by IBM or working in one of the few computer science labs that had a slot for an artist, my fellow would-be computer artists were all in the same position. This was one reason that the communities of like-minded artists began forming organisations such as ISEA, Ars Electronica, the SIGGRAPH Art Gallery, the Digital Salon, and Computerkunst.

The concept of the artist researcher might once have suggested white coats and experiments in a lab, and it is still difficult to think beyond the stereotype of the B-movie scientist. There is always the hardcore research by software engineers that drives the technology forward. But equally, there are the projects that look at the user as much as the laptop—that look, for example, at how we read, comparing the book page, the screen, and the PowerPoint lecture. (The PowerPoint experience of collective reading was one of Rich Gold's topics.) Software, even paint software, doesn't evolve in a vacuum. Developers don't throw in every piece of visual acrobatics just to show off. It is a synergy. The interface cannot be redesigned without an understanding of how it is to be used, and that use is determined by any number of social, economic, and cultural factors, which are in turn shaped by the ubiquity of computing. The clean-cut advertising that encourages us to upgrade is designed on those same machines. None of the 3D twirling boxes would be on my screen were it not for the "graphics" culture that makes it all possible.

As a mere user of software, you would ordinarily feel that programmers must be closer to the earth. They are engineering the fundamental grammar. They must have some insights into visual thinking. In my naïveté, I imagined that when an upgrade came up with a stunning new feature, the competitors bought the CD and stripped off that part of the code and fitted it into their own program. Not so. To my surprise, this was not how it was done. If you stole anything, it was the idea. In one case at a trade show, one such programmer saw a competitor demonstrate "tracing paper," and overnight the same feature was written in to his own product, albeit with an extra ingredient. When "artists who program" speak of code and algorithms, they can sound as if they have gone deeper than those of us who use the "surface features" of a program. We are playing with the novelties we pick up at the computer store; they are working at the core.

I recall a provocative exchange at a Eurographics conference in Milan in 1999. As in Britain, some of the most impressive 3D modelling in Italy was driven by the heritage industry, recreating virtual versions of ancient Rome, Michelangelo's *David*, Mussolini's Palace. In this case, a naturalistic reconstruction of medieval Norwich was being presented. Someone in the audience asked whether such amazingly detailed modelling capability could not be used more creatively: Instead of all this reproduction, this photorealistic 3D, couldn't it be orchestrated by artists, particularly those who were hot programmers? They could improvise forms unrestrained by gravity. The answer was short: yes, but generally speaking, artists are crap programmers. If they were to make a significant contribution, it would have to be as artists.

It has been said many times that the rows of 0s and 1s of binary code are neutral, and at the top level, you need the metaphors of file, desktop, brush, to help you make headway. One day we shall be looking back and wondering how we ever put up with the monitor and the mouse. In my case, I can get by without either: I normally use a drawing tablet and often project the image directly on a wall. Again, the fall in the price of the projector and the mobility that goes with the laptop have made this feasible in a painting studio. Only a few years ago, I would have been tied to a work station and would not have had the freedom to carry my studio around with me.

To be part of the research community, you don't necessarily need to be working at the "deep" level of computer code. There are roles for sociologists, psychologists, musicians, and artists. Computer scientists sometimes speak of art, of digital art or music, as the humanizing strain. I remember Jim Blinn making this point in an inspiring keynote speech at SIGGRAPH in 1998. He said that the presence of an art gallery was essential. It mediated between science on the one hand and the entertainment industry on the other. Three years before this, he had this to say on being an engineer who was receiving an honorary degree at Parsons, the famous New York Art and Design school:

> In the past years, the concept of using computers to create art and design has gone from being a crazy idea to a standard technique. Computer graphics is now cheap and powerful enough to satisfy the exacting needs of digital pre-press and Hollywood special effects. We talk casually of images thousands of pixels on a side and image files in the tens of megabytes. It is now no more unusual to expect that a graphic designer know how to use a computer than to expect them to know how to use a telephone. But I think that the most important result of the computer graphics revolution is not that it has provided better tools for artists. It concerns what has happened to the people involved. Engineers who make artists' tools have had to learn what artists DO. When they try to mathematically simulate lighting they've been motivated to go to art museums. When they try to mathematically simulate trees and clouds they've been motivated to actually go out and look at nature. Now, consider the artists and designers. They now wallow in operating system version numbers and file format conversion programs. Many designers write their own programs to produce unique effects. And I think that most of them have come to appreciate that mathematical equations can stand for geometric shapes. And that mathematics can be as beautiful as sculpture. I think that the most important result of the computer graphics revolution is that it has helped heal the gulf between Art and Science.

And how about my own personal odyssey through this? For the first 16 years of my career I spent my time developing the tools of computer graphics. But then I realized that few people remember who invented oil paints; most people remember the artists who use them. So for the past 12 years I have been using tools rather than building them. In my current projects I've become a graphical designer. I spend more time picking colors and balancing compositions than I do writing equations. Part of the reason I have been able to do this is that the creative process of mathematics and art are more similar than is realized by those who do only one or the other. In his book *The Illusion of Life* one of the great Disney animators Frank Thomas refers to the art of animation as problem solving. His problems were how to communicate the emotions and motivations of his characters, how to draw the eye to certain actions and so forth. This was a great revelation to me. I had always thought of problem solving in purely mathematical terms. But now I see it in more general terms.

So, now that the majority of the technical problems in computer graphics have been solved, I believe that the future belongs to those like yourselves who can actually use these tools to teach, to tell a story, to communicate, to bring joy. And now that I have been officially certified as being an artist, I'm proud to be one of you.[49]

Painters are constantly plying the metaphor. The delicate watercolour stain is not the actual sky. Painters could be understood to be researchers of a kind when, to make sense of their subject, they search through the visualisations that other disciplines invent. Whether the painters come up with interpretations in the form of conventional canvases or as screen images on handheld personal assistants is not the issue. What matters is their viewpoint, whether they can look at this material—this mud from the river—and see in it a creative potential that others have missed. I have sat through lectures on everything from astrophysics, brain scans, and car design to library cataloguing systems, the reconstruction of a cathedral, the physiology of pattern recognition, the creation of virtual characters in the *Titanic* movie, the creation of The Sims, the editing of a news report, literacy in Brazil, and animated typography. On these occasions I am no more than a wide-eyed dilettante, but there is a common language: It is all digital and it is all visual. Understanding even a fraction of how a 3D program works gives you the key to get into that particular frame of mind. Even if you know next to nothing about computers, it is enough just to stand on the bank of this river and take in the stream of images. Working out the connections can come later.

Carpets and Algorithms

In 1996 I began a spell of writing regular articles for *Computer Generated Imaging,* a high-end computer-graphics magazine. My brief was to report to this community what was happening in the milieu of digital fine art. One difference between then and now is that a higher proportion of artists were writing their own software. Bear in mind that Photoshop had then only been around for six years, and that if you have spent years learning and refining the way you work, you are not going to throw it all away at a stroke. There were also far fewer artists using computers. So the art part was essentially the generation of the image. The theory behind this was armour-plated—using off-the-shelf programs was out of the question—but there was no denying that "algorithmic" art had, and continues to have, its distinctive temperament. A further difference—these realisations creep up gradually—is that this was still an art form without an official label, not quite an underground art form, but not one that had been studied by academics, either. So when a succession of artists, well known within the computer-art circuit, passed through London, I approached art schools to invite them in to give a lecture. There was not as much interest as I had hoped— "perhaps they would like to see the student show." Nor did I have any better luck with galleries. It could be dispiriting.

Consequently, a recurring theme of the profiles I wrote was the improvised venue of the conversation. One of the more animated of these conversations takes place in the Pozzio coffee bar next to the Barbican tube. It is on the nature of algorithmic art. Apart from the two cappuccinos on the table, there is a lap-top, and scrolling across the screen is a Persian carpet. As it scrolls, it seethes, oscillates, and rearranges its symmetries like gauze over scurries of luminous ants. Jamy Sheridan is showing me his real-time magic carpet. It's character-based and fast— the letter D is assigned a little onion form—and wonderfully low-tech. At this scale, it's a deluxe screen saver. When fully realised, it runs as an installation where the image is projected down onto sand, with music by Sheridan's colleague John Dunn generated through the same program. The viewer gets inside the piece. As Sheridan elaborates on the symbolism of the carpets—the sacred gardens, the pools, fountains, trees, flowers, hedges—outside in Aldersgate the buses clatter by and the temps get their takeaway baps.

As we talk, I remember a wonderful exhibition of Persian carpets at the Hayward Gallery some years back, which in-cluded the giant Medici carpets. You could look in the dim light at the rambling octagonal geometry from a viewing platform. Behind me I listened in on a whispered conversation. Could this be the greatest work of art, in any category, ever made? The voices were familiar from the radio—the pianist Alfred Brendel and the art critic David Sylvester. I'd been lost in a parallel daydream, overawed by the dignity of the vibrantly threaded colour. It is a lost tradition, as remote to us as Greek sculpture was to the Italian Renaissance. But now, back in the coffee shop, Sheridan's rapid conversation is full of the meditative worlds, the stained-glass harmonies of cyberspace, the idea that these images, resonant with subterranean code, have a direct line into the psyche. Visual music. He points out that art forms have always involved systems, mechanisms. Even watercolour can be understood as a feedback loop through which a moving point delivers pigment suspended in liquid onto an absorbent surface. There's no break between the computer-generated and the human-generated; it's just that we're so used to the existing technology, we don't notice it.

As I listen and sip my coffee—we agree that the cup is technology—I'm putting several thoughts together. There is something elemental in the symmetry of these crimson and indigo diamonds. I think of the forms evolving centuries ago, with the women weaving row by row from memory, the glare and hassle of the desert outside. Maybe these quiet harmonies were therapeutic back then, too. Sitting there, I recall a conversation of a week before with a friend who is a senior nurse. She was speaking of an intensive-care course she'd done where she had to learn the cycles of checks—pulse, airway—so that she could run on autopilot in a real emergency. "On the bus home," she said, "people must have thought I was mad as I recited the algorithms." I pounced on the phrase, the analogies with the routines, the rhythms behind the patterns of art, be it painting, bowl, or rug.

Sheridan's involvement with computers goes back thirty-five years, and since the mid-1980s, he's been collaborating with fellow artist and programmer John Dunn. Dunn takes care of the underlying system software as well as the music. He wrote some of the first professional paint programs (including Lumena for the PC) and founded Time Arts Inc. of Santa Rosa, California. I first ran across their work in a dark cave of a room in 1996 on a visit to the University of Michigan, Ann Arbor, where Sheridan was teaching computer-based art—you might as well meet an astronomer working on the Hubble. In Britain it was hard to find a college that took painting with the computer seriously. Here was an art faculty with serious ambition—Frank Stella, the doyen of abstract painting, was an artist-in-residence. Like the curricula vitae of other artists whose work stands out, Sheridan's CV has its surprises, such as studying Chinese at Columbia University. Jasia Reichardt, who put on the pioneer "Cybernetic Serendipity" exhibition at the Institute of Contemporary Arts (ICA) in 1968, tells the story of meeting a group of electronic artists in Japan. They each recounted their background, and to her relief, none of them had studied art.

This is fine as an idea. Why shouldn't dentists, physicists, biologists, have a go? But on occasion I have had to grit my own teeth, not because of some supposedly beautiful piece of Spirograph-style drawing on a fluorescent violet background, but because the work has been made without any appreciation of context. Viewed alongside the comparable greats of abstraction like Mondrian, Kandinsky, and Gabo, the work is trivia. Perhaps this didn't matter, because it was a new context. Could a complete outsider make a significant contribution within the modernist canon?

Probably not. I wouldn't want an amateur working on my teeth, and I would prefer a dentist who kept up with the journals. But the postmodern canon, by supposedly erasing the distinction between expert and nonexpert, might occasionally appear to offer an opportunity to the amateur. "Slacker art," as it came to be called, was in fact a highly sophisticated form of mock amateurism. Artists were playing games. In contrast, computer art was earnest, like a footnote to the geometry of the pioneers of modernism. Quiet abstraction was not what the galleries were waiting for. Forget tasteful, forget modest, forget backward-looking. Forget the anonymity of computer code. We were moving into a phase when the artwork was becoming subordinate to the artist's persona; when the private became public, when the artist's personality was waving and shouting for attention. If there was an appetite for "raw art," it was for the utterly tasteless and outrageous. In London at the time, it was no accident that the most talked-about exhibition of contemporary art—at the Royal Academy, as it happens—was called "Sensation." All the same, in the mid-1990s, it did seem plausible that computer art might develop its own "raw" genre to challenge the mainstream. I saw plenty of work that was visually breathtaking—animations by Beriou, Chris Landreth, Troy Innocent, and Yoichiro Kawaguchi; performances by Stelarc; Sommerer and Mignonneau's bio installations; and these carpets. These works were creeping across the borderline between "computer art" and art and, in my view, could hold their own in the most testing gallery context. One difficulty was that they were presented as prototypes of the art of the future, as "demo art," a categorization that deflected the more thoughtful attention they deserved. Anything digital was seen only through the stereotype of cyberart. This could be confusing. At the time, I saw on the Web some news of a new digital gallery in London, part of the Backspace organisation. I checked its Web page—this was before the commercial online galleries really got going—impressive space, interesting installations. I rang up to find out the opening hours, and learned that the gallery is, um, virtual. I'm told, quite politely, that digital art only exists virtually anyway, on the monitor, on the Web.

This gets back to the question of whether the significance

of digital art lies entirely on the digital side, in the sense that it can exist and behave quite differently from art that is tied down to being "just" an object. So a show of digital art would emphasise this difference. For a while, digital art was a genuine novelty. I saw several "art of the future" exhibitions, which were full of interactive installations consisting of a podium with a mouse or joystick, and a projected screen, or a projected image on the floor. Without the art content, these exhibits would have been quite at home in a science theme park. In fact, a whole row of such installations, which just a few years before had been the star attractions at Ars Electronica and ISEA, were presented not as art but in the "Play" section of the ultimate theme park, London's Millennium Dome, in 2000. By then the projects were tested by the far more critical PlayStation generation. Initially, this had been *walk-through art,* that is, art that did things back to you if you waved your arms or shouted. It was fun, but also art—look, it was in the gallery! And if it was not art, at least it was entertaining and up-to-date. The ambience was the equivalent of the look-and-learn section of the science museum, except that here the devices weren't actually teaching you anything. They were like working models, interim artists' statements on the viability of interactive art, manifestos. "Serious Games" was the title of the show put on in 1997 at the Barbican Art Gallery, a brave attempt by the guest curator, Beryl Graham, to bring this underground into the mainstream institution. Relatively speaking, it was quite a tame kind of interaction. In 1920 at the Cologne Dada exhibition, you entered the show via the toilets and you'd be invited to interact with an axe.

"Revolution" and "Terror" were the themes of the 1998 ISEA conference held in Liverpool and Manchester, but there was nothing really subversive going on, just a lot of academics, curators, and new-media professionals and a bar called Revolution, with its decor themed on Lenin. It may have been interesting to speculate about outsiders breaking into the mainstream art world. But could this collective of insiders really direct the whole show from the sidelines? Significantly, theorists seemed to outnumber practitioners, and some artists must have felt that without a PhD, they would never get noticed. The imminent millennium, the technological optimism of *Wired,* and the need to believe in this revolution—a revolution never embarrassed by having corporate sponsors—all conspired to override common sense. You could not argue against the zeitgeist.

Round the corner would be "telematic art," where webcams and other sensors would facilitate connections between events witnessed simultaneously across continents. You can water someone else's garden. As the Web, the webcam, and reality TV shows have grown so fast since the mid-1990s, this no longer looks any more special than bidding on eBay. But at the time, the telematic artist had the painter in a corner. I recall such an artist waving his hand toward an ancient portrait that happened to be on the wall of the lecture theatre. We look at the picture, he says, we smile, we wave our hands. Nothing happens. (In his pieces, needless to say, all sorts of things happened when you triggered the sensors, and a parrot's head would swivel and track you around the room.) There it was, you sighed: painting, the obsolescent art platform.

Only a few artists bought into this vision of the high-tech avant-garde, and the majority may have been sceptical. But when digital art did receive any attention, it was because it promised this exotic experience. Art, by being launched into what was then called cyberspace, would emerge as something quite different, a new species. This was never a proper debate, because the conferences and exhibitions attracted believers rather than agnostics, and there was no brake of realism to rein in the fantasy. Rarely did anyone from the mainstream or "traditional" side say, Hold on a minute, an art form cannot be reengineered overnight. There is more to it than that. As with the Persian carpet, each genre of painting has evolved in its own way and is, in its own terms, an effective "technology." Speaking generally, painting has thrived during the emergence of photography, film, and TV, and paintings made in the 1970s and 1980s do not now necessarily look as dated—and dependent on extinct hardware—as does computer art of the same period. Seen in a glimpse, in what psychologists now call *thin slicing*, whereby the brain processes information in a microsecond, the visual field of a painting is the perfect solution. The 2D image may stand still, but your thoughts spin around it. The brain can only absorb so much, and you don't need to flood the system to get results. Understatement, simplicity, stillness, can work wonders. You do not need to be swamped in stimuli; you don't need sensory immersion. It is the same for poetry. It is hard to imagine how faster processors, smarter software, would necessarily lead to better poetry. Again, you would have to be completely engaged, a poet, and a long-time reader to spot where any difference was more than superficial. I recall a lecture in which a flipping electronic haiku generator was demonstrated. The nouns were vague and the random connections uninteresting. A librarian in the audience suggested it wasn't up to much as poetry. She was slapped down—"you're thinking traditionally"—as if it was out of order to question the oracle. Once you pass responsibility for the creative side to artificial intelligence, you have to switch off critically. Here is a possible symmetry: intelligent art for dumb spectators; dumb art for intelligent spectators.

Medieval Digital

The artists who established their way of working before the PC era and off-the-shelf software and who continue to write their own software identify themselves as *algorists*. They do not use the standard inkjet printers we take for granted today; they usually use plotters, on which a pen draws on paper controlled by instructions to move along *x* and *y* coordinates—left or right, up or down. The pen can be static while the paper moves, or vice versa. Instead of "printing out" an image created on the screen, the artist "generates" the image through the instructions, the algorithm. In other words, the image or pattern produced is grown, often by a long sequence of repeated strokes, from an initial formula. Algorists form a fascinating subgroup, because they remain committed to the procedure, despite the obsolescence of the hardware they need and despite the multimedia, interactive, and Web art "revolutions." Their plotters scratch away in studios and garages like medieval scribes.

Roman Verostko has been at the centre of this loose-knit group, which also includes Hans Dehlinger, Jean-Pierre Hébert, Manfred Mohr, Harold Cohen, Mark Wilson, and Yoshiyuki Abe. A fellow artist was visiting Verostko in his Minneapolis garage studio and, seeing the plotter drawings, exclaimed, "Com-

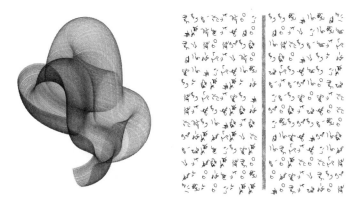

Roman Verostko, *Pearl Park Scripture—I*, 2004, 20" × 30" (52 × 76 cm), algorithmic pen and ink drawing with gold-leaf enhancement. Text: Nonrational glyphs. Format: 224 characters, 8 characters per line, 14 lines per column, 2 columns. (See also Plate 8.)

puter flowers!" Eventually the algorists are sure to be given the proper museum exhibition they deserve. They have been consistently rigorous and abstinent, monastic even, in the face of the psychedelic baroque. Seen as a whole, their art can find surprising connections. Once, when Verostko was in London, the connection he was after was in the British Museum, the Lindisfarne Gospels. This would not be so surprising if you looked at his delicate filigree drawings, with their woven patterns, their otherworldly stillness.

Verostko has been exploring computer graphics since 1968. He worked in Paris with Stanley Hayter (who taught Pollock) and also at the Massachusetts Institute of Technology. He was a monk for sixteen years. He edited the 1968 *New Catholic Encyclopaedia of Art and Architecture* and later lectured in China. He has trained his "scribes"—his plotters—to draw with Japanese brushes. In the pieces of the 1990s, each work is a series of improvisations, permutations on the gestural mark that the program comes up with. One analogy he likes to use about the power that an artist can get at in the computer is that of being at the controls of a crane. I recall one discussion we had about the spiritual in the setting of a rundown Charing Cross Road milk bar. On another occasion, we went round a Frank Auerbach show together, a Royal Academy retrospective, at a private view for artists, and he revealed how as a young man in Pennsylvania he was in total awe of this academy.

How would an exhibition of algorist art stand out in an exhibition of contemporary painting? I think it would look more like drawing. It might also look "ideological" in the same way that constructivist or systems-based art looks ideologically "pure"—intolerant of disorder, freedom, caprice, the random image. Its strengths lie in its limitations. When shown alongside the photo collages and "processed" images in digital exhibitions, the work of these artists does look more assured. They represent an older generation, too. But do they represent the way artists will use computers in the future? Not necessarily. In the first place, the basic premise is a half-truth, namely, that algorithmic art is "generated" by a program and thereby cuts out the aesthetic dabbling of the nonalgorithmic artist. In reality, these artists make aesthetic decisions all the way through—how to start a drawing, what materials to use, how to decide when it is complete, and which drawings actually work. Second, the material qualities of the image are not just incidental but absolutely crucial. In this respect, the drawings fit happily into a category of drawing, especially the category of machine or machine-assisted drawings, for which accidents and deviations from the plan are the attraction.

Jean-Pierre Hébert has made densely traced drawn circles where the hard pencil line seems to have built up subtle shifts of tone like a sand dune seen from above. They become like landscapes or moonscapes, not because they are meant to be but because one's eyes search out and interpret surface variations that way. At the 2004 SIGGRAPH Art Gallery, he showed a bluish plotter drawing of this type that had gone wrong:

> Since the 1970s I have been working with the conviction that to gain power and beauty, drawing should become pure mental activity more than gestural skill. I have endeavoured to make it so by banning completely the physical side of drawing. I create drawings by writing original code that will define the very concept for each piece.
>
> Running this code produces the path that guides the device that actually produces the physical proof on paper with pens, leads or brushes. . . .
>
> What makes it so rewarding is my continuing fascination with the slow mesmerizing apparition of each drawing on the paper and the anticipation of witnessing the correct

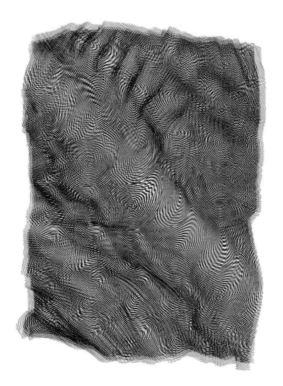

Jean-Pierre Hébert, *White Jojoba,* 1998, 5" × 3" (12 × 9 cm), virtual plotter.

unfolding of the proof. There is also the possible good surprise of a happy "accident", always tempered by the possible ink failure.

Here everything went wrong for the proofing, so much so that I annotated all the problems by hand afterwards.[50]

Over the years, I have noticed that doctrines come and go, and one surprise has been how the algorithmic position has softened. Nowadays the method used to produce a drawing almost seems irrelevant. Among my all-time favourite works of digital art in any category would be a selection of Mark Wilson's

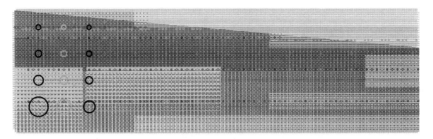

Mark Wilson, *VB3T134,* 2004, 24" × 72" (61 × 183 cm), archival inkjet print, edition of 5 on Somerset rag paper. (See also Plate 9.)

prints, which—uncharacteristically, for an algorist—are in adventurous full colour. He has carried his plotter methods over into large-scale inkjet prints.

Another of these artists who has managed to find a fresh approach is Hans Dehlinger. Dehlinger (see illustration on page 43) lives in Kassel, Germany, where for many years he was professor of product design at the University Art School. In 2003, he spent the summer working night and day on a lyrical series of drawings: rows and rows of tiny circles, each with a dot in the middle, all drawn by the pen or pencil held by his plotter, now an unfamiliar sight in a computer lab, as are his ancient PCs. An expert carpenter, Dehlinger built his studio himself, with immaculate plan chests and the edge of the woods at the bottom of the garden. His drawings convey the same patient respect for nature and natural materials: a complete craftsman. In these drawings, the circles are programmed to develop minute irregularities across each row. There are also the minute accents and variations in the behaviour of the pencil on the paper. Several of these drawings were at least three feet by four, and though they are the product of the program, what he terms "generative" drawings and in that sense are reducible to code, the set of instructions themselves would not be very interesting. (Elsewhere I have seen code exhibited, framed on the wall, to make the heavy-handed point that digital images pass through the system as binary numbers—the Homer Simpson answer to how to exhibit digital art.) Like other algorist artists, Hans Dehlinger is far from carefree about the physical expression of the code. It is actually the other way round. The only point of the code is to produce the drawing, and the way the drawing appears, the qualities of ink or pencil on paper, are absolutely critical. It is the minute imperfections in the drawing, the delicacy of the mesh of lines, that is the whole point.

In this case, Dehlinger was unrolling the drawings to show me after they had come back from being photographed by a trusted student. One problem for the algorists is that though they dig right into the system, the image itself is not a digital object but a physical one. You cannot convert such a drawing into a TIFF or JPEG file at the touch of a button. You have to photograph the physical object. On unrolling the drawings, we found—to Hans's distress—that the print of a hand had smeared right across the fine texture of the drawings. Two were effectively wrecked, hours and hours of work lost. Hans was sufficiently philosophical about this to reflect on the paradox of developing a way of drawing that was so independent of the human hand, yet could be wrecked by a single mark of the hand. A conventional drawing can be similarly wrecked, but there you can often retrieve an accidental mark by incorporating it or removing it. With a machine-made drawing, the human mark breaks the spell. I could only sympathise about this accident, but I also realised what a sensitive and potentially interesting question this touched on. The idea of the digitally pure—the otherworldly ideal—is unachievable. It is an illusion.

Matter and Spirit

A mediaevalist might well notice that much of the debate around real versus virtual, or object versus code, echoes the ancient division of matter from spirit. The body is material, corruptible, temporary. Spirit is pure and eternal. I mention this not to open up a metaphysics seminar—I've heard the Web itself referred to as "spirit," the collective mind of the planet—but because understanding the basic thinking behind medieval painting is quite a help, even for just a tourist wandering round a museum. Your knowledge of theological doctrine may have its limits, but it helps if you are looking at an altarpiece to know what is going on. Despite this truism, I found myself forgetting all of that; I was looking at early Renaissance painting with the blank stare of a camera; I was looking at the paintings as if they were computer graphics samples.

I became aware of the possible kinship between the digital and the medieval through spending many hours in museums in Cologne, Frankfurt, Hanover, and Berlin. I realised that constant use of paint programs, or thinking about how to paint with the given tools, had sensitized me to the way these paintings had been composed. The painters of the Cologne School, of which Stephan Lochner is the star, put great faith in the particulars of detail, the blade of grass, the ivy leaf, the buttercup, the satin, the velvet. Instead of the atmospheric unity of Italian painting of the Quattrocento and its feeling of a blended tranquillity or piety, this type of painting looks literal and everyday, not so much realistic as made up from fragments of ordinary life. The paintings, on wooden panels, are methodical, impersonal—no flourishes of improvised brush marks—and uncomfortably physical. To our eyes, used to mass-produced flat screens, these panels are visibly off-true and lumpy, and not just because of their great age. The rows of saints, biblical scenes, Madonnas, float like magical toys, half in this world, half in their own world.

One of the more peculiar paintings by Lochner—he died in 1451—is in the Städel Museum in Frankfurt. The painting consists of the wings of an altarpiece, two panels each divided into six sections, on which are shown in gruesome detail the martyrdoms of the twelve apostles. It is a smallish painting, hauntingly beautiful with the soft colours of the pink, lemon, and lime-green doublets and gowns of the torturers and their victims set against a gold ground. The poor apostles are being crucified, beheaded, clubbed, boiled, and skinned alive. Yet the

Stephan Lochner (1410–1451), *The Martyrdom of the Apostles (The St. Lawrence Altarpiece)*, 47" × 71" (120 × 180 cm), tempera and oil on walnut. Frankfurt, Städelsches Kunstinstitut. (See also Plate 10.)

participants are going about this quite calmly, like professionals, and the spectators don't seem at all upset. Strangest of all, the victims look unconcerned, and even Saint Bartholomew, lying on the bed on which he is being flayed, looks back at his butchers as if to check that they are doing it right. However, I was put right by a German art historian friend when I suggested this might have indicated a sadistic sense of humour. Not at all, he said. It shows that the martyrs had already detached themselves from pain and their material bodies. They are halfway to paradise.

These saints remain attached to their gold haloes even when their heads are detached from their bodies—a phenomenon familiar to anyone who has tested a virtual-reality environment before it has been completely debugged. I would not want to argue that there are parallels between Christian iconography and the icons of desktop and VR navigation, but it is interesting how different epochs manage to depict the unreal, or visions of the unreal. You could almost grade the weight and weightlessness of the figures. Sometimes the angels float as if in zero gravity; at other times their gowns waft gently downward. By the end of the nineteenth century, there were grand salon paintings in which the angels are fully physical—*embodied* is a word often used to express this—and were individual characters, with heavy costumes, complete with buttons.[51] When heaven becomes this literal, you have some continuity difficulties: Who made the buttons? Can the wings take their weight? The point is that painting can work as much through manipulating symbols as through flooding the eye with "embodied" form and Technicolor detail. Saying less can be saying more. That is not the most welcome of insights to come to mind when you have just upgraded an entire system. Show less? No way.

Meaningless excess and showy graphics are nothing new. In most museums, you can come across set pieces that are all show and no heart—this is always a debatable question and I take some pleasure in the kind of Dutch flower paintings that relish the dew on the petal, the wasps and flies half hidden on the tulip. These look quite artificial and remote from the values of contemporary art, whereas the Rembrandts in a neighbouring room seem to us to have psychological depth, though they are no less artificial. Somehow it is far easier to associate a "computer graphics" feel with clean-cut, "objective"-looking painting than with the murkier, romantic, and painterly. Seurat's great *La Grande Jatte* in Chicago's Art Institute looks digital because of its pointillist optical texture and its rectilinear armature. Monet's paintings generally look quite undigital, because they are emphatically painted, bonded together into wholes rather than broken down into particles and components. At the wonderfully superficial level that "painting" enters the repertoire of some demonstrators of paint software, both impressionists and postimpressionists have been the favourite source of novelty brushes and filters—the Van Gogh brush, or the harbour scene morphed into the mottled brushwork of "impressionism."

The polarities between the material and the immaterial, between the visual dynamism and disorder of the baroque and the clean harmonies of the classical, between, say, a Delacroix and an Ingres, the impure romantic versus the pure and ideal, were at work in painting centuries before anyone worried whether the digital was to be "all virtual." And obviously, too, these polarities are complementary and often intermingled. Spinoza defined passions as repressed desires. The purest and most neoplatonic elements, the vertical and horizontal lines Mondrian arranged on the canvas—first as paper tape—still had to be painted. For some abstract painters, the minute ridges of brushing between the black lines and the white are sacrosanct. And at the furthest limits of apparently reckless "painterliness" in abstract painting, as displayed in de Kooning's

243

paintings of the 1970s, there was rigorous discipline in the preparation of the brushes, neatly arranged in drawers. Even the freest painting needs a start point and a finish point. The problems digital artists feel they face for the first time may simply be traditional ones reappearing in a different guise. I would not argue that there are secrets buried in the "history" that might show how the digital and the physical could be integrated. But I would still agree with Reynolds that there is no better education than just looking at the best of what previous generations managed to achieve, and it is bizarre to act as if we have nothing to learn from all that accumulated experience, just because we've got an Apple G5. I am curious enough to speculate about how those painters might have coped if they had had a G5 or two in the studio, rather than teams of assistants grinding the pigment and whistling as they brushed in the boring bits of background foliage.

It is possible to come across the odd painting that has the cold facility of a 3D computer-graphics set piece—perhaps the equivalent of that 3D teapot that became a sacred icon to the SIGGRAPH community, except that the painters tended to start with something holy and iconic and turn it into 3D, rather than vice versa. Fully rendered 3D evolved from the primitive to the luxurious in painting, and when the "realism" is self-consciously paraded to the spectator like visual magic, you can find figures stiff as mannequins, every surface metallic and unyielding, the sky like an airless backdrop. My favourite example of a complete demo picture of this type is later than Lochner and his colleagues. It was painted in 1510 and, I admit, 450 years before the first paint programs came along: *The Adoration of the Kings,* by Jan Gossaert, in London's National Gallery. It is a tour de force of "high-resolution" detail, as if first composed in the vacuum of wire-frame drawing and then rendered in brick, brass, flesh, hair, fur, brocade, and other carefully transcribed material. In

Jan Gossaert, *The Adoration of the Kings*, 1510, 70" × 64" (177 × 162 cm).
Copyright National Gallery. (See also Plate 11.)

every corner of the painting, Gossaert is out to show you something top class—a line of angels receding into the distance in
perfect formation, jewels gleaming, the ornamental edging of
fabrics, a dog gnawing at a bone, the weight of the clothes, the
weightlessness of the clothes on the angels. The figures in the
drama of the nativity scene are peculiarly detached and unemo-
tional, unaware of each other, not interacting but alone in their
thoughts.

Initially I thought this was little more than a game, where you could wander round museums and imagine what "algorithms" the Sumerians were using, or whether Greek vases could have been made with wraparound plotters. As with Jamy Sheridan's carpet, thinking about how systems of repeated movement and variation build an image can open your eyes to qualities that you might ordinarily miss. Generally, the medieval and early Renaissance painters would use devices like stencils for patterns whenever it was feasible, and my guess is they would have used any mechanical or digital aid without hesitation if it gave them an advantage over their competitors. It would not have been rejected as artificial, because the way the paintings were pieced together was so entirely artificial in the first place. There is a further point. The art historian Erwin Panofsky observed that every "advance" in art comes at a price, and that as the Renaissance painters learned to model the figure more and more convincingly, so the less tangible, the more spiritual, qualities of painting receded. What you gain in naturalism, you lose elsewhere.

There could be a parallel here in that when you walk around a commercial computer show, you cannot help feeling that the ultimate goal of all these competing enterprises is to recreate the completely "there," 3D, real-time and interactive scene—the more "naturalistic" the better. Yet each time the technology gets close—hair, smoke, water, wrinkles—a new gap appears. I have some twenty-five-year-old SIGGRAPH Electronic Theatre tapes, the ultimate in realism for their time, yet they now look primeval. Realism is relative, but I cannot say that primitive equals spiritual in this instance, and no doubt Gossaert looked back at Lochner and his cronies with some condescension—one interpretation suggests that the crumbling ruin in which this nativity is set symbolises the disintegration of the old order. However, it intrigues me that the Renaissance still offers us a living visual grammar with some relevance; it may be no more than a detail of cross-hatching in a Durer that turns up in technical papers about perception and the fundamentals of computer graphics. Gossaert's prephotographic painting, with its schematic perspective, boxlike spaces, doll faces, and simplified lighting, is perfect for demonstrating how the eye interprets gradations, turning forms, roundness, and depth. Even a nativity can be—in part—a demo piece. I felt I should check up on my impression of Gossaert. Max Friedlander was one of the great scholars of Flemish painting, and when I looked up the painting in his *From Van Eyck to Brueghel,* which was first published in 1916, I was struck by what could also be a critique of computer graphics art as a whole. Gossaert, he says, only skimmed the superficial from the Renaissance when returning to Flanders from Rome:

In those critical days when tradition had disintegrated in the North, rationalism was an ever-present menace. The master was pre-occupied by particular problems of form and particular difficulties. And in working with arrogant pedantry to produce striking effects of perspective foreshortening and overlappings he loses the spiritual content. What was a means for an end for a Leonardo da Vinci became the end in itself.

The *Adoration of the Kings* is shown as a court ceremony. There is a complete lack of dramatic movement, and relationships between the individual, stiffly parading figures are scarcely established. Gossaert's talents lack dynamism. Self-conscious in expression, he is timid in composition, with only few ideas, and as a draughtsman he is sure of himself only when a life-model is continually available, otherwise, particularly in fore-shortening, at any rate in his early period, he is unreliable. The fact that the two dogs in the

247

foreground that seems so completely realistic are borrowed, and most adroitly borrowed, from engravings by Durer and Schongauer is symptomatic and instructive.[52]

The tone of this critique is excessively—and refreshingly—judgmental by today's standards, when art history is narrowly specialized and on a quite different track from art criticism, except when the art historians become critics. We go to the museum to witness the masterpiece, not to tear it apart. We read the labels and the catalogues, listen to the expert's voiceover, and feel inadequate if we don't appreciate what we are supposed to appreciate. We are not used to these sweeping and dismissive judgments that used to be traded off between connoisseurs. It is a little arch to compare the alleged failings of one master painter with the materialism of the iPod generation, the need to make everything compact, ultra hi-fi, and glisten with "reality" in the synthetic realism of computer graphics. But I think a point can comes across, just a glancing point perhaps, another question mark over the idea that digital art should be at some ultimate cutting edge. In a decade or two, another generation will be looking back at our dabblings in new technology and will be compiling some very nice satire.

Mathematical Flowers

This exhibition plotting the convergence between painting and computer graphics becomes more complicated if every "advance" proves to be short-lived, to be part of a larger cycle. Every move in one direction stimulates a countermovement, from extremes of naturalism to extremes of abstraction, from a generation of Net heads to a generation of paper tearers. There would be no simple-minded "big bang" as the origin of computer art, as if those plotted patterns came from nowhere other than enterprising lab artists moonlighting on the mainframes. There would be no arrow going back through machine art, Duchamp's contraptions, Muybridge's photos; no arrow going in the reverse direction showing new technology hand in hand with "new" art rushing into the future over the horizon. There would be no "this is tomorrow now" section. Without that time line, the premise of an exhibition on painting's digital future might fall apart. Take the futurism out of digital art, as we have seen, and you lose the backbone. It is hard to come up with any framework, any criteria at all—unless, that is, you use the same criteria, the same instincts, the same aesthetic muscles you would use in any other art form.

I am wary of the term *dialectics,* but thinking in terms of tendencies that pull away from each other might be a useful method. To return to the question of how the drawings of the algorists fit into the larger picture, they would be seen not as a historical curiosity—as much in a backwater as their plotter technology—but as perhaps the Quakers of digital art: the quiet conscience, the rational centre. I have heard Roman Verostko describe himself as a medieval scribe in an epoch of the mechanical press, and I have seen small pencil drawings by Hans Dehlinger, almost like musical notations, framed with the modesty of a Lutheran prayer, so this may be what has prompted this association. The modern household computer is faster than ever, networked to the Web, a media centre. For the algorists, the computer is a magnificent calculator, but for the modern household, the PC is what the salesperson might call a multimedia hub. With all these extra functions, a new genera-tion of artists would be bound to go for the full palette of sound, animation, and visual excess. Early computer art, work produced up to the 1980s, tends not only to be abstract but also to reflect the self-contained systems on which it is produced. There was no readily available way of inputting photographs or of outputting them, or of "drawing" on the screen. It is only in the last ten years that scanners, digital cameras, and printers have become affordable and at the same time much better at doing what they are supposed to do.

The Computerkunst exhibition has been held every two years since 1986 in the small town of Gladbeck, in Germany. The exhibition remains loyal to the concept of the computer-generated image, and indeed, the prize is the "Golden Plotter." But its resilient director, Wolfgang Schneider, has had to make sure the exhibition moves with the times, and now only a small proportion of the exhibition is "plotted." A word sometimes used to cover early computer art, including the work of the algorists, is *hermetic,* meaning the work exists in a sealed, airless space, like a mathematical space, quite out of contact with anything outside itself. In this respect, it is distinctive and a straightforward "output" of the "input" data that has been entered in as code. It is more difficult to identify the distinctive logic of the other works in such an exhibition, works that may be on either a minute or a monster scale, may be monochrome with tiny marks, or may be raucous photo collages. If the algorists are about restraint, order, and containment, then the rest can at first strike you as unconstrained visual noise.

The difference now is that the user has to bring in the structure, the equivalent visual logic, from outside. If the only digital material available—going back to the mud metaphor—is an eight-by-eight grid with two colours, your structure is given. You don't have to invent your restraint; your limitation is staring at you in the face. There is only so much that you can do. The equipment tells you this. It is like a chessboard, and most of the rules are already there. When the complexity of the system increases to the extent that you become quite unaware of how it works—you can no longer see the pixel with the naked eye—you have a new difficulty: There is too much choice. If through

250

cameras, scanners, and Wacom tablets, your raw material becomes anything you can see, anything you can draw, you have to invent your own way of making sense out of it. This might mean plotting it all into a grid, thinking up a looser set of constraints, or going for something freely improvised. If variation and deviation from the expected is at the core of algorist drawing, the "paintbox" artist has to find the metaphor, has to find a workable system, a containing form, a matrix. This is, again, comparable to the argument between the classical, with its order of ideal form, and the romantic, with the drama of "real life" that touches the viewer's emotions. It is a dichotomy in painting, but it also comes up in music:

> As he told Sibelius at the two men's famous meeting, Mahler thought the symphony as a medium should be all-inclusive like the world. But his unflagging endeavor, torn as he was by spiritual and consciously racial conflicts of schizophrenic magnitude, was to reduce the teeming contrasts of that world to some kind of order.[53]

It was also part of the argument of Rauschenberg's "all-inclusive" collages and assemblages in the 1950s and 1960s against the perceived austerity of the abstract expressionists.

Putting *world* on one side and *idea* on the other is a gross simplification, and as epistemology, it is, well, rudimentary, but as a conversational starting point, it is useful—and it illuminates the difference between Rauschenberg's combines and Stella's stripe paintings. My first inkling of how the dividing of world and idea could be useful in deciding my path through digital painting came in the bizarre setting of the midnight midsummer arts festival in 1994 in Helsinki. I was at the ISEA festival and had been struck all day by the contrast between the electronic exhibits on show in the museum and the paintings from the early 1900s next door. The ISEA exhibits included works by Stelarc and Verostko, and though I could appreciate and enjoy them, I was not moved in any way. I knew quite a few of the exhibiting artists, and knew of their different characters, backgrounds, and their sense of humor, but when looking at their work, I was looking at or through an interface without a personality.

A glass door at the end of a corridor led to the permanent display of paintings by Finnish impressionists and realists. Passing through, I felt immediately that I was in contact with a human being, seeing what they had seen, feeling the cold of the snow, the relief at the beginning of spring—a tiny painting of a fir tree emerging through the thaw. I was aware that this was a forced comparison—the shivering artist painting the self-portrait in the log cabin was much more of a story than a mathematical formula visualized as a pattern. But the point was that this was much richer and more memorable as art. The images had a point to them—the women fishing through a hole in the ice.

That evening, I went to a concert of electronic music, part of the ISEA symposium, at the Sibelius Academy, and my embryonic theory was soon in pieces. The Japanese American composer and violinist Mari Kimura played some of her compositions with tremendous passion, and you could tell that the audience was taut with the feeling in the music, not just registering that it was happening. Some years later, I was able to see exactly how she worked by integrating acoustic and electronic violin. I found parallels with the trials I had gone through in trying to connect real and electronic paint. Some of the structural ideas happening on her laptop screen were close to what I would do in a paint program. As a performer, she had kept in touch with the classical repertoire and saw no contradiction between being both acoustic and electronic.[54]

The audience at the concert was small, and the only ISEA face I recognized was that of Yoshiyuki Abe, who had works in the museum's exhibition. His pictures are instantly recognizable in that they consist entirely of gradated colour, sometimes striped, but more often silky and dreamy. He is an algorist in that he writes his own programs, but the pictures are more paintings than drawing. They are sensual colour fields, but hard and chilly like perfect jewels, deep pools with infinite echoes. He speaks of them as essentially mathematical spaces, with no right way up, no up and down, very distant cousins of Kandinsky and Malevich. He speaks of periods of quietness, getting in the right frame of mind. He sets the parameters for his 2D ray tracing, and tries out a few variations. He works them in real time, he says, because he thinks of the computer as his collaborator. He wants to imbue the images with his own sensibility, his own sense of the metaphysical. He trained as a photographic engineer and has worked as a translator for a computer-graphics journal. At that time, his whole life was spent with his two PCs running nonstop—mailing, editing documents, programming, translating, administering the mail server for the Japanese branch of ISEA. He does everything on the computer, he says, except eat, sleep, and take a bath. His art is in that same dimension. For the record, he had never even tried Photoshop—I remember raising this question in 1997. He dismissed my theory that the idealised spaces in his images compensate for his confined Tokyo workspace.

In Helsinki, we somehow managed, amid the mayhem of the "night of the arts," a conversation about the ideal versus the real. I made the point that in reading a gradation, the eye fills in any missing tones, and that a suggested smooth surface can look more convincing than one that is completely "filled in"— we were talking specifically about Vermeer's View of Delft, in which the water is actually made up of quite a broken texture.

He maintained that his images needed to be perfect in themselves, objectively and I suppose absolutely. Seeming right was not the same as being right. In fact, I learned a year or two later how far he took this, because he had found that a London bureau could print his Cibachromes for a third of the prices he paid in Japan. When it came to checking proofs for flaws, he certainly was a perfectionist. Over the years, we have touched on the debate around computer-generated images versus some more painterly alternative, once over fish and chips in Upper Street, Islington—the only plausibly authentic English food I could think of amid all the trattorias. After that meal I wondered again about how his work could fit into an exhibition, an exhibition perhaps called "The Transcendental: Visual Rapture in Techno Art." I happened to be flipping through my copy of Hans Richter's classic *Dada* and stopped on the page where Huelsenbeck, one of the founders, in 1918 says: "We hated nothing so much as romantic silence and the search for a soul."

Random Flowers

During this period, I did get to know other artists who were not algorists and who one way or another sought to bring "life" directly into the equation. Sometimes this could be quite literal and personal, with family histories, diaries, softly wafting in layered spaces, such as Cynthia Beth Rubin's evocations of Jewish memory.[55] Some were closer to a documentary mode, such as Annette Weintraub's collaged patterns of photographs of her New York neighbourhood—work that was also in the Helsinki exhibition. Weintraub had been a painter in the 1970s, and soon after this series of printed work, she became one of the first artists to move over to the Web. Among other pieces, she made a marvellous travelogue about Times Square and its seedy subculture, with floating snapshots and anecdotes spoken in a

Cynthia Beth Rubin, *View from the Women's Window,* 2005, variable dimensions, inkjet print. (See also Plate 12.)

gravely voice. Joan Truckenbrod has been another who has worked in a wide variety of materials and technologies since the 1970s—she began with photocopiers—always with a narrative thread. One of her most ingenious methods for manipulating colour came from a technique improvised before scanners and printers were available. She simply upended the monitor onto a photocopier and copied the image. Later she had the idea of filling a fish tank with water and placing it over the colour scanner. She then dropped dyes in the water and gently moved them around—and scanned the result. In the paint program, she inserted into these clouds of blue and red stains primitive-looking masks and figures linking arms.

Coming up with an umbrella term for this more painterly and, I suppose, romantic approach is difficult. The manner in which the material is composed is only "random" in relation to the tightly determined structures of the algorists. These artists are not linked by common influences, ideologies, preoccupa-tions. They just happen to have exhibited together. Generally, they are less hard-core, are less committed to being exclusively "digital," and blend more readily with the mainstreams of art. It may be telling that there are more women in this grouping, whereas there are few among the algorists. The women have been more flexible, keener to improvise using off-the-shelf soft-ware, taking advantage of the fall in price of the equipment.

Pioneer is a relative term, and it can be misapplied to artists who merely took advantage of technologies invented for quite different purposes. One of the more interesting by-products of the growth of digital art as an idea has been the recovery of a history of the inventions behind today's industry. For many attending the computer-art conferences, the high-lights have been well-illustrated talks by Erkki Huhtamo, Lev Manovich, Bruce Sterling, and Charlie Gere on the "archaeol-ogy of media." In their different ways, these speakers have shown how everything from optical illusions shown at fairs to magic lanterns, peep shows, panoramas, early cinema, radar, bomb aiming sights, and national defence networks are all the ancestors of our ubiquitous computers. I cannot see this becoming a compulsory subject for students studying digital art, nor do I see why they should be confined to looking at com-puter art as if it has its own isolated history. All the same, the black-and-white photographs of the first mainframe com-puters, racks of wiring like an old telephone exchange, or photographs of radar operators during the cold war do give a historical perspective. In some respects, no work of art can compete in terms of the frisson of novelty or pure ingenuity with the hardware itself. At SIGGRAPH, there is usually one section that is the art show; a section of emerging new technologies with their possible applications; and by far the largest section, the commercial exhibition, with displays of new hardware and new software. Lev Manovich suggested that in terms of what was really interesting, it was usually the commercial show first, then the emerging technologies, and the art show last. I had to agree, and I recalled how many times I had run into artists like Perry Hoberman on the commercial floor as fascinated as I was by the sheer creativity of the industry itself. You cannot compete as an individual "techno artist." All you can do is stand aside and feel the heat, and also feel a little humbled. What on earth can you do with this stuff?

Eco Artists

The equipment the digital painter needs is no longer specialised or outrageously expensive. Comparing Macintosh 1990 prices with 2005 prices suggests you could now buy a Mac Mini for a twentieth of the price of the fastest Mac IIfx of that time, and yet have something thirty times faster. But the magic only lasts so long before it too becomes obsolete. As digital art has gained ground as a respectable academic subject, and advertisements for posts for lecturers in its history appear in the educational section of the papers, I notice a ten-year-old Mac LC discarded on the pavement. The uncomfortable part of throwing out old equipment is that you know that it still works. It is not that the older printer lets you down; it is that your eyes have got used to the finer quality of the new one.

This is not quite how developments happen in painting.

257

There are not "killer applications" that wipe out the previous style. You often can go back. Picasso and Braque's cubism borrowed its cut-through facets from African masks then regarded as primitive. On the other hand, there are subtle alterations in the ways we look at paintings—the word for this would be *sensibility*—alterations that make us break with old allegiances and find something "new" elsewhere. At one period during the late 1970s and early 1980s, for example, the seriousness of austere "minimalist" painting was challenged, first by New Image painting, then Pattern Painting and then by what came to be known as neo-expressionist painting, led by Julian Schnabel and Georg Baselitz. Critics wrote of this as high modernism being replaced by postmodernism, but whatever the terms used, and whether you agreed that this was significant or new, the change was undeniable. The centre of attention had shifted. The previous generation began to look stale.

One side effect was that abstract painting was marginalised, not because there was any overall decline, but because the taboo on representational images had been so successfully broken. Abstraction was deprived of its raison d'être. The new painting was full of recognizable images, decorative effects, and was bursting with its own energy. It was clearly much more of a challenge to received taste than a white-on-white monochrome installation. For some years paintings without imagery of any kind had seemed to be pushing against something, defying some orthodoxy. Now, apparently, a painting with just two colours and two squares was just another "abstract" painting, pleasant or unpleasant, no more a sting for the eye than a bowl of fruit. An abstract painter might have felt quite at home with the interface of the 1984 program MacPaint, because it offered the fundamental forms, circles, squares, lines, fills, and patterns, albeit without colour. But for abstract painting in general, that visual language had lost its meaning.

After the 1994 Helsinki ISEA symposium, I went over my impressions and decided that I should give my digital works much more of a local identity. Pure geometry, or mark making, was inadequate. I felt that the works should at least have a texture and a sense of the temperature, that this would tie them to a particular place. The lack of place was something that disturbed me about most of the digital pieces I had seen—and also the works I had produced. They could have been made anywhere—Cairo, Los Angeles, London, Beijing, Helsinki, on the moon—it was all the same. It may have been an unfair reaction, but at least it was a reaction. I resolved to include basic local information in my digital work, just the texture of a wall, to make clear I lived on planet earth, in a particular part of London. I took digital photos of a local railway arch and, through manipulating the contrasts, discovered traces of old signage about motor lorries. The signage was invisible to the naked eye, but became visible when manipulated photographically—more or less the same technique used to access data from shots of Mars. I soon realised I could train my eyes to pick up ready-made clues that could feature in possible paintings—from No Parking signs, to wandering tourists. It was going to be Zen painting. One project that did not work out as I planned—probably because the source material was always going to be more interesting than any treatment I could give it—was a derelict café, slowly crumbling on Hackney Road. Fittingly, it was called Victory Café.

What had also set me on this course was my response to a painting exhibition called "British Abstract Painting," which I saw right after returning from Helsinki. I knew these artists in the exhibition, and their work was very familiar to me, but now I was looking at it with digital eyes. I was making the same demands that I had been making of the digital pieces in Helsinki. I again felt something was missing, as if the painters were simply going through the motions, going through familiar routines, each with his or her own special repertoire, but with nothing very much at stake. It was academic, unconnected to anything that mattered. Of course, it would have been arrogant to have voiced this opinion openly, when I could do no better myself. Nor did I think that the equivalent "figurative" painting was inherently stronger, or that "imagery" was of itself the solution. The truth that dawned on me was that for all its obvious shortcomings, the digital-art community put itself through a much more gruelling critical examination. No one was sleepwalking.

If nothing else, the constant changes in equipment usually prevent digital artists from repeating the same work from decade to decade. I confess to having several generations of printers in my attic, some of which might still work. Perhaps one day I can go back and produce some work for an exhibition when a smart curator thinks up a title like "The New Archaic: Digital Primitive." Perhaps I could revisit the Okimate printer that never got anywhere close to the sixteen colours that I saw on the screen but seemed state-of-the-art when it spooled out a four-by-six-inch print on paper so thin it was transparent. This was advanced in that only a few years before, there had been no convenient output at all. It wasn't till the 1990s that any printer really came on the market specifically targeted at the "fine artist." Computer-aided design was for engineers or architects, and the plotter was designed for precision drawing. Early paint programs were for graphic design, for page layout. Monitors were sometimes vertical and black and white only, in a page format, or arranged for video games. You could say making life too easy for the painter—with an intuitive, easy-to-use paint program and perfect print just like what you see on the monitor and on proper watercolour paper—is counterproductive. It cuts out the creative part—the experimenting with odd techniques,

the problem solving, the anxiety. It eliminates the grit, the resistance. There are alternatives. Some artists avoid the slick
solution and go the long way round. They underline their connection with nature in all its muddiness and decay.

Lane Hall and Lisa Moline have long worked together and
have often preferred retro print technology, not out of perver-
sity or nostalgia, but because it is more in tune with the processes that interest them. At one stage, their principal resource
was their Milwaukee compost heap. They have made huge
prints by customising dot matrix printers, the predecessors to
the inkjet, which used tiny spikes to imprint rows of dots. They
have mixed this technique with traditional woodcut, and the
images have been both microscopic and cosmic: bacteria, plants,

Lane Hall and Lisa Moline, *Post-Parasites*, 1999, Post Gallery,
Los Angeles.

Lane Hall and Lisa Moline, *Gut*, 2001, height 28' (8.5 m), print installation.

insects, birds, star maps. The improvised and cheap technology has been part of their "guerrilla print" concept, their idea of a public, democratic, and sometimes mural scale form of print. Their projects are well documented on their "Bad Science" Web site:

> We are interested in the non-sentimental depiction of nature—primarily animals and their traces—and seek to explore the boundaries between the "natural" and the technological. The act of collecting, visualizing and categorizing natural specimens is often the genesis of this work. Our collection serves as the database for many of the projects we create. From cosmological maps and astronomy, radical

Lane Hall and Lisa Moline, *Bug Box*, 2004, 9' × 15' (274 × 457 cm), tiled laser print installation. Photo by Hall/Moline.

enlargements of bacteria and parasites, to the flora and fauna of the suburban landscape, we explore issues of scale, representation, and the mapping of knowledge.[56]

They produced their work *Gut*, a 28-foot-high laser print of a scanned pig's intestine, for the Muybridge-centred exhibition, "Silent Motion," in Kingston in 2001, pasting the image on the wall from sheet after sheet of A4 pages. It turned out to be like an elegant vertical brush mark on the end wall of the gallery: "As we created the work, we were surprised by the textural range, subtlety and amount of beauty in something as generally gross as an intestine."[57] The economy, the lightness of touch, the depth of research, the humor, was typical of their work. One of the few other artists with such a crisp conceptual

263

elegance is Perry Hoberman. In comparison, there are all too many digital artists who are fine at being creative but not so good at being critical. They end up looking excessive, self-indulgent, and humorless.

Temperamentally, I may prefer the work of artists who are half in and half out of the "technology is our salvation" camp. Perhaps I share their ambivalence. Perhaps it really is necessary to stand outside such a make-believe world now and then. Or put more simply, the thought that all the significant art in the future will be made by people sitting at desks staring at flat screens is not very appetizing. Or would it be so dispiriting if I had no knowledge or memory of an alternative? I once tried making the point to David Roberts, a senior "ease of use" designer with IBM, that one of the limitations for a painter using computers had to do with peripheral vision. In a studio, the painter can have a dozen variations on a theme pinned to a wall, and a pile of half-finished canvases lying around. Without needing to stop to think, you can tell at one glance where you have gone wrong, what you should do next. On a computer screen, you can display a dozen images at once, but only in a contrived row of shrunk versions. Roberts's point was that the only thing holding back, say, the construction of the wraparound studio, with a dozen or more screens, is cost. Once an economy brings down the cost, the fully electronic studio will be feasible. Would I really want it? Would I want my bookcase replaced by virtual book covers? I keep returning to the thought that as much as I love working on the screen with "paint," it is when I get up and go for a walk that another part of the brain becomes properly engaged. Writers speak of being blocked, but also of how important it is for them to feel the weight of a book in their hands, to run their fingers across the spines of the books on the shelf and open one at random.

264

In practice, artists, like writers, are often driven personalities, and when you see artists' work, compelled as it is by their obsessions, you don't think about it being inkjet on canvas, acrylic on canvas, or a video projected on a screen. You just take it in. You forget about the medium. The first Anna Ursyn work that I saw was a print, almost a diagram, depicting in 3D an enigmatic pattern of horse silhouettes on a carousel. I wanted to buy it. Or arrange a swap. Almost twenty years later, we were presenting at the same "Ozone" session. This fringe section of SIGGRAPH is run by Kevin Kane and Stewart McSherry and gives a platform to people taking an individual, or individualist, line. I realised then how the horse worked as a symbol, a symbol both of energy that is controlled and of energy free and wild. All her work—sculpture, paintings, lithographs—was based on principles of control and freedom. She has long been based in Colorado. Sometimes she speaks about her Warsaw background,

Anna Ursyn, *Horsing Around, Flying High*, 1996, 12" × 24" (30 × 61 cm), photo-silkscreen, photolithograph. (See also Plate 13.)

of her parents telling her of the history of her country. In this talk, Anna showed a painting called *Monday Morning*, which is all about what she called the Zen of driving in traffic. In a statement for this picture, she writes:

> Mondays emphasize the typical routine each of us goes through during the work week, as after the weekend everything starts over. The cycle repeats itself with greater empathy, less efficiency and even less energy. All commotion, turmoil, confusion, and individual interests are then expressed and perceived with greater intensity.[58]

She reflects on commuting, on the monotony of the repeated journey, how drivers may actually enjoy this monotony, which gives them the mental space to unwind, to think through their problems. She showed sets of pictures of wild horses, beautifully scattered and galloping across the open terrain and set in contrast to the grids of the city. I am tempted to say that she had found a metaphor, something like the free spirit breaking from the cage of a system, but not only does that sound trite, it would not be at all accurate. Presenting in the same session was Carlo Sequin, professor of computer science at Berkeley, an expert on 3D printing technology, an amateur sculptor, and a successful competitor in the annual snow-sculpture competitions held also in Colorado. In the snow-sculpture event, the competitors worked against the clock to produce extraordinary structures some twelve feet high, and Sequin's team, of course, was building the "impossible" 3D twisted geometry. There was nothing dispassionate or dehumanizing about that, but again as the snow threatened to collapse, it was very much mind over matter, idea versus nature.[59]

Ken Huff would make the perfect case study for someone researching the possibility of a purely digital artist. He didn't study art but anthropology, and dropped out after a couple of years. His father had a print business in Orlando, so Ken had access to SGI machines, the top range of computers in the early 1990s, when he began. He is one of the few artists in this field who gets by without any teaching or other income and survives from the sale of his prints. His images are instantly recognizable and are quite obviously computer images, categorizable almost as cyberart.[60] (See illustration on page 94 and Plate 5.) The forms could be plants, or machine made, patterned or symmetrical, coiled in spirals like the bud of a fern opening up. Everything is constructed in 3D with obsessive attention to the detail of texture, so that the tendrils or applelike nodules have the substance of real plants. They recall some of the bizarre coiling "evolutionary geometry" of William Latham, which worked best as animations, or the wonderful psychedelic forms of Yoichiro Kawaguchi. Kawaguchi, in fact, is far from being a "purely digital" artist only interested in algorithmic forms. He is obsessed with nature, travels in South America, and makes vibrant colour drawings close in spirit to Miró or Léger. The subjects of these drawings are the exotic fauna of the reef, including the intricate patterns of corals, nudibranchs, and sea cucumbers. Huff finds more of a connection with a "green" artist such as Andy Goldsworthy. Huff also photographs and draws plants, and takes his cues from that faithful old friend of the painter, nature. Weird as his work may look, and weird as the idea may be, it would actually make sense to frame a whole exhibition of digital art around the theme of ecology. Artists using high tech seem much less embarrassed about connecting their images to the natural world than do mainstream painters. Pure landscape painting—other than the leisure painting approach—seems implausible without underlining the fact, with an ironic shrug, that all we can see is a representation.

Chapter 8 **The Silver Thread**

Choosing the Course

Funny how, when you have the freedom to do anything
you want, you end up doing so little. Infinite choice seems
to translate into no choice at all.

—Jonathan Coe, *The Closed Circle*

Art students beginning their studies undertake a one-year foundation course, both as a general introduction to a way of life in which visual thinking will be uppermost and to decide on their degree specialism—fashion design, fine art, graphic design, product design, film, and so on. They may have only a week in each special studio before they make their choice. So the perceptions these students pick up—some students are impressionable eighteen-year-olds—is an interesting place to begin thinking about the future role of painting. For many artists, the first few months of the foundation course remain the most vivid of their studies, and for the tutors, it can be the most challenging kind of teaching they ever do. When I went through my foundation course, there was not one art ideology, but several: The younger tutors were in tune with what was then called *basic-design* thinking, whereas the oldest, those close to retirement, were keen on teaching anatomy basics for life drawing. Today's colleges face something similar, with several competing ideologies—traditional painting, conceptual, activist, new media. Today, a foundation course has to be organized much more carefully. Instead of eighty students, there are eight hundred.

So if I were eighteen again but had the benefit of knowing what I know now, how would I decide? The terms, the concepts, can be confusing since "multimedia" may look attractive and cater to my leanings, except that this would mean joining graphic design, alongside typography, commercial art, and photography. "Fine art media" include digital media, but painting would be just another section of 2D, alongside printmaking, drawing, and video projection. Painting would also be the "traditional" part of fine art. It would attract the more timid students. It would be difficult to choose to be both a digital specialist and a painter. I could choose media and do painting as a sideline, or be a full-fledged painter with a hobbyist's understanding of Photoshop. I doubt that anyone has deliberately sat down and planned a college's curriculum to make sure that painting and computer graphics were kept apart. It is a habit of thought that has become normal practice, which after a while becomes institutionalised. Someday this arbitrary division may disappear, and the student applying for a place on a painting course could be required to be proficient in 2D software, just as a graphic designer cannot be classed as professional without a working knowledge of Photoshop.

I never had to make those choices. Apart from a basic induction into the mysteries of lithography, etching, and screen-printing, and enough photography to be able to take reasonable slides of paintings, I never had to give technology—new or old—a second thought. Painting was painting, and that was about it, apart from the dissident murmurings of conceptual art. I am glad that I have never had the responsibility of designing a curriculum appropriate for the next generation of painters. Would students be better off if they studied digital painting on its own, exclusively, with just a dash of new-media theory here and there? No, because the ideal study program would contain everything it could to inform the student about painting, past and present, technical and intellectual, as well as all that was necessary to understand computer graphics, digital culture, software. That is asking a lot, and finding a balance between technical knowledge and theory, between the historical and the contemporary, would mean calling in a time-management consultant.

At some point, too, the practitioner and the theorist must part company, but not just yet. The painter's job is to produce decent work, one way or another, and to get on with the next project and not to worry about what goes on in a seminar on the aesthetics of new media. While they must know the background of their interest, painters cannot be expected to read everything that touches on their subject. A painting is not an academic paper. All the same, painters are entitled to speak up when they come across preconceptions that have become so ingrained as to be accepted as facts. I can, for example, agree wholeheartedly with critics who argue that painting cannot be taken for granted as an art form, and that we must be aware of its diminished status, its limitations, its abuses, the barrage of polemics it has had to endure, and the competition from new display systems, and, of course, from digital paint. But I cannot accept the—to my mind—lazy assumption that within a few years the conversation will be over, and "digital" art of one sort or another will triumph. The evidence is just not there.

What evidence there is points to a different conclusion. When Christie's auction house put on a sale of early computer memorabilia in February 2005, there was no mention of any art. Original documents, business plans, are the true collectibles. On the same day that I get news of this auction, I come across a news item that a vast canvas in Thailand had been sold for $30,000. It looks vaguely like a landscape, but the selling point, or what makes it highly collectible, is that it has been painted by specially trained elephants. There is actually a site where you can purchase smaller-scale paintings, in an *art informel* abstract manner, by elephant artists such as JoJo.[61] I would not want to bring auction prices into a discussion of the relative appeal of early computer art versus equivalent painting made in the 1960s and 1970s. But were there to be this all-encompassing exhibition about the impact of the computer on painting, it might not be so absurd to have a section comparing paintings made by "intelligent" machines, with paintings made by chimps and elephants "trained" to paint. The point it might illustrate is that while the images may be pleasant, or passable, what really interests us is that they are not generated directly by humans. If we saw the paintings without that information, we would not give them a second glance.

Matching the Best

Can I imagine going to an exhibition of digitally produced paintings that had the impact of the greatest Picassos, the steely presence of Goya portraits, or the indifference of Warhol? No. It is too much of a stretch. But such a show could happen within a decade or two, once the category of *digitally produced* becomes meaningless because almost everything we see and touch has been designed and processed that way. Saying that most things you see in your room started life as drawings used to be a device to jolt students into thinking about drawing. My hope is that one day, it will seem as ridiculous to speak of a digitally assisted painting as a drawing-assisted painting.

For the present, we tend to be inhibited and self-conscious in our response. Instead of the "free play of the imagination"—which was how Kant described aesthetic experience—the digital response has to follow the script. The experience is a package with instructions attached, and the instructions are written in the language of the artist's statement telling you what to see and feel. It is as if you had never come across a painting before and needed to be told what to do, just as you might need help using a new scanner.

Experienced painters, on the other hand, expect their work to balance out in a ratio of successes and failures. They know there can be quite a gap between what you think you are doing and what you actually do. If they need corroboration, they pick up signals from colleagues, and sometimes from reviews in the press, but most of all by being part of a milieu. This milieu of fellow artists, gallerists, curators, critics, enthusiasts, the occasional collector, is not the same as an "audience," especially the tame audience hanging on every word of the carefully crafted statement. At the nuttier extremes of interactive art, the recipient is expected to be quite unresistant, a completely noninteracting and obedient empty vessel, like an experimental subject in a lab. Like the rat in the cage, the subject has to be trained to press the lever in response to the stimulus. And like the rat, the subject is not supposed to have any independent ideas about art, memory of other art works, or any opinion about the quality of this piece. Just walk though the experience, please. If I flip through my collection of catalogues of digital shows, I find it is a litany about nonlinear narratives, artificial-life algorithms, virtual bodies, data surveillance, telematic environment. Were a Martian to spend a few hours at one of these "experience" shows, would he or she or it learn anything useful about what it was like to live on planet earth?

I have on my desk three recent surveys: *Digital Art* by Christiane Paul, *Internet Art* by Rachel Greene, and the more substantial *Information Arts* by Stephen Wilson. The premise of these books—which are very necessary and comprehensive—is that digital art exists as a distinct kind of art. Few exhibitions have examined the field, and there is much ground to make up. True. Not surprisingly, painting or drawing are scarcely mentioned. As art forms, they would have no more relevance than aromatherapy, in other words, just modes of "delivering" sensations. A student ploughing through all these names would have a hard time working out how any of the artists would be connected, if at all, to major figures such as Joseph Beuys, Gerhard Richter, Bill Viola, or Santiago Sierra. It is as if digital art exists on a different map, or in a complete cultural vacuum. The anthologies have as much of the air of lab reports as of critical writing. The writers see their task as cataloguing the subdivisions—Internet art, telerobotics—and reporting the gist of what each artist has done. That is it. No "I liked this but not that." There is no real testing of criticism, no weighing one contribution against another, no saying who influenced whom, no personal or emotive response. It is "objective," academic, and neutral—straightforward "documentation." Of course, much is implied by what is included and what is excluded, by the dominance of references to sociology, the sciences, and the digital lifestyle over references to the leading lights of contemporary art.

274

It is as if art criticism had never been thought of, as if no dialogue were possible, as if performance art, installation, and video art were too pretech to be in the frame. The photos—black-and-white in Wilson's book—are similarly "objective" documents, populated by "subjects" sheepishly negotiating interactive installations or wired up as though they are undergoing tests in clinics; the background is often pitch black, as the photos are of video projections. In other words, we are looking at other people experiencing the art, sometimes in a trance and sometimes embarrassed, and sometimes the artist is there in weird costume as the experimental subject. The ambience of these books is a throwback to the deadpan "documentation" mode of 1970s conceptual art, where the artist would do something provokingly banal like walk round and round a room in circles for twenty-four hours. At that time, the aesthetic was crafted to look like a nonaesthetic. It was a reaction, a mirror image, and in fact a duplication of what was called *formalism*, the reduction of art to a sensual blast of colour and form. Except it was deliberately vacuous, like a sensory-deprivation experiment. The difference now is that there is little irony and little wit. Instead, these artists are laying down markers for posterity: the first deep VR submarine experience! The first virtual-body project! The first webcam on a wasp! But despite these breakthroughs claimed for "art," it is like prepackaged history that never had to go through a reality test, and all that we are left with is the archive. Hal Foster called this "hindsighting the present."

I experienced—usually after waiting for some time in line—some of these experience installations. Some really were amazing, some remarkable, and others of not much consequence at all, just part of a theme park built by an enthusiast. Yet within a year or two, the muscle required to keep the virtual reality afloat was itself superseded. The top hardware made by

275

SGI for a while was called the Reality Engine. Once office PCs began to approach the performance of these monsters, the essential cutting edge was lost. Already, a trail of new-media highlights are known principally on trust as third-party events, "experiences" that you read about and see photos of but that are no longer live. If they are restaged, the effects would now look unacceptably crude because we are acclimatised to smoother pixellation, and most of us have played The Sims. At ZKM in Karlsruhe, Germany, you can see some of these installations, and to my eyes only a very few pieces—Jeffrey Shaw's bicycle, Mignonneau and Sommerer's *Interactive Plant Growing*—survive their metamorphosis into old tech. At that "science art" museum, you can peek through to the regular art museum, and I confess to rushing over with a sense of relief to look at some paintings of Sigmar Polke there. The pieces had not become dated at all and were still "live," though according to the new-media textbooks, they were in a noninteractive genre and should have been consigned to "history." Someone must have thought he or she had the answer: Wheel some workstations and video projectors into a gallery, immerse the viewer in Sensoround spectacle, deliver a knockout "art experience," and it is game over.

The way art is talked about has not kept in step. It is convenient to separate digital and traditional art as if they were distinct and even polarised alternatives. From the 1960s on, there was a scattering of articles and exhibitions on art and technology themes, but these were intended as "art of the future" showcases, not so much science fiction as science art. In *Studio International*, the science-art reports were on a rougher kind of paper, like cardboard; "computer art" was seen as a by-product of the lab, something synthetic that may occasionally look like an abstract painting, but is no more part of the "serious" mainstream than those paintings made by the chimps and elephants.

Through the 1980s and the early 1990s, up-and-coming critics began using word processors and enthused about the cutting-edge of contemporary art, but few of them saw any significance in painters using paint programs. Phrases like *cyberspace* and *virtual art* gained currency, but again this terminology expressed the idea of going beyond the everyday world into something immaterial and otherworldly, as if the "new art" would use the same gadgetry as *Star Trek*'s teleporter. It was not something you had to know about in any great depth. And yet by the 1990s, critics, whose home territory was art history or English literature, suddenly found themselves confronted by an exhibition of Internet art. I recall one art history lecturer at the Tate, also a critic and an authority on the Web, explaining what a Web site was by projecting 35 mm slides. It is only during the last few years that any firsthand user information has begun to creep through into the general conversation.

For most of the period that many of us have been painting "assisted" by software, the whole subject has been poorly understood, in fact, misunderstood—no, better to say, "misdescribed." The phrase *computer art* suggests that an image is being generated by an electronic box, while someone in a white coat stands beside; *digital imagery* suggests neon pixels; *virtual* or *cyberspace* suggests some sort of fluorescence hovering in the air, unconnected to the world we live in—that dog on the pavement outside; *interactive* suggests that pre-electronic art is inactive and fails to engage its audience sufficiently; *new media* suggests that there is also old media; for that matter, *new media* has been around long enough to now be *old media*.

These misperceptions are forgivable, given that some twenty years ago, the typical image would be blocky and "programmed." Whatever you produced through a computer would certainly have a computer look about it. In movies, the trick was to convince the audience that the melting chrome of

Terminator II was the way the future would look—just as the fourteenth century's way of conveying supernatural space was the shimmering gold-leaf background. Today, 3D animation software is much more capable and doesn't have to avoid skin, hair, water, and smoke; its repertoire is no longer restricted to aliens, dinosaurs, and insects. Nor are artists confined by the technology to use relatively primitive resolutions and simple objects. Increasingly, the medium merges seamlessly with previous technologies—photography, video, printing, painting, collage—and the issue of being or not being digital should drop away. At the same time, it becomes quite hard for a painter who has studied in the traditional way to comprehend just how far the ground has shifted; if the "paintings" that impress them turn out to have been digitally assisted—and are indistinguishable from the real thing—that could be unsettling, more troubling than having to contend with an art form that was openly "different" and didn't claim the same territory, the same inheritance.

Drawing Redefined

Drawing may not be the first topic that springs to mind when we think about the digital in painting. While the existence or nonexistence of authentic "digital" painting can be debated endlessly, we all know that drawing exists. We know what it is. Drawings are used in all kinds of occupations and circumstances— medical diagrams, a map showing how to get to the nearest station, plumbing, pavement pictures, identikit portraits, artillery range-finding, garden design, engineering, preschool playtime, Pictionary. The ability to draw, or rather to draw well, is held to be a natural gift. The art store has a rack of how-to-draw books, covering everything from farmyard animals to aliens. Drawing is generally acknowledged to be a good thing. In the

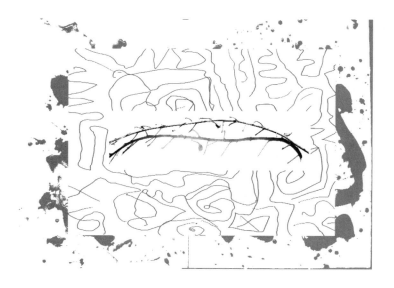

James Faure Walker, *Found, Drawn, Painted,* 2005, 27" × 36"
(69 × 92 cm), inkjet print. (See also Plate 16.)

UK, there have been successful "Drawing Power" campaigns,
with public events in Trafalgar Square, celebrities, and millions
of schoolchildren covering acres of paper. In colleges, new institutes and BA and MA courses have been set up—I helped set
one up at Kingston University. Competitions attract thousands
of entries. In New York, the Studio School is famous for its
drawing marathons.

But look closer, say the wrong thing at the private view of
one of these competitions, check what they say in the catalogue,
and you realise this could also be described as the period of the
drawing wars. How so? I recall a colleague, an art historian,
scanning one such catalogue and saying, Surely it is just a question of style; there are just a number of ways of making drawings these days: thin lines, thick lines, abstract, traditional,

experimental, digital, and so forth. In other words, artists can do their own thing, express themselves however they want. It's up to them which style they choose. One artist present almost exploded. It is not about style, she said, it is about belief.

In drawing, style is not necessarily a choice. If you were a professional illustrator, you might have a repertoire: a soft wispy manner for heritage commissions, a crisp line for a classic look, and a splattery punk style for a "youth" subject. You would switch between these, depending on your client. But independent artists would often maintain they do not have a choice in the matter. The way they draw is dictated by their nature, their temperament, their idea of what drawing is, or what it should be. The divisions between modern and traditional, romantic and classical, the polarities between the smudgy tonal drawing and precise line, have grown up over centuries. To be seriously engaged in drawing nowadays—like it or not—means you are part of the argument. You have to be aware of the positions even if you do not take them yourself. Is drawing a natural process, a blending of observation and intuitive response through pencil on paper? Or is it something more detached and self-conscious, where the artist has a strategy and calculates the effect on the viewer? Is drawing a means to an end, part of the working-out process, or is it an end in itself, an autonomous art form? Can machines actually draw?

There are echoes of the divisions within digital art: Can painting through the computer ever be "natural"? What does it mean for art to be objective? How important is the human touch, the mark? Through the centuries, there have been drawing machines, systems, and child geniuses who make nonsense of the idea that excellence in drawing can be taught. At one extreme you have the fluid brush drawings of Rembrandt, at another the mannered precision of Ingres. In the drawing classroom, you may have one teacher encouraging spontaneous expression, and another enforcing the laws of perspective with rulers and erasers. The ubiquity of computer graphics has played its part in disrupting the traditional formulae. It is not so easy for a master draughtsman to demonstrate complete command of complex perspective when we are used to seeing 3D architectural walk-throughs. Nor would it be easy to persuade an art student that a sketch made on the spot is better than a click with a camera phone.

As with painting, clever gadgets do not of themselves replace drawing, but they do serve to stir up the atmosphere. We may continue to draw as much as ever, but we make some adjustments. Dozens of features that are routine on most paint and draw programs are now indispensable for those who draw "on the computer": the ability to undo a whole sequence of actions, the automatic right angles, the snap-to-a-grid feature, exact measurements, exact circles, Bezier controlled curves, the copy and paste functions, 3D wire-frames, the ability to resize photographs, colour correction—the list is endless. In themselves, the individual features may amount to no more than a drawing aid like a compass or set square, but when working fluently together, they allow a draughtsman to build structures without all the stops and starts of working on paper. Whenever I have to make a large-scale drawing with accurate geometry, even something as simple as a grid on a canvas, I realise what a chore it is without the automation. It may be good for the soul, and good to get away from a computer desk for a week or two, but do "real materials" enhance creativity? Would drawing in general be better off without these digital assistants?

Computers have indirectly played quite a part in prompting the drawing renaissance, sometimes by prompting an instinctive reaction, the "return" to the handmade, to the traditional—or to something that can stand in for the traditional. It may be that architects bored with their computer models want to recover some of the informality of the sketch. (Ironically, some programs, such as SketchUp, can do this for you by roughing up the lines.) Another impetus has come from the computer-graphics community itself, in that the commercial exhibition space at SIGGRAPH has been colonised by various art schools that attract future students by offering a free life-drawing class—do the drawing, get the T-shirt. Surprisingly, even the most doctrinaire digital artists who teach tend to insist that their students first learn to draw, that is to say, draw from observation, in order to learn the basics of how to frame and compose a subject, recognize the constituent parts of a form, learn about light and shade, and learn to describe a shape in perspective. There is such a thing as a basic visual grammar, and drawing is as good a method as any for picking it up.

This is not the only role, or even a major role, that drawing can play in a college where every student has a laptop. Occasionally I have an interesting talk with a mathematician. Sooner or later the mathematician points out that real math has much more to do with the manipulation of concepts and symbols than with actual calculations. There must be a parallel here for the use of calculators. Far from replacing the essence of math, they liberate the imagination. In drawing, digital processing affords a similar opportunity to reconfigure the whole subject, to ask much more of it, to see how far the subject can reach. Instead of feeling trapped by the old chores, the old divisions—tone versus line, accurate versus expressive, abstract versus representational—we should feel free. One way or another, drawing is not what it was.

From Prince to Peer

I mentioned the drawing wars just now and how easy it is to say the wrong thing. I have done this more than once, and unwittingly caused offence. At a public panel discussion at the Prince's

Drawing School in Shoreditch, London, some of the postgraduate students I teach went along. They were taken aback by what they felt was the conservatism of the audience and surprised that there was no mention at all of digital drawing—these students were not particularly keen on digital, by the way. One member of the audience who pointed this out was airily dismissed. I had not attended, but I did know the chair of the discussion. When I mentioned this, he said, oh no, not true at all. They only heard what they wanted to hear. I should go along myself and see the school's own MA students' exhibition.

The Prince's Drawing School was set up in 2000 to encourage drawing, particularly drawing from observation. It runs life-drawing classes and lectures and offers a number of courses, including the MA "drawing year." So I felt I owed it to my friend, Timothy Hyman, to go along and see the exhibition. It was certainly remarkable, in that it consisted entirely of life drawings and drawings of stations, St Paul's, and other London landmarks, all drawn in a manner familiar to the art student of the 1950s, even of the 1920s. There was no abstraction or deviation from the concept of the fine-art drawing, the well-made life drawing. Some of the drawings were excellent of their type, but I wondered what role the quiet, well-made drawing could play. Such a drawing was not being used to help with a painting and could never recapture the allure of a seventeenth-century "old master" drawing. What also struck me was the incongruity of seeing these drawings with the background noise of a soap opera the attendant was watching. It jarred because the dialogue in the soap, *East Enders,* was contemporary but the drawings were in a language that needed the ambience of trench coats, pipes, and London smog: the 1940s B movie.

I was a little perplexed that such a well-heeled institution, strategically placed in the trendiest part of London, should have such a wayward idea of what drawing was—the view would not be eccentric at all, of course, if you believed that modern art as a whole was a misguided adventure. These students did not appear to have been challenged at all by any alternative to the stereotyped idea of good drawing, an idea discarded by all but the most feebly conservative colleges. The overall standard was not impressive. The only radical work—perhaps *radical* is too strong a term—was the student who made conventional drawings but on old brown envelopes. Strangely, the building was set amid numerous Hoxton galleries, which rightly or wrongly must have felt they had no connection whatever with what this institute was up to.

Walking along the street outside, I realised that what I had thought was a half-open shop was in fact a gallery, a new one I had not expected to find in a row of depressed-looking shops. Looking into the window, I saw it was a drawing exhibition, and I recognized the artist as David Austen. Pressing the buzzer, I was told the gallery was actually closed. I asked what its name was, not seeing any sign. I was told it was called Peer. The drawings inside—yes, I was peering in—were all the same size and framed identically in three clusters: 160 drawings in all. They were all drawn in a self-consciously "bad"—or "slacker"—style: thick, rudimentary, gloopy outline. There was no revision, just a handful of lines. They were mostly of naked bodies, couples, close-ups of genitalia. I did not respond to either the erotic or the pornographic imagery, simply because this is quite a familiar indication that the work has "edge." It is cool not to notice, just to accept.

After some minutes looking through the window, I wandered off and reflected that neither of these concepts of drawing—traditional or edgy—really convinced me, but both were symptoms of a minor identity crisis. No one knows what drawing *is* anymore. What else can we do with it? What is it for? How can it be made fresh? The Peer exhibition was repetitive, but I could see that drawing the same kind of subject over and over again—which they were also doing at the Prince's school—was like a compulsive activity that was its own reward. But it was more provocative than innovative, and too self-conscious. Drawing should be something you get lost in. You make a world. You forget yourself.

If drawing had the defined role it once had in the past, such as preparing a composition in a painting, making a quick sketch of a cloud formation, or simply visualizing an idea, then we would not be having these worries. Drawing was the natural way to show what something looked like, how it worked, how to put it together. It was visual problem solving, but now the range is greatly diminished. If we make drawings as ends in themselves, whether as exhibitions of draughtsmanship or as expressions of our art-world strategy, then something is not quite right. It is like trying to shock people by swearing in Latin.

A combination of photography and paint programs now takes care of many of those tasks, like capturing the look of the town centre in wet weather, visualising a scene, and planning a composition, though this does not mean that drawing declines so much as it shifts sideways into a different role. In fact art schools are already coming up with new categories, a term like *graphic fine art,* which puts drawing alongside printmaking and digital media. Drawing can be a section within the all-embracing term *fine-art media.* Yet drawing, like painting, does not seem its proper self, sparely defined as "2D still media."

Imagine, then, another panel discussion, a discussion on the future of drawing, where as far as possible all the main positions were represented. In a neighbouring hall would be an expertly curated exhibition, with fine examples of many kinds of drawing: academic studies by Degas, contemporary Chinese calligraphy, Hergé's Tintin illustrations, delicate drawings by Paul Klee, heavy graphite works by Richard Serra, Escher puzzle pictures, Durer engravings, Rembrandt brush drawings, Harold Cohen's AARON drawings, technical computer-aided design (CAD) drawings, Roni Horn's work, Daniel Clowes's comics, Quentin Blake's drawings . . . If the panel members could not agree about what was and what was not drawing, they might agree that it was one of the most informal and spontaneous of the arts, yet also one of the most exacting. Looking at the range of drawing, and the range of opinions you would probably get on such a panel, you would immediately think that any kind of computer-assisted drawing would be relevant where precision, geometry, or perspective was demanded. In other words, what used to be called *technical drawing* would now be *computer drawing*. The softer, tonal, washy, or nonlinear kinds of drawing, the sketchier varieties, would be less easily absorbed.

Dictionaries published as recently as the 1970s have surprisingly little to say about technology, let alone new technology, and this is a reminder of how so many of these questions have only come to the fore in the past decade or so. It does not mean that the visual vocabulary of repetitive forms, patterns, geometry, symmetry, stencils, optical aids, and numerous other tricks of the trade only appeared when commentators began speaking about technological art. I chanced upon a fascinating 1985 article by Doug Stewart about the teaching of "visual thinking" at Stanford and MIT. The principal idea was to stimulate the industrial-design students to come up with creative solutions, and the strategy was to make the familiar unfamiliar, to think laterally. Edward de Bono's method had been referred to in art schools in the 1960s, and I recall him discussing "sculptural thinking" with Anthony Caro at St Martins. The projects Doug Stewart reported were all ingenious: making shoes play tunes, making sitting "machines" from cardboard, Ping-Pong ball vacuum sweepers, power tools for a hypothetical planet with twelve times the earth's gravity. Students are given comparable projects today, but rarely within a computer context, as the computer is perceived as itself the solution. At the end of this article, the professor, Scott Kim, mentions the newish handheld device of the mouse, and conjectures on the effect of the newly produced Macintosh: "Computers are the answer to getting visual thinking recognized." He would be proved both right and wrong.

The term *creative* is horribly overused in cookery books and in graphics sales talk and usually means no more than a wacky gradient filling a typeface, or the capability of software to simulate a complete range of squidgy paints. It doesn't have much to do with problem solving. The "Get Creative" manuals to guide you through the complexities of Photoshop give you the solution—the watercolour from the photo—but not the problem. Professors of computer art have expressed their frustration. They can teach the students the software—some say that you shouldn't need to teach Photoshop, that the students should come with that knowledge as a given—but what they cannot teach is the ability to think in a creative way. Students imitate the solutions they see. The professors are under pressure to provide technical training, but by and large, students who have developed broader problem-solving strategies and who can adapt and think independently pick up software skills more easily. That happens to be the "fine art" approach.

As a victim of digital marketing and the upgrade syndrome and to some extent a victim of the digital-art cult, too, I would still maintain that an addiction to computer graphics does not of itself make me any more or less creative, more or less able to produce interesting, expressive images. By the same logic, switching to traditional art materials won't of itself increase or diminish my creative potential. If instead of buying a software upgrade I spend the same cash on piles of Saunders watercolour paper—I do this all the time—all I am doing is keeping an alternative channel open. No one, to my knowledge, has decreed that once a painter goes digital it is against the law to continue painting with conventional art materials. In my case, the move from one medium to another often nudges me into rethinking a picture. In fact, the issue of how to move between the physical and the digital, even to integrate one with the other, is one of those tantalising problems that hangs around to keep us thinking.

Choosing a Colour

One thought that keeps circulating in my mind is one I have mentioned already, about paintings and windows onto knowledge. The encyclopaedic reach of Google, the ingenuity of The Sims, the entire industry that simulates and animates, all this represents something colossal, something that dwarfs the civilisations of Greece and Rome, a dimension in knowledge that never existed before. Within all this extraordinary network of communications, the art of painting still carries on, or rather, new generations learn about it, continue trying to renew it, keep sending their pictures to competitions in ever-increasing numbers. As an art form, it is less marginalised than poetry or jazz, and some painters enjoy celebrity status. These are not the symptoms you would expect of an obsolescent art form. What drives it forward is not the ever-improving graphics card but the willpower of the artist: mind over silicon.

This all-too-simple thought returned to me after I had spent much of one week attending meetings and seminars on research, that is, research in university art faculties, where the question is how "practice" can be dealt with as research. At one small conference, the talk was mostly about managing research, a strange subject to raise in what was once an art school priding itself on an informal atmosphere where students could mix with practising artists, drop round each other's studios, throw ideas about, have heated arguments, and make up in the pub. The management consultants have appeared because universities and colleges are funded according to how they perform on league tables. The research managers are supposed to help the staff achieve the maximum points according to the scoring systems of the auditing body. So their strategy is shaped by the possible audit as much as any need for enquiry or spontaneous curiosity. It was like a seminar on filling in a tax return.

The following day, I attended a meeting of actual researchers from a wide range of the arts—dancers, novelists, musicians—and many had a digital slant. But there was other common ground. Most of us felt uncomfortable with this way of framing the arts in terms of such dreadful phrases as *research outcomes, practice-led, knowledge transfer, supportive environment*, and *moving forward*. As soon as some of these individuals began showing what they were working on, the meeting came alive. It might have been Patrick Kieler who had assembled a DVD with the earliest footage taken in the UK (a tram ride through Trafalgar Square taken sometime between 1890 and 1910); or David Toop speaking of how, yes, it also made sense to speak of the medieval digital—such as bell-ringing—in music.

In these two days, I had seen the impact of the digital from two sides: the corporate side, with everything reduced to a database of quantifications; and the researchers' side, digging through the material and worrying about it. I had realised acutely the need for free thinking, to hang on to the live threads of ideas, to be allowed the freedom to roam. How easy it was to sidestep the questions of value, how easy for a society intent on quantifying "knowledge transfer," and slotting the arts into that role, to throw up a management system that actually snuffed out just the initiatives it was supposed to stimulate. Major exhibitions are now corporate sponsorship events, and for all the benefits of the funding, it does engender a culture of passive appreciation rather than one of dissent and argument. It is not café culture—though the Hayward Gallery does now have a Starbucks in the foyer so that you can rest with your shopping and look at the catalogue. But I had other reasons for focusing on what I meant by freedom—call it my silver thread—and whether I was being sucked into a digital culture that gradually blotted it out. I was thinking about a talk I was to give the following week on research methods.

I had to drop in at John Lewis, the Oxford Street department store where our household was on the point of committing to a new carpet. I wanted one last check to make sure we had chosen the right colour. Leafing through the swatches, I found to my relief that, yes, I chose the same colour again. I then had some time to kill before an appointment, so after buying a couple of books—one, *Haunted Weather*, by David Toop, with whom I had just been chatting, and the other, yet another one on Internet art—I decided to wander round some galleries. In a short while, I found myself fascinated not only with some superb Picassos and a late Braque still life called *Echo*, but with the incongruous situation I was in. I had picked up the price list, and some of these paintings were as high as $6 million. Normally, I would not have blinked at this, but it must have been the combination of a challenging research meeting, the worry of agreeing to pay quite a large sum for so many square feet of carpet, and my constant use of the Web as a reference point for paintings. In any case, I wondered whether this was really such a normal way of feeding off a work of art. These galleries were in Cork Street, an exclusive part of Mayfair, but no longer the centre of the art world as they had been twenty years before. The galleries had kept to the same opening hours, closing at 5 or 6 and open only on Saturday morning at the weekends. It occurred to me that one way of explaining the pricing would be to think of the paintings on the wall as real estate. Just as Mayfair was an exclusive and enormously expensive neighbourhood, whose apartments were valued accordingly, so was the exclusivity, the rarity, of these modern masters—as much as their inherent quality—what accounted for the price tag. I was not thinking of this with any moral disgust; I was just pleased with myself for seeing a connection between the layout of the gallery and a real-estate office—the female receptionist, the polite browsing, the unimaginable prices. The system worked because it was about scarcity, about exclusion.

When I returned home, I saw a pattern in these thoughts, enough to suggest how I might lay out some principles in a talk on research methods. Without realising it at the time, I had been doing something akin to research, or at least the groundwork that over a period might lead into a project. Or put the other way, without roaming from such different spaces as a carpet showroom, an art gallery, or a research hothouse, I would never have got the stimulus, the challenge, to look for connections. It is a way of sniffing around that cannot be done at a desk surfing the Internet. Just as the piano tuner can instantly distinguish the real resonance of wood from the synthetic and sampled sound of the electronic keyboard, so there is a difference between an Internet search and the things you find roaming around. What had irked me about the language of the managers—who meant well—were the implicit analogies. Acquiring knowledge was like an Internet download; transferable skills were like switching programs; supportive structures would be like technical support; and at any stage performance indicators would be as clearly visible as processor speeds. I returned to the thought that the best instrument we have is the human mind; the last thing we should do is tie it down to imitate the behaviour of the printed circuit.

Nature Speaks

One real difficulty for the painter is the prestige of painting, the unimaginable prices that leading artists can command and the social elitism of the celebrity artists, gallerists, curators, and collectors who populate the international art fairs. It would be fine to speak to eighteen-year-olds about the amazing history of painting, the subtlety, the rebelliousness of a Polke, but if those students visit such an art fair, they cannot avoid also noticing the VIP lounges, the calculators held up to the well-dressed clients explaining currency exchange rates. On the *Today* radio program, a New York dealer at the Frieze Art Fair was asked what there was for the "ordinary person" at his gallery. Embarrassed, the gallerist replied that this was not art for the first-time visitor to an art show, but for the experienced art aficionado; trying to say it was not just for the rich, he said the prices went all the way from $5,000 to $250,000. If students were listening, they might find even the lower price a little hard to reach, but if money and fame were the driving force, they might well get busy. Even the moderately successful painter is caught up in market forces, the pressures of galleries, clients. The Net artist, in comparison, is a free spirit.

The handmade—or "hand-brushed"—painting comes to seem something special if shown alongside mechanically produced works, paintings that have the anonymous surfaces of inkjets on canvas. But what if artists can produce much better prints than originals? Given the miracles of paint programs, this should soon become more and more the pattern. With such "paintings" being 100 percent digital, they would also be 100 percent reproducible and therefore available in editions and, in some cases, different sizes. To its credit, the digital-art community has among its number many who prefer the low-cost distributed forms, the Web, the print, the public mural or projection, to the preciousness of the handmade, the snobby wall ornament in the gallery. I can't see this as a reason for holding back from making "originals," and I can't say that what claims to be outside the system is always genuinely outside. The "system" immediately cottons on to whatever it can find, and constantly presents its "discoveries" as if they have emerged from a wild underground scene. Every other gallery at the elite art fair likes to think it has the most dangerous artists on board. The galleries juggle with the same A-lists, they read the same magazines, they attend the same parties. Where there are signs of digital art breaking through into this very competitive world, it is not as a category but through the original twist an artist achieves within a familiar genre. Being or not being digital is irrelevant.

The difference does matter in the painter's mind. Thinking about this more broadly, it would be a great pity if the flood of images and new ways of making images—the digital river— were to flow by and leave the painting world untouched. You do not have to believe that the future is digital, or that new media will replace old media, to see that something vital and immensely creative has been let loose through computer graphics. So when, at an art fair, I stopped and compared impressions with an old friend who is now a critic, and we concurred that the overall mood was "art lite" and "snazzy," in the sense that it should not mean anything too much, that stylish indifference to effort and cool were the thing, I mentioned that I was not really wholly there; my digital self was otherwise preoccupied. What I was trying to say was that for all its faults—my friend dismissed the Internet art book I had just read as if it weren't worth a second look—digital art had a life of its own. It was not patrolled by the living dead, or the dead living. It had its own beating heart. It can be colossally naive and pretentious, but here and there, I had come across people who were truly exceptional—not necessarily artists, but programmers, inventors, amateur artists, professors of geometry.

I have wandered round art fairs playing different roles: as an exhibitor, as an artist on the make, as an art journalist, as a potential customer, and as a nobody. I do find it puzzling to know how to connect. It is not enough to say I am just there to see the art, because the context is as virtual as an airport departure lounge. I often find myself distracted, watching people and their dress codes as much as I observe the art. The Frieze Art Fair takes place in a huge marquee in London's Regents Park. Interspersed among the galleries were spaces given over to "projects" by less official artists, supposedly to bring the spice of alternative culture to the smooth cool of the occasion. Consequently, extraneous noise or yelps could be mentally assigned to "projects" rather than hard-sell installation works. One "piece" consisted of an artist starting a queue by a door that led nowhere, and sure enough within minutes a long line established itself. Everything is about showing, and being there, being part of it. Compared with the constant questioning, the arguing, and the mix of computer science, entertainment, art, and the collective mind of a SIGGRAPH session, the Frieze was all about conformity, a crowd sleepwalking through a market. Amid these slow-moving art fair visitors and the blur of conversation, there was a deeper, rumbling sound ending in a sharp crack. For a moment we forgot where we were and looked round, wondering whether this was a super-surround-sound piece. We did not want to be caught out or miss the main event. But no, it was thunder.

The manifestos, the prototypes, the demos, hoping to establish digital art as a viable alternative to this mainstream have had little effect. So far, it does not look as if art has really gone digital at all, not if you watched the merchandise being shipped though the art fairs, not if you looked through the schedules of upcoming museum exhibitions, not if you polled the latest intake in art schools. The picture would be inconclusive. The alternative digital-art world is not going to supplant this world of collectors and tangible collectibles. It may be my painter's prejudice, but in the end, I feel more comfortable with an actual object than just an apparition, a half-object on a screen. Yes, I remain enthusiastic about the whole digital project and hope to keep an open mind, but sometimes I reflect that this may all go down in the histories as an exceptionally creative period, a coming together and fusion of disciplines. But what was at the centre was not art, but a whole range of experiments in interface design. In a science-fiction creative-writing class, a standard question to students would be, What would happen if gravity were switched off? These questions about a different kind of art are similar "what if" questions: What if we had never had art before, what would it be like if we only had computers to produce it? Switch off the reality of "art as it is," and off you go.

After messing around with this metaphorical river, its mud, its quirky ways, its backwaters, its illusions, what conclusions have I reached? I don't think I am any the wiser, except that I now realise that one of the essential problems is that the substantial art that this digital tribe might invent has not actually been made, or not made yet. The conditions are right, the energy is right, but perhaps the thinking—certainly my thinking—has been awry. A little more respect for history, a little less chasing after the phantoms of ghosts from the future. Perhaps, too, a glance sideways at what might come from downstream, from the spreading of the previously closed world of expertise through democratising software. The real innovation could be electronic folk art, and perhaps that is what will be sold at airports. As for painting, I do feel there is—forgive the metaphor again—this silver thread that connects pictures from the past to the present, and that thread of inspiration matters more than whether the medium is a scratch in the clay, a tempera panel, or Photoshop XXII. Meanwhile, I must stop looking out the window and meditating on this imaginary river, and get back to drawing, to photographing it, stretching it in software, scraping through it in those grey turquoise streaks of paint.

Complex Waters

I began this book with a quotation from Ruskin about getting to know your local river, and Rich Gold's suggestion that we make our art out of the mud of that river. Well, I have obediently been watching my local river, the Thames. I have been photographing it, studying what Turner, Whistler and Monet have made of it, and wondering whether any kind of art can match the experience of just watching it.[62] Possibly not. I have been using the river as a metaphor, and it is time to abandon the metaphor. I should admit that the river—water in motion, shaped by currents, surface wind, the wakes of river craft, the sparkling light reflected on its surface—has such complexity, has such inner harmony, that to reduce it to an illustration, to a line, to a squiggle on a map, or to a digital simulation is always a long way short of the real thing.

On the other hand, it would take someone like Ruskin, with all his quirkiness, and then generations of painters, photographers, filmmakers, to remind us of that visual richness. And not only Ruskin. I was proudly walking into the Royal Academy's Summer Show on "varnishing day" (proudly, because I had never got a work accepted into this show before) when I found myself confronted with a masterwork of "river painting." In fact, it was a suite of lithographs, each a different texture of swept horizontal brushstrokes. They were stunning, some crisp, some sluggish, some just moody. They turned out

296

to be the new 2005 set of *States of the River,* by Ellsworth Kelly, an honorary Royal Academician and an artist whom I have long admired, especially for the works made in Paris in the 1950s and derived from shadows falling on stairways.[63] This had no direct connection with digital art or digital painting, but it was again a reminder that the simple dragging of a brush loaded with ink, just black on white, could bring out the visceral essence of the subject. A month later, I came across another

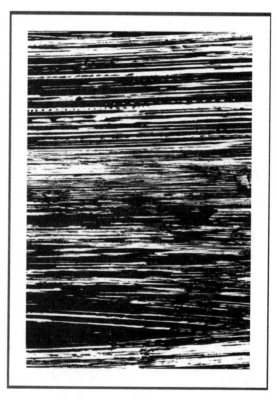

Ellsworth Kelly, *The Thames,* from *States of The River,* 2005, 45¼" × 32" (114.9 × 81.3 cm), from a suite of eight lithographs on Arches cover. Overall size framed: 47" × 284" (1.19 × 7.21 m) (AX.318–X.325). Copyright Ellsworth Kelly and Gemini GEL LLC.

depiction of water. I was at the small Foster Art Gallery trying to figure out how a picture of water currents had been made. A voice beside me broke in, saying, "Shall I tell you what it is?" The voice belonged to an old friend, the artist Shelagh Wakely, better known as a sculptor and an installation artist. She told me how it had been stitched together in Photoshop from a video she had taken standing a few feet above the sea in Lamu, South Africa. Again, the picture had nothing whatever to do with the digital ethos, yet it was uncannily similar in that it was a nature-inspired image that had been shifted into unfamiliarity. It was also disorienting. I thought I was looking down on water from a hundred feet. The fractal experience.

A book and an exhibition could be made on the theme of rivers, or the depiction of water, with Leonardo's drawings at the centre. It would not matter how artists managed to produce

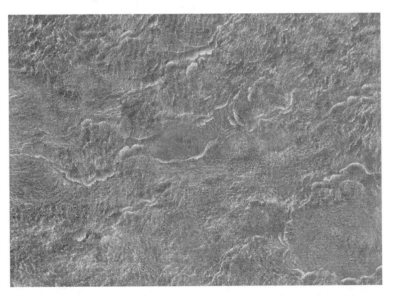

Shelagh Wakely, *Five Seconds—Lamu*, 1999, 34" × 48" (87 × 122 cm), inkjet print. (See also Plate 14.)

the work—whether they used water or oil as the medium for the pigment, drew with a pencil, or mixed pixels around. Given such a theme, or given just a decade or two for a "new" medium to settle and become an accepted medium, and these distinctions would be forgotten. For years, digital artists wanted to be both the far-out avant-garde and to be acknowledged by the mainstream. Unfortunately, this is not how the world, or at least the art world, works. The Royal Academy is no longer as conservative as it used to be, but it is still where the Establishment compares notes. The intermingling of social and artistic hierarchies in Jamyn Brooks's *Private View* carries on today much as it did then, and perhaps the cognoscenti of our times are just as insular, just as ingrown in their taste, just as incapable of recognizing innovation. The Summer Show is no barometer of new trends, being full of works by amateurs (prints of cats tend to sell out on the first day) as well as by professionals, but it does demonstrate what some would call a middlebrow consensus. Serious critics give the show a wide berth. Earlier in the book, I mentioned how the phrase *mechanical/technological intervention* cropped up in the announcement for this exhibition.[64] Sure enough, there was at least one whole room of digital prints and installations, and as far as I could see, no one was complaining. What interested the audience was finding that roomful of neo-pop art works by what till recently were termed the YBAs—the young British artists—who are now in their forties, and, yes, some of them are Royal Academicians, and yes, they use "technology."

What of the promised revolution, or has it happened without anyone noticing? Perhaps the period of anxiety is over, and the digital artist need not fret about recognition. We may not be locked into the digital universe of those 1990s manifestos—that particular future hovered over us, hung around a while, yawned, and went away—and art has not, so to speak, become so different from what it was before. Do I regret being drawn into all that soul-searching? A simple thought comes to me. Even if I were never to touch a computer again—unlikely—I have learned an immense amount about painting that I would never have learned any other way. And were I to abandon my physical studio and go completely digital, then I know how to set my sights, what to aim for. No more excuses. No more "hold on, the technology is not quite there yet." Perhaps I have learned why we need art in the first place, why we need to be critical, stay alert, and not put up with the second-rate. I suspect there must be many painters like me who initially hesitated and then took a similar journey and came back—dare I say this—better artists.

Notes

Preface

1. Ruskin said, for example, "I would rather teach drawing that my pupils may learn to love Nature, than teach the looking at Nature that they may learn to draw." John Ruskin, *The Elements of Drawing; in Three Letters to Beginners* (London: Smith, Elder & Co., 1857), preface, p. xii. See also Rupert Shepherd, www.oxfordtoday.ox.ac.uk/features/07.shtml; and ruskin.oucs.ox.ac.uk.
2. Over the past few years, I have tried to keep to a routine of making at least one drawing a day (usually painted on the floor using Pelikan Plaka black on 22-by-30-inch Saunders Waterford paper). Part exercise, part relaxation, part a resource for finding a motif I can photograph and feed into a paint program, this habit helps keep me in touch with the more fluid and sometimes incoherent aspects of painting. Though never intended as illustrations, some of the drawings did seem obliquely connected with themes of this book and thus became part of the design for the chapter opening pages.

Chapter 1

3. PAIR stands for PARC's artist-in-residence program.
4. "Art and the Intelligent Lunch-Box," *Modern Painters,* spring 1994.
5. Stephen Wilson, *Information Arts: Intersections of Art, Science, and Technology* (MIT Press, 2001).
6. "Computer Graphics and Computer Art," *Page,* 19 (December 1971): p. 2.
7. *GHz* is the abbreviation for gigahertz, or one thousand million hertz, and *MHz* stands for megahertz, or one million hertz.

8. The best examples of blocks of colour looming forward in this way can be found in the paintings of Hans Hofmann.

Chapter 2

9. He continues: "The possibility of making studies from such results would have had an influence on my work that I can only guess at from the use I can still make of them, even in the limited time I can devote to detailed study; photography provides a palpable demonstration of nature's true pattern, of which otherwise we have only the most imperfect ideas." Eugene Delacroix, *Selected Letters 1813 to 1863*, edited and translated by Jean Stewart (Eyre and Spottiswood, London 1971), p. 321.
10. Joy Hakanson Colby, " 'Post-Digital Painting' Pumps New Technology into an Aging Art Form," *Detroit News*, Cranbrook Art Museum, Mich., 30 January 2003, www.detnews.com/2003/entertainment/0302/03/c02-72045.htm.
11. Ben Schneiderman, *Leonardo's Laptop*, (MIT Press, 2003), p. 10.
12. David Em, introduction, *The Art of David Em* (Abrams, 1988). See DAM Web page, www.dam.org/essays/em01.htm.

Chapter 3

13. Henry Jamyn Brooks, handwritten account of the painting in the National Portrait Gallery, London, 1914. See www.npg.org.uk/live/rp1833a.asp.
14. See, for example, Caryn and James Faure Walker, "The Activity of Criticism," parts 1 and 2 (interviews with Max Kozloff, Harold Rosenberg, Rosalind Krauss, Lucy Lippard, Roberta Smith, Darby Bannard, etc.), *Studio International* (March-April and May-June 1975).
15. Nelson Junius Springer, "New York," *Studio* 94 (1927): 302.
16. "Mondrian in Disneyland," www.snap-dragon.com/mondrian_in_disneyland.htm; and Charles Harrison, "Mondrian in London," *Studio International* (December 1966).
17. "Is Modern Art a Sham?" *Studio* 112 (1936): 295.
18. Ibid., 315.
19. Norman Klein, *The Vatican to Vegas: A History of Special Effects* (New Press, 2004).
20. See Cher Threinen-Pendarvis, Painter Wow! Book series (Peachpit Press) and Jeremy Sutton, Painter Creativity series (Focal Press); see also www.pendarvis-studios.com/ and www.paintercreativity.com.
21. Anne Morgan Spalter, *The Computer in the Visual Arts* (Addison-Wesley, 1998); Stephen Wilson, *Information Arts* (MIT Press, 2001); Lev Manovich, *The Language of New Media* (MIT Press, 2001); Peter Lunenfeld, *Snap to Grid* (MIT Press, 2000); Christiane Paul, *Digital Art*

(Thames and Hudson, 2003); Rachel Greene, *Internet Art* (Thames and Hudson, 2004); Karin Schminke, Dorothy Simpson Krause, Bonny Pierce Lhotka, *Digital Art Studio* (Watson-Guptill Publications, 2004); Bruce Wands, *Art in the Digital Age* (Thames and Hudson, 2006).

Chapter 4

22. *Guardian*, 20 January 2005, p. 19, online at www.guardian.co.uk/online/ story/0,3605,1393747,00.html.
23. Sir Joshua Reynolds, Discourse XII, in *Discourses on Art*, edited by Robert R. Wark (Yale University Press, 1975), p. 210.
24. Ibid., p. 217.
25. Alvy Ray Smith, "Digital Paint Systems: An Anecdotal and Historical Overview," IEEE Annals of the History of Computing, p. 14, online at http://accad.osu.edu/~waynec/history/PDFs/paint.pdf.
26. From the introduction to Stuart Morgan, *What the Butler Saw*, edited by Ian Hunt (Durian Publications, 1996), p. 13.
27. SECA: Society for the Encouragement of Contemporary Art.
28. Exhibition Review, SFMOMA/ISEA96, http://mitpress2.mit.edu/ e-journals/LEA/REDESIGN/BKISSUES/TEXT/LEA4-10.TXT.
29. www.lacda.com/exhibits/bauer.html
30. Ray Smith, "Digital Paint Systems."
31. "Silent Motion," exhibition at Colville Place Gallery, 2001, which included the work of Victor Acevedo, Anne Baker, Andrew Carnie, Hans Dehlinger, James Faure Walker, Lane Hall, Lisa Moline, Rejane Spitz, Annette Weintraub, Jody Zellen, and Eadweard Muybridge, online at www.kingston.ac.uk/picker/archive/silentmotion/indexb.htm.

Chapter 5

32. The gallery was called Artists' Market and was located at Earlham Street, Covent Garden, London WC2, in 1973.
33. Other examples of compass point marks in the British Museum include vases by the Princeton Painter (540 B.C.), Myson (500 B.C.), and the Niobid Painter (460 B.C.).
34. Workplace Art Gallery, Studio G1, Tea Building, 56 Shoreditch High Street, London E1 6JJ, online at www.wacart.com.
35. Sol Le Witt, "Paragraphs on Conceptual Art," *Artforum*, June 1967.
36. See www.art-exchange.com.
37. See www.theprintstudio.co.uk.
38. See Gill Saunders and Rosie Miles, *Prints Now: Directions and Definitions* (London: V&A Publications, 2006).
39. Notice to Artists, Royal Academy Summer Exhibition 2005, London.
40. See http://news.bbc.co.uk/1/hi/technology/4228569.stm, 2 February 2005.

41. Peter Schjeldahl, Stuart Morgan Memorial Lecture, Tate Modern, 19 October 2004.
42. The term *VJ* is a twist on the older term *DJ*. VJs can be considered video jockeys, or video artists. For more on VJing, see www.vjs.net.

Chapter 6

43. For a photograph of Derry with Rauschenberg, and a useful account of Painter's philosophy, see John Derry, "Of Pianos and Oranges," *ZoneZero* e-zine, www.zonezero.com/magazine/articles/derry/derry.html.
44. Bruce Wands, www.schoolofvisualarts.edu/grad/index.jsp?sid0=2& sid1=28.
45. James Adley, letter to the author, July 2003.
46. Robert Storr, *Gerhard Richter: Forty Years of Painting* (MoMA, 2001), p. 307.
47. Ibid., pp. 297 and 288.
48. Clement Greenberg, interview with author, 1974. For a full interview, see James Faure Walker, "Interview with Clement Greenberg," *Artscribe* 10 (January 1978); republished in Clement Greenberg, *Clement Greenberg: Late Writings,* edited by Robert C. Morgan (University of Minnesota Press, 2003).

Chapter 7

49. Jim Blinn, Graduation Address at Parsons School of Design, New York, 2005, online at http://research.microsoft.com/users/blinn/parsons.htm.
50. Jean-Pierre Hébert, SIGGRAPH 2004 (Los Angeles) Electronic Art and Animation Catalogue, p. 51. The drawing referred to is illustrated.
51. I was first made fully aware of this by examples in the Palais des Beaux-Arts, Lille, but similar cases can be found in other regional museums in France.
52. Max Friedlander, *From Van Eyck to Bruegel,* vol. 2 (Phaidon, 1969), p. 103.
53. Bernard Jacobson, Mahler Symphony V, Pentatone Classics, sleeve note.
54. We planned to collaborate on a live "performed" paint/music animation, but never managed to get round to it, as Mari lives in New York.
55. For an excellent account of the beginnings of painterly digital work, see Cynthia Beth Rubin's article: http://mitpress2.mit.edu/e-journals/LEA/LEA2004/ez.features4.htm. (The image illustrating the article is not attributed but is actually *Happy Circle,* 1988, by James Faure Walker.)
56. See www.badscience.org; and www.criminalanimal.org.
57. Ibid.

58. Anna Ursyn, artist's statement for *Monday Morning,* www.ursyn.com.
For her *Commuter's Tunes,* Anna Ursyn adds her poem:
And again you commute
stable and roaming
sitting quietly while driving in a haste,
attentive yet unobservant.
So distinct in your glass case
yet immersed in milieus
urban and rural anew,
too familiar to disturb.
Composing tunes you whistle
listening to yourself
learning what you want for sure
enjoying the company of you.
59. See www.cs.berkeley.edu/~sequin/SCULPTS/SnowSculpt05.
60. See www.KennethAHuff.com.

Chapter 8

61. See www.hqartgallery.com/viewall3.html.
62. On Turner, Whistler, and Monet and the Thames, see Katherine Lochnan, ed., "Turner, Whistler, Monet" (catalogue for Tate Britain's exhibition) (Tate, 2004).
63. These prints can be seen at www.joniweyl.com/v2/prints_current.asp_artistid=23&more=1.htm.
64. See page 166.

Index